The Young Black Leader's Guide
to a Successful Career in International Affairs

The Young Black Leader's Guide

to a Successful Career in International Affairs

What the Giants Want You to Know

Aaron S. Williams
Taylor A. Jack
Jennifer M. Brinkerhoff

LYNNE
RIENNER
PUBLISHERS

BOULDER
LONDON

Published in the United States of America in 2022 by
Lynne Rienner Publishers, Inc.
1800 30th Street, Suite 314, Boulder, Colorado 80301
www.rienner.com

and in the United Kingdom by
Lynne Rienner Publishers, Inc.
Gray's Inn House, 127 Clerkenwell Road, London EC1 5DB
www.eurospanbookstore.com/rienner

Library of Congress Cataloging-in-Publication Data
Names: Williams, Aaron S., 1947– author. | Jack, Taylor A., author. |
    Brinkerhoff, Jennifer M., 1965– author.
Title: The young Black leader's guide to a successful career in
    international affairs : what the giants want you to know / Aaron S.
    Williams, Taylor A. Jack, Jennifer M. Brinkerhoff.
Description: Boulder, Colorado : Lynne Rienner Publishers, Inc., [2022] |
    Includes bibliographical references and index. | Summary: "An essential
    guide for Black Americans interested in pursuing a career in
    international affairs"— Provided by publisher.
Identifiers: LCCN 2021062896 (print) | LCCN 2021062897 (ebook) | ISBN
    9781955055567 (Hardback) | ISBN 9781955055574 (Paperback) | ISBN
    9781955055581 (eBook)
Subjects: LCSH: International relations—United States—Vocational
    guidance. | Diplomats—Vocational guidance—United States. | African
    American leadership. | Career development.
Classification: LCC JZ1238.U6 W55 2022 (print) | LCC JZ1238.U6 (ebook) |
    DDC 327.296/073—dc23/eng/20220213
LC record available at https://lccn.loc.gov/2021062896
LC ebook record available at https://lccn.loc.gov/2021062897

British Cataloguing in Publication Data
A Cataloguing in Publication record for this book
is available from the British Library.

Printed and bound in the United States of America

5 4 3 2 1

Contents

Foreword

It might be the most famous commercial for the Peace Corps: "The hardest job you'll ever love." I remember seeing it as a little girl. It showed people of different backgrounds teaching, working in agriculture, and so forth. I was captured. So by the time I was eleven or twelve, I knew I was going to be a Peace Corps volunteer and have an international career. I just thought, "Who doesn't want a challenge? And who doesn't want to love what they're doing?"

I was a mediocre student, in all honesty. My mom used to yell at me, "I know you can do it!" So I had a lot of pressure. I mostly ignored it until I decided I really did want to go to college. I knew that once I focused, I could excel. It's so important to believe in yourself, to know where your strengths are and what you need to do to tap into them. I'm a great commencement speaker. I give comfort and hope to parents because I say, "Listen, I was a C student. Let me be clear, I was a C student. Help your child to find their passion, and they will excel."

When I was ambassador to Malta, I had to fight with the Bureau of European and Eurasian Affairs, saying, "I need more diversity at this post." And I can see why we have struggled with this for so long: because people want what they want, and they're not thinking about inclusion and diversity. The State Department was telling me, "No, you need to take this person." The department makes the assignment decisions, but the ambassador can say no. So I said no. Either they were not going to send anyone, or I would have to wait for whoever was left—all the people who didn't get assigned, designated "over-complement." And I said, "Great, I'll wait." I've been on that over-complement list myself several times in my career. And even brilliant people are often on overcomplement for a variety of reasons. Maybe they didn't want to go where the department was trying to send them and decided to take their chances. Maybe the handshake fell through, mom got sick, or they needed to leave an assignment to do some family care . . . there are all kinds of reasons why great people are on overcomplement. Not once in my career, when I gave someone a second chance, along with the support and guidance they needed, did they turn out to be unsuccessful. Not ever.

This suggests to me the following. First, you have to find your passion to do your best work. Second, you have to be your own best advocate to fight—or take risks—to get to where you believe you belong. Third, you need to also fight hard and take risks to support others if we are ever to attain a truly representative, diverse, inclusive, and maximally effective foreign affairs apparatus. And fourth, we need to do more than just get people in the room. We need to support them and provide guidance so they know what success looks like, how to achieve it, and how to survive the inevitable setbacks we all face in a career over a lifetime.

This fourth objective is the primary purpose of this book. It provides a guide, from one generation of foreign policy experts to the next generation and those to come. The many unsung, unknown giants featured in the book want the next generation to climb onto their shoulders and reach the top. Within these pages, I hope you will find clarity about whether or not you have or may develop a passion for international affairs—for other cultures, languages, and cross-national policy engagement—and that you will find the guidance and support you need to make a go of this extraordinary career.

—Ambassador Gina Abercrombie-Winstanley
Chief Diversity and Inclusion Officer,
US Department of State

1

Invitation to a
Meaningful Career

Not everybody can be famous but everybody can be great because greatness is determined by service.... You only need a heart full of grace and a soul generated by love.

—Martin Luther King Jr.,
sermon at Ebenezer Baptist Church in
Atlanta, Georgia, February 4, 1968

We want to encourage Black Americans to pursue and succeed in careers in US foreign policy and international affairs so that these fields come closer to reflecting American society. Through a multigenerational dialogue, we knit together (1) the experience of individual "giants" who blazed a trail in US foreign policy and international affairs and (2) the needs of young Black Americans. We ask trailblazers to reflect on how they navigated challenges to reach their great achievements—what you, the next generation, want and need to know—rather than what they may naturally want to focus on.

Achievements are important but may not always provide the full story. Trailblazers might overlook forgotten challenges or prefer not to dwell on painful experiences. Or they may simply find the implications and challenges of their skin color to be so commonplace as not to be worth mentioning. Perhaps the struggles associated with their race were so unexceptional at the time they experienced them that they might not think about the need to discuss them as a particular set of challenges.

But these are precisely the experiences you may need to know about so you can gain the courage you need to pursue this professional career and understand how best to navigate your own challenges when you confront them.

Who We Are

■ *I'm Aaron Williams. Throughout the book, I will "speak" to you in the slanted typeface that you are reading now. I believe the greatness of America is clearly found in the rich diversity of our citizens. This diversity will continue to be the foundation for our nation's progress in all aspects of our society and a pillar of America's role in global leadership. Black Americans are so unrepresented historically in terms of diplomacy and international affairs that we need to build a corps of leaders to present the true face of America as we interact with the rest of the globe. The more diversity you bring into the C-suite of the foreign policy halls—where the highest-ranking senior executives work—the bigger the cadre of people who have a different perspective on the world and how we should interact in it. And so, you have a better-informed dialogue and policymaking capability.*

I was blessed to be born in an era of amazing progress in interracial understanding and societal change. This was achieved thanks to the great sacrifice, measured in blood, sweat, and tears, of the giants of the civil rights era. This led to expanded opportunities in terms of education and career opportunities for Black Americans across our nation. I was determined to pursue such opportunities and have been fortunate to have had a career that led to leadership positions in government, business, and the nonprofit world. As an integral part of my career, I sought every opportunity to assist and mentor Black professionals, to help them in achieving their career goals—to "drop the ladder down" for those coming behind me.

Thus, I wanted to write this book as a pathway for the next generation of Black leaders in the foreign policy arena. This book illuminates for them—for you—the rich and often unknown history and pioneering life experiences of the giants who blazed the trail of excellence in diplomacy and international affairs. They, in turn, seek to both encourage you and offer you lessons from their careers.

▶ My name is Taylor Jack. Throughout the book, I will speak to you in the sans-serif typeface that you are reading now. I became a part of this project when I was completing my master's studies in international development at George Washington University. Writing a book was the furthest thing from my mind, but my curiosity and need to always "unpack" things led me to be the other voice speaking to you today. From the moment I decided to pursue a career in international service, I knew I wanted to tackle the issue of the lack of Black voices in leadership in US foreign policy and international affairs. Jennifer mentioned this project that she was starting with Aaron Williams. Based on my professional background and interest, and because I represent the audience for this book, she invited me to sit in on a sample interview with Aaron, just to test out some questions and then reflect on what we should be asking the giants.

Meeting Aaron was kismet. His reputation precedes him. Having the opportunity to observe his sample interview changed my life in more ways than one. During those two hours, I broke every rule I learned in my research and design class. My observation lasted for all of ten minutes before I interjected and asked Aaron to elaborate on a trying time in his long and decorated career. I could see that my questioning was unexpected, but to my surprise he leaned in and answered my questions fully. Aaron framed the book as a gift to my generation, as a way to impart his wisdom and to share not only the triumphs but also the struggles that he and his colleagues and peers experienced pioneering this career. As a member of his target audience, I saw it as my duty to push for the questions that I know many students and young professionals are anxious to get the answers to.

Fortunately, my audacity paid off, and we ended up having a really good dialogue. Aaron and I discovered we have a lot of similarities. We are both from the South Side of Chicago—we grew up, albeit at different times, roughly two miles apart. We went to similar high schools. We were both Peace Corps volunteers. Our connections made it easier for us to have these conversations as he probably saw something in me, and I saw Aaron, a son of Chicago, who had reached heights that I could only dream of. After that day, I became a part of this team. I've been very honored to get the chance to hear these stories and ask the questions I think you would ask if you were in my place.

I'm Jennifer Brinkerhoff. I won't be speaking to you directly, but I want to introduce myself. I've had the honor of facilitating this project. My husband, Derick Brinkerhoff, and I had profiled Aaron in our 2005 book *Working for Change: Making a Career in International Public Service*. When Aaron retired, he approached me about writing a similar book specifically targeting Black Americans. I embraced Aaron's proposal immediately. I am from an immigrant family and am of its first generation to be college educated. When I moved to South Central Los Angeles to pursue my graduate studies, I realized just how privileged I am as a white woman who attended a great high school in a wealthy suburb. The 1992 Los Angeles civil unrest exposed me to the depth of that injustice. Until our public sector—both domestic and international—reflects our society, too many voices will be unheard, too many perspectives ignored, and too many opportunities missed to ensure this great country is a just one for all of us. When we speak to you together, we will write in the front that you are reading now, Times New Roman.

Why We Wrote This Book

So why did we write this book? We want to inspire young people who already have an interest in international affairs or to spark that interest in young people who perhaps have not thought about a career in this field. We want to ensure that Black students and early- and mid-career professionals have the guidance they need to succeed. We want your talent to be represented in the United States and around the world. When Aaron first joined the diplomatic service, only a limited number of opportunities existed for Black Americans to be engaged in international affairs, such as the Peace Corps, for example, which was his ticket. But now you can join Google or work with Goldman Sachs. You can volunteer with international NGOs. You can do a wide range of things. Because of that, we need to encourage this next generation to consider public service.

▶ We want young people who have had no exposure to international affairs to pick up this book and say, "I see myself in this book, and I represent the very best of the United States." I didn't start my journey in this industry blind. I knew that I would be the only one in the room more often than not. But if I can do my part to make the journey easier for those who follow behind me, then I have served a greater purpose. We have the opportunity to occupy spaces and claim a seat at the tables that were previously denied or rationed out to the many hidden figures of US foreign policy and international affairs. This book is a symbolic passing of the torch from one generation to another, and it is up to us to make sure that there is no void of Black leadership in international affairs.

One of the things we've observed in working on this book and from our own experience in George Washington University's Elliott School of International Affairs is that the majority of Black Americans expressing interest in international affairs and participating in important fellowship programs are first and second generation. It is so inspiring to witness how many see the disparities between their heritage places and the opportunities they experience living in the US and want to make a difference. We want to also make sure multigenerational Black Americans see the importance of serving internationally, whether it's in diplomacy, development, business, or the military. Taylor is a multigenerational Black American. At Howard University most of her classmates were first-generation immigrants. The Black American trailblazers in US foreign policy were both multigenerational and more recent immigrants. We want to ensure that all of these important voices and experiences are represented in our foreign policy.

When Aaron first approached Jennifer, he had the idea of profiling the trailblazers because they're his people. He knows so many of them.

But a lot of profiles are already out there. People do their oral histories, and they're available on the Internet.[1] We knew we wanted not just to attract people into this field but to help them succeed. So we organized the book around themes, or guideposts, that will help you understand what challenges you may encounter and how to work through those challenges. ■ *We need to have role models to show people what we can do on the world stage. And to the extent that we can encourage young people to pursue these types of careers and accumulate and compile the types of experience that bring them to positions of power and influence, I think that's a worthy aim.*

This book builds on the experience of the giants who have served in the international affairs arena. It is a means to open up the world of diplomacy and international affairs to the next generation and encourage you to enter the game.

Public service is about serving others. Related careers are usually associated with government work or nonprofits. This book is about international public service specifically. When we talk about US foreign policy, we most often think about service in the federal government—the State Department, US Agency for International Development (USAID), Defense Department, Millennium Challenge Corporation, Foreign Commercial Service, and Foreign Agricultural Service, among others. US foreign policy is also executed by a range of private and nonprofit organizations: those who work under contract with the government but also those who remain independent nonprofits that nonetheless represent the values and interests of the United States abroad. The Carter Center comes to mind, for example. Whichever sector (government, nonprofit, or private) or specific organization you work in, the business of US foreign policy is about representing American values, as expressed in policies and programs, abroad. Throughout the book, we will use the term *US foreign policy* to refer to the United States' participation in international affairs broadly.

Why should you care about US foreign policy? And why now? What's so great about a career in US foreign policy? And how can this book help you on this journey? This introduction begins to answer these questions and provides a road map for the rest of the book. The book is crafted as an intergenerational dialogue—both between Aaron, a giant, and Taylor, who is at the beginning of her career, and between you and all of our giants. Throughout the book, you will hear directly from the giants—those who blazed the trail of excellence in diplomacy and international development—in their own words. The appendix contains a complete list of the Black Americans we consulted, through our direct interviews, their own writings and records, and biographies of additional trailblazers. Like Taylor, we invite you to sit at the feet of those who went before you, some of whom are still navigating toward their giant status in this arena. Welcome to the conversation.

We'll start by addressing why this intergenerational dialogue is so important. We'll tell you about who our giants are. Then we will address the many reasons why your participation matters for US foreign policy. We then take on the tough question of why this matters now, given the many challenges and injustices we face at home in the United States, and how the quests for justice at home and abroad are not necessarily mutually exclusive pursuits. The next section presents the many factors that make a career in US foreign policy so appealing. Finally, we briefly present what we learned from our many conversations on the road to this book and introduce the chapters to follow.

Crossing the Generations

■ *In the aftermath of the George Floyd murder in Minneapolis, it's clear that multi-generational, multiethnic thousands, if not millions, of people have decided that things have to change. I think young people in this country have demonstrated, over and over again, that they are fed up with the status quo. And it's not just in terms of racial injustice, but also in terms of limited economic opportunity. So they—you—are in the forefront of all of this. My role and that of my generation is to inspire you, to serve as a catalyst and to let you know that the door is open. I think you're not convinced that it is. We have to listen to you and follow your lead. I think our role is to give you space and encouragement to actually lead. We have experience. We understand how to exercise power. And we have the alliances that are needed to make change in this country. We've got to share that and help to build new alliances.*

▶ "You know where you have been, but you don't know where you are going." My grandmother, who escaped a life in the Jim Crow South with a tenth-grade education, lived by this creed. This standard of humility has laid the foundation on which I walk to this day. We have to be students of history to inform the decisions ahead of us and to honor the ones made for us. "I am because you are" becomes more relevant every time any Black person ascends to new heights. Many of the names in this book are ones that most people will never know, but their contributions are timeless and are deserving of our gratitude and recognition.

Speaking truth to power is one of the many mantras that my generation lives by. There is beauty in pain and restoration in the truth. We get fired up. Aaron and the other giants in this book have been through so much, and now I want to take that on. I want to run with it. So I needed to be able to ask those tough questions that no one has ever asked before and to say, "Look, I'm about to walk into a storm, and I have no idea how to navigate this world. Now that you've had four-plus decades of experience, what is something that you would tell your twenty-year-old self? Or what is something that you wanted to know back then?" So that's what I wanted. And it's what I want this book to give you.

This book provides that important bridge, giving you, younger generations, access to the great voices of experience, achievement, and courage—voices you might not have otherwise imagined accessing. Maybe you don't even know these accomplished individuals exist. And we ask the tough questions, what we think you want and need to know. We didn't just rely on Taylor to learn that. We also held focus groups with our Black graduate students and with recently awarded fellows of the Pickering, Rangel, and Payne programs.[2] We have doubled down on those salient issues that we first heard about from our focus groups and also from more than one of the giants we talked to.

Our intergenerational approach speaks to the needs of all of us and to the challenges of our time. As civil rights leader Ruby Sales (2020) put it, "There is a hunger that young people have, to be claimed, to be a part of an intergenerational—a trans-generational experience, to know people, because without knowing another generation, they feel incomplete, just like I feel incomplete without knowing younger people. And so we are incomplete without knowing each other."

Meet Your Giants:
The Many Voices in This Book

So who are these giants? Some are undoubtedly already giants; others are giants in the making. We wanted to make sure that we captured experiences over time. This enables us to understand better those issues that are timeless, those that are particular to a stage in one's career, and, in some cases, those that are unique to a particular time but from which we can still learn. They are all giants in their own right.

■ *Let me tell you something I truly believe. Typically, when you're at a senior level in an organization in the United States and you meet a peer, someone who is a person of color, in any organization, you can be pretty sure, without a doubt, this person is an exceedingly good leader, a competent professional, and has achieved a lot. Because they've had this journey. Nobody handed it to them. Very few of us have ever inherited a situation. I have pored over the personal biographies of many, many people of color in business, government, and the nonprofit world. Everybody had to fight their way up. There was no "Hey, I want you to be my protégé and I'm going to bring you along." Very rarely does it work that way.*

▶ What I know to be true is that a leader doesn't ascend to the heights that they have without being relentless, unapologetic, and bold: relentless in their pursuit of excellence, no matter the cost; unapologetic about who they are; and bold enough to know when to take the risks that no one else will take, to speak up, and to serve a greater purpose.

If we were to ask you who the Black American giants in US foreign policy are, would you be able to name them? Don't worry if not. Our focus group participants maxed out after just a few names. This is the point of the book. And it's not just to introduce you to the most famous, the few who come readily to mind. If you look at the history of the US foreign policy arena, you will note that despite there having been significant leaders who were people of color, they are not represented in the literature. They are almost invisible. They are invisible because, first of all, they are few in numbers and, secondly, because, with a few exceptions, they have not had the opportunity or been in the right circles to write their story. Most people, for example, would never know that Frederick Douglass had been a US diplomat. He's known for his antislavery work.

We want to introduce you to those who have never received the publicity or accolades they deserve, who work both quietly and not so quietly both behind the scenes and on stage. We want to expose you to their diversity: their many origin stories, their varied paths, and the many different ways they have worked to advance US foreign policy across the sectors (government, business, nonprofit, and military). Just knowing who they are may boost your confidence. We want you to see yourself in them. And there are many more than those who appear in this book. Time and space prevented us from including them all. We hope this book will inspire *all* of the giants to share their stories with the next generation beyond the pages of this book.

■ *In our interviews, I found confirmation of what I have seen in my career. There was a commonality there. And especially the more deprived a person's early background was, the more incredible the transformation that allowed them to be emblematic of the American dream. I certainly had no clue, growing up in the South Side of Chicago, what a foreign policy career was. I didn't even know what a Foreign Service officer was. People like you have done this, and you can also be successful.*

▶ I have seen a piece of myself in every person we have had the honor to interview. Much like Aaron, growing up I didn't know anyone who was in the Foreign Service or had an internationally focused career. What I did have were parents who were dedicated to making sure that I had every opportunity to excel and see the world. Without their belief that I could be extraordinary, I would not have the confidence to even dream of a career in international affairs.

Some of our giants came from very humble backgrounds: from the South, like Edward J. Perkins, James Joseph, and Linda Thomas-Greenfield; from Philadelphia, like Johnny Young and Sundaa Bridgett-Jones; from New York, like Bob Burgess, Harry K. Thomas Jr., and Paul Weisenfeld; from Chicago, like Aaron Williams, Johnnie Carson, and Ertharin Cousin; and from Boston, like Alonzo Fulgham and Verone Bernard. Some benefited from early and significant exposure to the vibrant cultures afforded by historically Black colleges and universities (HBCUs), where their parents taught, like Aurelia E. Brazeal and Katherine Lee. Others benefited from typical middle-class upbringings. Some were raised in families with high expectations that they pursue higher education and succeed. Many are multigenerational Black Americans, and others have roots in the West Indies.

They include some of the firsts in their field. Like Aaron. ■ *Of course, in my career, because of my age and my generation, I was always the first in just about every case—in business, in government, and in the nonprofit world, because I've worked in all three sectors. I was always the first or part of the first group.* At USAID, Aaron was a pioneer in public-private partnerships, the first Black person to lead the Latin America and Caribbean Bureau and to serve as mission director to South Africa (when Nelson Mandela became president). And after his career at USAID, he was the first Black person to hold the following positions: vice president of the International Youth Foundation, executive vice president of a business group at RTI International, and the first Black male director of the Peace Corps.[3]

Our giants' firsts include the following:

• Ambassadorships: Australia (Edward J. Perkins), Bahrain (Johnny Young), Bangladesh (Harry K. Thomas Jr.), Brunei (Sylvia Stanfield), Federated States of Micronesia (Aurelia E. Brazeal, who was also the first US ambassador there and the first Black woman US ambassador to Kenya and Ethiopia), the Philippines (Harry K. Thomas Jr.), Slovenia (Johnny Young), South Africa (Edward J. Perkins), the United Nations Agencies for Food and Agriculture (Ertharin Cousin), Malta (Gina Abercrombie-Winstanley, who was the first Black female US ambassador there), and the first and still the only Black female career ambassador (Ruth A. Davis)

• Other essential posts in the State Department: the first Black American male (Edward J. Perkins) and female (Ruth A. Davis) directors general of the State Department; the first (and only) Black American executive secretary of the State Department (Harry K. Thomas Jr.), the first Black American executive director of the United Nations World Food Programme (Ertharin Cousin), the first Black deputy assistant secretary for East Asian and Pacific affairs (Aurelia E. Brazeal), the first Black woman to head the Australia, New Zealand Affairs Office (Sylvia Stanfield), and the first woman to head a diplomatic mission in Saudi Arabia and the first chief diversity and inclusion officer (Gina Abercrombie-Winstanley)

• At USAID: the first Black USAID director of South Asia, mission director for Afghanistan, and acting administrator (Alonzo Fulgham), the first USAID HIV/AIDS coordinator (Dr. Helene Gayle), and the first Black mission director in South America (Paul Weisenfeld)

• The first Black American assistant secretary and director general of the US and Foreign Commercial Service (Lauri Fitz-Pegado)

• The first Black president of CARE International (Helene Gayle)

• The first Black American to serve as the US Army's director of the Human Resources Policy Directorate—Pentagon (Barrye Price)

• In the international business and consulting world: the first person to lead a corporate social responsibility program at a major international corporation (James Joseph at Cummins Inc.); the first, and until he retired, the only Black senior executive in the manufacturing operations of GTE Sylvania (and its successor companies) (Bob Burgess); the first Black president of the Disneyland Resorts in Anaheim, California (Ed Grier); and the first Black senior vice president at a major international development consulting firm (Victoria Cooper)

Most of the giants are also firsts of another sort. Like Aaron, they were the first in their families to pursue international careers. Aaron was even the first in his family to leave the South Side of Chicago other than to join the military.

The interviews were an opportunity for Aaron to express to many of his friends and former colleagues, ■ *I'm just proud to know you, to be your friend, to have walked down a couple of these roads with you, and to be able to stand back in awe of you and watch you as you carried out your business.* Some of our younger giants were just as awed by Aaron, like Chris Richardson, who said, "I've got to tell you guys, I am so excited to be here with Mr. Williams. I don't think I can ever call him Aaron. . . . You're such a legend in the State Department and in global, international affairs. It's a real honor to be here with you." Thanks to helpful referrals, we all met some giants for the first time.

▶ It was special for me to see Aaron and the giants look back on the times they have worked together and see how they have come full circle breaking down barriers as they go. One thing that will never escape me is that I had the chance to question, probe, and even challenge some of the greatest leaders, visionaries, and trailblazers in this industry. It was a privilege that I know not many will ever experience and a wonderful demonstration of mentorship from Aaron as well as trust. He empowered me to push the giants and unpack stories they may have never revealed. They have attributed their success to mentors and sponsors who guided them, spoke up on their behalf, and gave them tough love when they needed it the most. Aaron has walked so I could run, and I will forever be grateful.

We intentionally talked to giants from all three sectors—government, business, and nonprofit—as well as the military. Several of our giants worked across more than one sector, including Aaron, of course, and James Joseph, Dr. Helene Gayle, Dr. Jacob Gayle, and Lauri Fitz-Pegado. Some moved from government service to the nonprofit world, and even back to government, including Ambassador Ertharin Cousin, C. D. Glin, and Sundaa Bridgett-Jones. We talked to military leaders (General Barrye Price) and those who moved from the military into business (Bob Burgess) and government (Edward J. Perkins).

Some of our business giants were skeptical about why they should be included in a book about US foreign policy. As Aaron explained when recruiting former Disney executive Ed Grier, ■ *As a global executive, you are an ambassador for the United States. It just comes with the territory. As a matter of fact, what you do in a US business overseas is much more important in many ways than our diplomacy, because you have a bigger footprint, more resources, and are listened to. The official donor-funding flows that used to be the primary source of assistance to developing countries have been surpassed by direct foreign investment and trade flows. Due to this shift over decades, clearly global business leaders are now key diplomats in the world. So, I thought it was important to have this perspective.*

Our giants, especially the firsts, want to make sure there are seconds, thirds, and hundreds, with you among them.

Why Your Participation Matters

As noted above, US foreign policy is about representing American values, as expressed in policies and programs, abroad. One of those fundamental values is democracy and, relatedly, upholding the US Constitution. Ours is a representative democracy, and the quality of that representation matters greatly. George Mason argued that our representatives should reflect our society as a whole. He put it this way: "To make representation real and actual . . . [r]epresentatives ought to mix with the people, think as they think, feel as they feel, ought to be perfectly amenable to them, and thoroughly acquainted with their interest and condition" (Elliot 1836, quoted in Kenyon 1955, 32). This is well worth repeating: representatives "ought to mix with the people, think as they think, feel as they feel."

There are so many reasons why your participation matters. We'll start with the greatest one of all: fulfilling the intention of the US Constitution. Your participation also significantly enhances the effectiveness and efficiency of US foreign policy in several specific ways.

Fulfilling the Intention of the US Constitution

Quite frankly, your participation in US foreign policy fulfills the intent of the US Constitution. No one illustrates that more beautifully than Ambassador Edward J. Perkins, to whom this book is dedicated (see Box 1.1).

Box 1.1   Edward J. Perkins: Living the Constitution

"Foreign Service officers have to make sure that the Constitution is adhered to in everything we do, and also take it to the community. I spent a lot of time in Black communities when I was Director General [of the State Department]. Not because I wanted to achieve a certain point, but because I needed to have myself there, and never to forget it. I wanted them to know that there was a tool [for them] somewhere in the government. I remember being in a place called Houma, Louisiana, one afternoon. I have a cousin who was working there in the state government. And she asked me if I would meet with all of her supervisors, who were all white. And she said, 'Well, here is my cousin. He works in Washington, and he helps to get things done. And he helps to get your things done, but you don't know about it.'

"And it was a look-see moment for these people, all white men—something that they had not ever considered before. And one of them had the nerve to ask me, 'What do you consider to be the most important thing that you're doing?' I said, 'The most important thing is never to forget that I am a citizen of the United States, and the Constitution of the United States, which I'm sure all of you have read.' And I knew they had not, right? 'That's for me and for you too. And that's the good thing about it.'

"No one said a word. They looked at me in astonishment. And so that astonishment told me that we have a long way to go. And we aren't talking just about Black people. We're talking about other people as well. We all have got to understand, this Constitution is a living thing. You have to make it. You have to keep it living. To keep seeing it. It takes a lot of people. It takes the population to make it live."

Black Americans have a particular experience that needs to be a part of making our Constitution a living thing. Speaking in the aftermath of the George Floyd killing, Chris Richardson, former State Department consular officer, elaborates, "People of color have both a realistic and optimistic view of the United States that other people may not necessarily have. They have the ability to tap into both the good and the bad of America, and to explain America in a way that I don't necessarily think a white colleague would be able to, especially when you have moments like this." Chris wants to tell you to "keep that optimism that you have, but also be willing to explain America in a realistic way, because I think what's missing from the State Department, and from foreign affairs, is a willingness to call out America, and explain America to people who aren't Americans in a way that's realistic and practical." When your experience is not represented among policymakers, our policy is debilitated. For example, the Ronald Reagan administration completely missed the tenor and potential influence of special interest groups regarding apartheid in South Africa because it was not "in tune with the minority population of the United States" (Perkins 2006, 248).

Your participation provides the example our Constitution aspires to present to the world. During Perkins's confirmation hearing as ambassador to apartheid South Africa, he said, "Our nation is strong. That strength . . . comes from our diversity and our inherent tolerance of all people. But above all, I believe we are strong because of our respect for the dignity and worth of the individual, our encouragement of individual excellence, and our insistence that each person enjoy the right to achieve the highest of which he or she is capable. We are far yet short of perfection, but no one who knows us can doubt that we are committed to ceaseless striving for it" (Perkins 2006, 268).

Enhanced Foreign Policy Credibility

As you enact our Constitution through your presence and the important posts you will hold and execute, your participation makes our foreign policy more credible. Ambassador Harriet Elam-Thomas shared, "Though I thoroughly prepared for each new assignment, I am certain the key to making a contribution toward a credible articulation of US foreign policy was the fact that I had the opportunity to serve and felt included" (Elam-Thomas 2017, 4). Your presence also may be essential to the credibility of particular foreign policy agendas. Katherine Lee, retired senior officer of the US Information Agency and US State Department, worked to promote greater equality in Brazil. She reported, "By bringing in US speakers who could show how the US Black situation had advanced, we were giving hints to them of what they could do to progress" (Lee 2005). C. D. Glin, president and CEO of the US African Development Foundation (at the time of our interview), similarly fulfilled a role only a Black American could. He was part of the first Peace Corps group to serve in South Africa after Nelson Mandela came to power. The group was carefully assembled to showcase diversity as a strength. He used the experience as an opportunity to promote pride in the Black identity (see Box 8.4).

Better Understanding with Other Peoples

Your participation enhances understanding abroad. Our giants have been very well received in their work overseas, precisely because of their Black identity. Whether its "oppressed people around the world who identify with our aspirations and our activities" (Ambassador James Joseph) or "people [who] see our struggles aligned with their struggles" (Dr. Helene Gayle), many of the giants experienced what Alonzo Fulgham shared: "I've always had more support and empathy from foreign policy leaders in other countries because of who I am, because I'm not one of the normal, usual suspects. I think it has always been an asset." As Ambassador Edward Perkins reported of his meeting with Albertina Sisulu, copresident of the United Democratic Front and wife of Walter Sisulu, who was imprisoned with Nelson Mandela, she said, "Mr. Ambassador, I guess you're wondering why I am here in view of the boycott of you by the Black leaders. It is very simple. You are a Black man. You can't be all bad" (Perkins 2006, 310).

▶ What we have learned from the Black Lives Matter movement is that our world is more interconnected than ever and that this is not our fight alone. Sectors within the broader international affairs community are having a racial reckoning, forcing them to have the tough discussions about institutional racism and its roots in colonialism. This point in time has allowed us to have true and honest conversations about the roles that we have played and to dispel the narrative that international organizations are not racist. Though it took the world to be confined to their homes (during the Covid-19 pandemic) to understand the linkages between police brutality and systemic racism, we now have their attention, and I hope that the collective "we" uses it to further dismantle the structures preventing the global community from achieving true change.

Bringing International Understanding Home

Your participation also enhances understandings that are brought home to the United States. Victoria Cooper put it this way: "Every voice needs to be represented when we are outside of our shores to ensure people in those countries understand our diversity, as we work to understand theirs, and bring this broader experience back to the US. If everything is filtering only through one layer, then you're not getting a true story, you're not getting a true reflection."

■ *When you have truly representative, diverse individuals engaged abroad who bring their unique perspectives and rich experiences back home (e.g., Peace Corps volunteers, business executives, or development experts), they will enrich their domestic organizations. Their contributions routinely inform the mission and improve the results of their respective organizations and make them stronger. They see the global chessboard as multidimensional, understand the challenges and opportunities presented, and have the nuanced experience to respond effectively.*

Accessing High-Quality Talent

Fundamentally, your participation is required to ensure that US foreign policy is crafted and executed by the best talent available. George Shultz, former secretary of state, said of Ambassador Edward Perkins, "The fact that he is extraordinarily capable reinforces the message that talent knows no racial boundaries" (Shultz 2006). ■ *We need to be able to tap the talent of all the people in our country. It's a mistake for us to not have access to the best and the brightest across all groups of people and to limit our ability to, together, strive for success. And it will handicap the United States in terms of its ability to compete in the world. For far too long, we have been hindered in our ability to capitalize on the vast strength of the American people because there's been this inherent limitation, stated or otherwise, legal or informal, in being able to do that.*

As US President Franklin Delano Roosevelt famously said, "No country, however rich, can afford the waste of its human resources" (Roosevelt 1934). Eighty-five years later, Susan Rice, former national security advisor, lamented, "All too often we fail to leverage our greatest strength. By choice, we are battling to defend our people and our interests in a complex world with the equivalent of one hand tied behind our back" (Rice 2019, 428).

Enriching Policy Creativity and Innovation

Your talent, and the talent of our giants, does not stand alone. A crucial contribution comes from how your talents, ideas, perspectives, and experiences mix with others' and contribute to the stew that becomes innovation. Your participation expands the range of ideas and creativity.

McKinsey & Company's 2020 report *Diversity Wins* shows that highly diverse leadership teams have a higher return on investment, no matter how you measure it, in the for-profit world and the nonprofit world. Diversity brings a rich variety of experiences to look at the world and to build stronger teams.

Our giants confirm this fact in the foreign policy context. As noted above, you bring a different perspective. Dr. Helene Gayle confirms, "If our voices aren't there, our foreign policy is not going to reflect a different way of thinking that sees people differently because we do have a different lens." Susan Rice reports that the diversity deficit in our national security agencies "troubled [her] mainly because [she] found that people from similar backgrounds—for instance, white male graduates of the Ivy League—tend to approach complex issues in similar ways. They might miss nuances of language and gender, while dismissing insights that others from different backgrounds might more readily embrace" (Rice 2019, 428). Diversity is fundamentally about different ideas. As Ambassador Reuben Brigety II urges, "We have to be able to engage with each other. Not so that we can be a bunch of balkanized groups who decide how we're going to divvy up the spoils amongst our various tribes. But so that we can achieve the true promise of America, that our country is a nation based on ideas, not based on backgrounds."

Ambassador Perkins worked tirelessly to expand diversity within the State Department. And he used the efficiency argument to do so. As he relates in his autobiography, *Mr. Ambassador: Warrior for Peace*, his early and successful advocacy efforts with Secretary of State Henry Kissinger rested on the argument that "bringing in more Blacks and minorities [would] help him better manage foreign policy" (Perkins 2006, 156). Later, when he was director general, Lawrence Eagleburger, then deputy secretary of state, asked for his help in ensuring the State Department remained relevant in government. Ambassador Perkins's answer? Diversity.

In these times, the salience of this diversity could not be greater. Ambassador Aurelia E. Brazeal—Rea to her friends (pronounced Ree)—provides this analysis: "I don't believe that white Americans have the coping skills to know how to be a minority. . . . You have to win an argument on its merits. You can't bring in the political argument and say, well, that trumps everything. . . . American diplomats are going to be reduced to ordinary garden type of diplomats along with every other country in the world." What makes your participation matter in this? She continues, "White Americans, in particular, will not know how to adjust to that. I think the fact that we've been a minority and we know how to be a minority gives us inroads to other cultures that are more astute, more analytical, more on target, than our other fellow Americans who may not have that experience."

Why Now?

The evidence is clear, as outlined by Ambassadors William J. Burns and Linda Thomas-Greenfield (one of our giants): "After four years of relentless attacks by the Trump administration and decades of neglect, political paralysis, and organizational drift, US diplomacy is badly broken" (Burns and Thomas-Greenfield 2020). They call for reinventing US diplomacy for a new era. They identify the lack of diversity in the diplomatic corps as "a national security crisis." This lack of diversity, they argue, "not only undermines the power of the United States' example; it also suffocates the potential of the country's diplomacy."

■ *It's hard, especially at this inflection point in our society, to convince people of color to think about the outside world, because we have such an amazing array of problems and challenges that we face in the United States.* Dr. Helene Gayle agrees and adds, "Because these issues are front and center. They're right in your face. They're things that affect you so very personally because of your own personal experience, and so it makes it harder to think about, 'Why should I be focused on the rest of the world?' But I think as the world is getting smaller and these issues are becoming more intertwined, there is even more of a reason for a young person of color to think about a global career." They—and all of our giants—believe you can integrate public service and justice work in both areas, overseas and at home, by pursuing a career in foreign policy.

► We can't stop the fight on equal and fair housing practices. We can't stop the fight on predatory lending. We can't stop the fight on better schools for our inner cities. This is just one of many things that we have to keep pushing. You have to find your space in the movement that fits you. This is a movement about much more than just police reform. This is about changing the culture of our society, breaking down systemic barriers everywhere. Our fight is multifaceted, layered, and does not end when we achieve justice for one of the many things that has oppressed Black people for generations. ■ *We're focused on police brutality today, and the reform of law enforcement, because that was the match that lit the most recent flame, but a flame has been burning for a long time because of gross inequality across our society.*

Ambassador Ruth A. Davis wants you to see "the importance of not being turned off of public service by systemic racism. It's everywhere in this country. You've got to deal with it. So you might as well deal with it when you're making a contribution to the betterment of [hu]mankind."

Justice at Home and Abroad

There are several ways you can engage in public service and justice work both at home and abroad. Justice work comes in many forms. Your particular brand may evolve over time. Ambassador Ertharin Cousin started out working domestically for legal and social justice as a lawyer in the South Side of Chicago. Emerging opportunities led her to Washington to work on a national scale, and then she was offered the opportunity to work as the White House liaison to the State Department. Her commitment to justice has not changed, but the context and particular focus have evolved with her experience and learning.

Your work for justice at home can be enhanced by your experiences working in foreign policy. All experience produces learning; you can bring lessons home. Dr. Helene Gayle says, "I'm better in what I'm doing today—which is very locally focused and really focused very much on issues of inequity in Chicago and, by extension, the United States— because of the work that I've done globally. And I think it doesn't have to be a trade-off. I think I see things differently because of having had the global experience."

You may be able to structure your assignments so you can work on domestic justice on your own time, as Ambassador Rea Brazeal did. Reflecting on her first overseas assignment from 1968 to 1971, she shared, "I would be thinking, why am I in Buenos Aires writing about the price of beef when it looks like my country's burning down?" She managed to get posted back to Washington, DC, so she could be closer to what was happening. She continued her professional work in the Foreign Service and worked on civil rights in the United States after hours.

We believe this book and its aims are important because everything we do on the global stage connects with what we do at home. We want you to walk away from this book understanding that you can have both. ▶ What you do on the global stage you can bring back to your community in a number of different ways. The fact that I know how to design programs and certain interventions for global communities is an asset that can't be overlooked. I want us to understand how this career leads to endless possibilities. You can touch upon your need to be an activist in your community and also have a voice in broader global communities. ■ *Yes. It should not be an either/or situation. You can do both. It's a matter of which direction you go in and how you find ways to complement those dual experiences.*

In the wake of the 2020 Black Lives Matter spring and summer, as we write this, more doors may be opening for your participation in US foreign policy and beyond. Aaron has received several requests to help federal agencies or development organizations in the international affairs arena to strategize about how to address today's issues concerning diversity and inclusion. Every institution is now expected to take responsibility for opening its doors. If you look at any of the statements from all the major corporations now, they're not just talking about the boardroom and management. They're talking about recruitment across the board. They're talking about supply chains, how they present themselves, their mission statements, and what they present to the world in terms of their marketing strategies.

Appeal of an International Career

Our students wanted us to ask the giants what makes them proud to be in this space. What makes them excited about being there? Ambassador Ruth A. Davis responded, "Where else could you take part in nation building? . . . Where else could you say that I was taught three or four different languages? And where else could you say that I moved and lived all around the world? And also, in all of that time, contributing to the image of the United States?"

■ *Amen to that. The chance to have a fantastic career and to see things and do things and make a difference in the world is pretty unique. The opportunity to represent the United States has always been a distinct honor for me, illustrating both the promise of America and the historical reality as a minority in our nation. I often found that my perspective was both appealing and a source of surprise and admiration for my foreign counterparts, and this was especially noteworthy during my tenure as Peace Corps director during the Barack Obama administration. As it was expressed to me in Africa, Latin America, and Asia, they believed that "I heard them" and could relate to their problems and dreams for the future; and I was perceived as a reliable partner or respected adversary.* Ambassador Davis adds, "Anybody who knows me, knows that I say that there's nothing that I would have rather done with my career." Stacy D. Williams, deputy director for the Office of the Haiti Special Coordinator at the State Department, sums it up: "There is no greater service than serving your country and seeing the world. . . . You will not find another career like this. It's hard to get in, very easy to walk away, but the experience is overwhelming and life changing completely."

You are likely to be motivated and inspired by more than one aspect, as we and our giants have been. Whether it's the personal experience of adventure, learning, and developing cross-national friendships; your own personal exploration and growth; the ability to enlarge your footprint and legacy; or the challenge and mission itself—careers in US foreign policy have a lot to offer you.

Curiosity, Seeing the World, and Living History

Some are attracted by curiosity and the opportunity to see the world and live history. It can be as simple as curiosity, as it was for Katherine Lee: "I remember as a teenager seeing a picture of a young African American lady in *Ebony Magazine* who was a Foreign Service officer in Europe. I was so impressed that she was representing the United States abroad and imagined she must be leading a very exciting life." Ambassador Johnny Young's first overseas experience sold him on the idea of an international career. He traveled to Beirut, Lebanon, representing the YMCA at a YMCA/YWCA conference at the American University of Beirut. He was awed by meeting people from all over the world, seeing their different ways of dressing, and trying different foods: "I just found that exhilarating. . . . It literally penetrated my soul at that point. I was determined from that point on that I was going to do something in the international arena."

Building relationships across these cultural differences is a large appeal. Our giants have deep friendships across the world that continue well after they leave their posts or retire. When Stacy D. Williams organized retirement celebrations for his mentors, some reported they would miss the people the most. This is true for Valerie Dickson-Horton, who reported she would most miss "helping people, seeing the world, and learning how important it is to put human upliftment above politics" (USAID 2013). She added that this career "gives you a much deeper appreciation about what the world has to offer and it allows you to grow into someone with a broader understanding of the human race" (Ibid.).

Ambassador James Joseph wants you to know that "you're a part of the larger world and you need to be engaged. [Global engagement] provides the cultural experience that I think is critical to life in the world in which we now live. And it provides a relationship and an understanding of parts of the world which we have to deal with as we move into the future." And, who knows? Perhaps you will find yourself sitting on the front lines of history as General Barrye Price describes in Box 1.2.

Box 1.2   Barrye Price: On the Front Lines of History

"I served in a unit called the Blackhorse, which was border Cavalry. It had the interzonal border that separated East and West Germany in the most likely invasion route through the Harz mountain coming into Fulda, Germany. It was the most remarkable experience, because that's really where my focus came on what it means to be an American, how special a privilege it was to be a US citizen. I really learned about American citizenship through the lens of my German counterparts being on that border. I was on the border leading a patrol when freedom prevailed on November 9, 1989.

"All of these bands were lined up at the border and there was nothing that came in from higher headquarters that told us what was going on. And then they opened the gates. But it wasn't tanks or MPs or motorized armored vehicles. It was civilian cars. There were all these blown bridges, and in subsequent days there would be an oompah band on the West side and an oompah band on the East side, where they couldn't reach each other. One would play a song, and then the other one would reciprocate. I was like, 'God, everything I had believed about the evil empire . . .' They were only East German because that's where they were when they determined the demarcation line. And it separated families. It was a perfect time to be there and to really glean a great lesson in being a great ambassador for a nation, a great lesson in citizenship and the privileges that are afforded to you as a citizen, and a great time to be an American."

Expressing Your Identity

Building relationships and expressing yourself fully may be particularly meaningful for you. Sundaa Bridgett-Jones shared, "In other contexts, I can be so many groups of people around the world. I can be Latina. I can be Brazilian. So that experience that I've received around the world where I'm not initially judged in one way or another allowed me to gain confidence. I see people celebrating African American culture around the world. Why don't I just go in and be myself? You don't have to feel like you dot every *i* and cross every *t* in these situations."

After a somewhat nomadic military upbringing, C. D. Glin shared, "Some of my siblings settled down, and, literally, once they got to a place, they wanted that sense of settling in and not moving every three or four years. And for me, it was the exact opposite—in part because I could remake myself again. I could become like a new person. I could continue to build my skill set, change personality, sort of adapt to new arenas." ■ *Given that few people of color work in global organizations, I was usually in the position of explaining America and its posture in the world, in terms of both global issues and local host-nation issues. I found that being my authentic self was always the best approach for representing the United States and the basis for forming long-lasting and worthwhile relationships.*

Opportunity for Impact

Of course, a huge motivator for a career in US foreign policy is the opportunity for impact. Working in the development arena and still in the beginning stages of her career, Verone Bernard described, "I'm part of the group of individuals who have the exciting job of being able to conceptualize and try to come up with solutions to the development challenge that has been presented to us by USAID—which is a super exciting task because it really forces you to be creative, to research and identify models that have worked in other places, and to engage with stakeholders on the ground and local partners. I love what I'm able to do every day. . . . While I remain cynical about development and its effectiveness, I am still inspired by some of the work we do, and I have been able to see firsthand how the work that we do really does transform lives."

Alonzo Fulgham, reflecting on his first experience in Haiti, still conveys that deep excitement: "You love it, or you hate it. And as you can tell by my enthusiasm, I caught the bug. Especially as a private-sector officer, because you have an opportunity to add value. . . . You start to realize what AID was trying to do in Haiti was the right thing: to build institutions, but also, while building institutions, to simultaneously create opportunities at the lower end. It was a totally integrated approach to trying to solve the problems in a country that was in desperate need of moving forward, from a development perspective. It's where I started to romanticize about what the US government could do, if you were to apply the right resources, get the policy, and you had the right leadership."

General Barrye Price lives by the dying words of his father: "'Seek impact versus impression.' What does that mean? I'm twelve years old. So my journey since then has been a life of living that purpose that he gave me. And it's a remarkable gift. Over the years I realized that impact has more to do with legacy; and impression has more to do with experience. Impression is short-lived. It's a fleeting event. But impact is me going back to Fort Polk, Louisiana, in 2015, where I started my career in 1985, and people remember me. It's making a difference. It's changing a circumstance. It's making history in people's lives." Ambassador Sylvia Stanfield put it simply: "Do you want to work for value? Or do you want to work for the bottom line, the money?"

Careers in US foreign policy afford opportunities for unique impact. Ruth A. Davis, in Box 1.3, shares one of many such opportunities from when she served as ambassador to Benin (AFSA 2016).

Influencing Policy

Some of the greatest impact comes from influencing policy. Ambassador Johnnie Carson shares his vision for what working in foreign policy means: "I, for one, do not believe that diplomacy is a passive activity. I believe that diplomacy is deeply activist in its definition. Diplomacy should be about advocacy, about advancing fundamental American values and principles, advancing US foreign policy goals and economic and commercial policy. And, fundamentally, it should be about advancing the interests of our country—those that are enshrined in our Constitution and its values and those that are sometimes transitory but very important. I think that one should be as active in speaking out on these issues as one can be, recognizing that we should always be in a listening

---

Box 1.3   Ruth A. Davis: A Lasting Impact in Benin

"My very able USAID director, Thomas Cornell, and I chose helping to restore the devastated Beninese education system as our principal aid project, with the caveat that Beninese girls, who were previously excluded, should be included in the education equation. This, of course, had a profound impact on the lives and prospects of girls and an impact on the social fabric of the country. Among many other important undertakings, we assisted in the creation of Benin's Constitutional Court and the country's equivalent of our Federal Communications Commission, in addition to supporting Benin's restructuring to a free and open market economy.

"What an exciting, extraordinary time it was for me! It was like being in the United States with Mr. Washington and Mr. Jefferson, when they were building our country and defining American values. Where else, except the Foreign Service, could I have had an impact on the evolution of democracy in a developing country?

"And if that's not enough, serving in Benin put me in touch with my ancestry. In West Africa, I visited ports from which millions of slaves were shipped to the Americas. In Ouidah, Benin, I visited the Tree of Forgetfulness, around which slaves were forced to march in a symbolic severing of ties between themselves, family, and Africa. I marched around the tree, but I did it backwards because I never want to forget."

and understanding mode first but never in a passive mode. Diplomacy is not a passive activity."

Victoria Cooper stresses that such policy influence can come from the business and citizen side of things too: "When I was president of the American Chamber [of Commerce] in Ghana, as well as helping to just build that chamber after Ron Brown came and encouraged us to do an American chamber in Ghana, I learned that congressional delegations listen to Americans overseas. They want to hear the American voices. So there are many ways to get involved. . . . You can come at this from different angles and add the foreign policy component to it." There is a great variety of work you can do in US foreign policy, in the State Department and beyond, including technical work, such as environmental engineering or climate specialization, private-sector development, religious freedom, and the arts, to name a few.

Our giants want you to engage around US policy. Alonzo Fulgham believes young people "have a responsibility to ask the questions about how they want policy for the United States government to be made in the next twenty to twenty-five years. And if they want to be a part of the process, then they can't just sit outside and scream and holler. They have to come inside, participate, and do the work." Ambassador Sylvia Stanfield asks, "Don't you want to make some of the decisions? Don't you want to have a seat at the table when we negotiate the trade agreements or intellectual property?"

Greater Opportunities for Success

Working overseas can also present greater opportunities to be successful than what you may find working domestically. Speaking to students at Southern University, one of Jennifer's former colleagues from Rutgers University, Felix L. James, stated simply, "Open the box. Open the world to yourselves. If you think the space is small in the United States, think global and look at global careers." Bob Burgess, retired senior executive at GTE Sylvania, agreed wholeheartedly: "I think that my career was made because I went overseas. I went to Trinidad and Tobago and I learned about manufacturing. And I wasn't an accountant anymore. I was the manager. I was a leader. I was the innovator. And I loved it."

Valerie Dickson-Horton says international experience just sets you apart: "Say you have somebody who is in engineering, but they also went out as a Peace Corps volunteer someplace. So, they have a technical skill that's unquestionable. And then they go out and pick up some experience through Peace Corps. And you automatically get thrown into a different category." It doesn't just set you apart; international experience is the key to leadership, as Dr. Jacob Gayle explains: "I think it's important for our Black leaders to know, whatever sector they're in today, in order for them to be in that C-suite—in that senior-most leadership—they have to take on the global world. And so whether it's doing a two-year stint in the Bahamas, or whether it's a year in China, or if it's just learning a foreign language, in order to be the leader of tomorrow today, global is the answer in every sector."

The Challenge and the Mission

Many of our giants were attracted to US foreign policy because of the challenge and the mission it represents. Representing the United States overseas includes advancing national security and economic interests, as well as values, such as human rights and democracy. It includes serving American citizens abroad. And it encompasses working with other nations to address cross-national and global challenges, such as global health, environmental degradation and climate change, and terrorism and crime. It is varied, complex, and challenging. And it inspires a sense of purpose in those who take it on.

When asked about his service as a Black US ambassador in apartheid South Africa, Edward Perkins responded, "I accepted the president's offer as an American, and as an American who believes that we should not stand as cheerleaders on the sidelines of the great issues of our time, but that we should have the courage to engage ourselves in them. I accepted this assignment as a Foreign Service officer who took an oath to go where needed, when needed" (Perkins 2006, 271–272). Ambassador Ruth A. Davis summarized her sense of purpose: "I love this country. I love it profoundly. And I always wanted to serve my country. So putting in that confidence, that love of country and not being afraid of hard work—I think that those were basically the characteristics that helped me succeed." As an ambassador, Harry K. Thomas Jr. reported being challenged daily, and every day brought something new (Xi 2013).

Managing Your Expectations

Of course, it's important to enter this arena with a realistic perspective. Katherine Lee (2005) shared that as a career counselor of new officers, she could usually tell who would last beyond one or two years in the Foreign Service. It was all based on their reasons for joining. If it was only love of travel, they might become disillusioned by the bureaucracy.

They might join hoping to serve their heritage country, but you cannot spend an entire career in one place. It's important to join the US diplomatic service because you believe in the mission described above. That sense of purpose will enable you to be flexible and provide greater opportunities for achieving a meaningful life and career. In recruiting for the Foreign Service, Ambassador Ruth A. Davis reported, "I do not sugarcoat the many challenges of a career in the Foreign Service, but tell them honestly that it offers a unique opportunity for public service that makes a difference in issues with global impact" (AFSA 2016). Despite the challenges, as the great Elijah Cummings said, "So many people come to government knowing that they're not going to make the kind of money that they would make in the private sector. But they come to government to feed their souls, to help other people, to lift them up, to make their lives better. And that's you and you and you and you" (quoted in Davidson 2019).

What Have We Learned and What's Next for You?

Collectively, our giants cover decades of much progress, setbacks, and continuous struggle. ■ *I told Ambassador Ruth A. Davis, "It struck me the challenges you took on, because you saw this whole thing evolve from the 1960s and the height of the civil rights movement to where we are today. Of course, you've faced many of the same challenges once again because these battles are, as you know, generational. You win a battle of one generation, new leadership comes in, a new generation, you've got to fight the battle all over again." From all the interviews with people I mostly have known for many years, what struck me was how much commonality there was between their journeys to the top, what they had to deal with, and how they addressed it. The commonality of the Black experience. And the fact that most of us use the same skill set to maneuver in these treacherous waters and still stay afloat, persevere, be successful, and also come out at the other end not bitter but very positive and forward-looking.*

▶ While everybody's had different experiences, their pursuit of justice, their pursuit of excellence, and the service that they've led with their entire lives are all the same. And they've all had some level of risk. And they gambled a little bit with pushing back on authority, saying, "No, we need to do this." Everything that they have been through and sacrificed allowed me to get to this moment.

The people we interviewed not only stayed true to themselves but amplified who they are, as they navigated these spaces. And they used that to their advantage in the way that they built relationships and persuaded people, especially some of the women whom we interviewed. Most impressive was their resilience: their ability to withstand the assaults and not just do their job but excel and become role models and leaders for all of us.

How do we begin to tell their stories in ways that will help you succeed? We start with where the giants' journeys began. General Price emphasized how important that is for really reaching you, our readers. As he put it, "It's very important to start with the guy who left Gary, Indiana, in 1980. Because that's the guy that they can identify with best. If they don't go through the progressive and sequential journey of my life, they can't see necessarily becoming that somebody." We cover our giants' first exposure to international affairs, the birth of their careers, the things they've accomplished on behalf of the United States, and the exquisite role models they have been and continue to be.

Their many stories and advice are organized around guideposts to help you succeed. Chapters 2 and 3 address starting out and building confidence. We review the potential sparks that can light up your interest in this career path and explore how to get there—including a discussion of the comparative advantages of attending an HBCU, various internship and fellowship opportunities, and family support. Chapter 3 looks at what happens when you arrive. What is it like to be the only? What is imposter syndrome, and how can you manage it? Our giants provide advice for gaining confidence. Chapter 4 is about how to benefit from others: networks, role models, mentors, and sponsors. Who can help you as they helped our giants? How can you find, or recognize, and accept them? What is the difference between mentoring and sponsorship? And what are your responsibilities in a mentoring relationship? In Chapter 5, we draw from our giants' advice and experience to describe how you can navigate your foreign policy career: the importance of having a vision and how to hold the reins of your career, create and seize opportunities, and make strategic choices—including taking on what may look like undesirable jobs. We will also address when race is a factor in navigating your career and how to manage performance-review processes.

In Chapter 6, our giants describe specific experiences, cautionary tales, and demonstrated skills for knowing when to fight discrimination, jerks, and other injustices and how to endure and sometimes triumph in the face of these and other challenges. In Chapter 7, we emphasize that you are not alone. Facing these challenges and life stresses requires intentional effort to construct a balanced life with support from others and beyond your job. We pushed the giants to address that tired old stigma against talking about mental health to share with you their coping mechanisms. They stress the importance of seeking support when you need it, connecting with your peers, building support networks, and nurturing your life outside work. In Chapter 8 we address how to do all of the above and also be all of who you are: how to understand and capitalize on the advantages of your identity, how to balance your professional and personal identities, and how to be your authentic self.

Chapter 9 addresses the triumphs and challenges of leadership. In sharing their own stories and experiences, the giants illustrate the components of skillful leadership: being responsible, building your team, innovating, and creating a followership. They provide guidance on how to sustain the right attitude to be successful, to weather inevitable setbacks, and to be resilient. Chapter 10 is the giants' and our final gift to you. We summarize the elements of success gleaned from these many experiences. The giants then provide their charge to you—what they expect from you as you pursue and excel in following their path of meaningful careers in international public service. We conclude with a symbolic passing of the torch to you and your generation. Aaron will present his final charge to you, and Taylor will have the last word, responding to that charge and making one herself to you, her peers.

The giants are inspiring, no doubt. But, as Taylor intended, some of this is tough stuff. We are so grateful to the giants for their willingness to share their strengths and vulnerabilities. Every one of our giants shares a commitment to supporting the generation coming behind them. Several of our giants have served as diplomats in residence and/or served in universities to mentor in other ways. For some of our giants in the making, the project has afforded an opportunity to give back. Aaron had already modeled for them what it means to support the next generation. C. D. Glin said, "To be asked and to just know that this is such an important project by such an important man whom I have called on in every instance of transition probably over the past fifteen years in one way or another, it definitely was humbling and an honor." In reflecting on Aaron's mentorship of her and others, like Paul Weisenfeld, Sundaa Bridgett-Jones shared, "We need to do that for Taylor and others— invite them in our homes and let them see both our achievements and our vulnerabilities."

Our giants—no matter how old or experienced—have one very important thing in common: They all want to see more of you in this arena and in leadership positions. They want to see and help you succeed. And so they were willing to talk about the good, the bad, and the ugly. And they were willing to move outside their comfort zone to do so. Ambassador Johnny Young told us, "I hate to talk about myself, really. There's nothing that I dislike more." We told them, we want this to be informal, like you're talking to friends. You don't know that they are your friends, but by the end of the book, we want you to feel like they—our giants—are your friends. This book is their gift, and it is our gift to you.

Notes

1. See "African-American Ambassadors," Association for Diplomatic Studies and Training, April 2016, https://adst.org/african-american-ambassadors.

2. These are foreign service recruitment programs offering graduate school assistance, paid internships and special trainings, and a guaranteed job for qualified participants. See Chapter 2.

3. Carolyn R. Payton was the first Black director of Peace Corps (1977–1978), when it was a part of ACTION, a consolidated service agency that included Peace Corps, Vista, and other service programs.

2

Starting Out

New things lie in front of moving feet.

—African proverb

Thinking about the giants and their achievements can make the prospects of a career in US foreign policy seem daunting. That's why General Barrye Price stressed the need for us to lead with the beginnings of their stories. When our giants started, their situations were not much different from where you are now. There was a time when they had no idea about the rest of the world. They might have developed some interest in the broader world but never imagined they could make a career from that. Even as they determined they wanted to explore the possibility, many faced the challenge of getting their families on board—it's hard for parents to contemplate their sons and daughters venturing into waters they themselves are unfamiliar with, especially onto paths that take their children far from home. Our giants confronted the familiar choices of where to go to college and, notably, whether or not attending a historically Black college or university (HBCU) would help them on this particular professional journey. And once they graduated, like all of us, they faced the question "Now what?"

Starting out in international affairs begins with a spark to light your interest, extends to deciding where to go for college and graduate school, and encompasses accessing study abroad and other internship and preparatory experiences. Of course, it also includes figuring out what to do once you graduate from college. And you may also be wondering how in the world you can convince your family this is a good idea. We address each of those topics in what follows.

The Spark

Collectively, the giants represent many common experiences. The sparks that ignited their interest in international affairs include the influence of early experiences and exposure in childhood—perhaps from their heritage, travels abroad, and news and current events—and the enthusiasm and support of key teachers, professors, and family members.

Some of you may have already had early experience traveling overseas and being exposed to how people live differently. C. D. Glin experienced that through his overseas military upbringing. Others, like Verone Bernard and Paul Weisenfeld, experienced it through connections to their heritage. Still others, like Ambassadors Johnny Young and Rea Brazeal, benefited from overseas leadership programs at an early age. Such early exposure can spark a curiosity and even a passion for learning more about how things are done differently in other places. And meeting our counterparts abroad can also inspire us to aspire to do more, as was the case for Rea Brazeal (see Box 2.1).

Box 2.1   Rea Brazeal: Meeting Youth Leaders Abroad and Aspiring to Be More

---

Ambassador Rea Brazeal had the opportunity to participate in the Encampment for Citizenship (EFC) in Puerto Rico in 1963. EFC, according to its website, is a residential summer program designed to give youth leaders "a compelling experience in democratic living, with emphasis on critical thinking and social action." She reported, "I was taken by the fact that the Latin American attendees could stand up in front of the group and say, 'As a future leader of my country, I'm here to tell you X, Y, Z.' And I would sit there and say, 'Hmm, now I don't feel I could stand up and say, as a future leader of my country.' So what makes these people tick? What cultural values do they have that they would feel that way at age 17, 18, 19, or however old we were? And so I became interested in Latin America and Latin American studies. That opened the door early in my life."

In some cases, early exposure to international affairs may inspire questions about why some people abroad—perhaps including relatives—don't experience the same quality of life and opportunities as you may have in the United States. Witnessing depravation firsthand can simultaneously inspire a desire to help and a sense of pride and privilege as a US citizen. Verone Bernard shared, "My parents grew up very poor, both of them orphans at some point in their childhood or in their adolescence. They both came to the US from Haiti, searching for the American dream of a better life. My earliest recollections of knowing there was home outside home or a world larger than the neighborhood that I lived in are vivid memories of my mom recording, rerecording, and sending cassette tapes back to her sisters in Haiti to share *nouvels* (news or gossip). It was years later when I realized they recorded tapes instead of writing letters to share stories because they all struggled with literacy. It was also around that time when I realized that it was likely my family were direct beneficiaries of USAID and other international aid."

Paul Weisenfeld reminds us, in Box 2.2, to take these experiences and inspirations and also to be flexible in finding the best fit for you in terms of how you will express related service objectives professionally.

**Box 2.2   Paul Weisenfeld:
            Early Experience and Redirection**

Paul Weisenfeld had an interest in international affairs very early on. His mother is from Trinidad and Tobago, and as he put it, "She used to send us down to Tobago to get disciplined from her mom when we were young." He also spent summers in Tobago and learned how differently people live in the world.

His specific interest in an international career was sparked by the antiapartheid movement while he was at Queens College. The movement inspired him to become a lawyer. While in law school, he met Navi Pillay, a South African lawyer who was on a one-year master of laws program at Harvard. After his first year of law school, in 1985, Paul spent the summer working for her in South Africa. Hers was a human rights law firm, and they were suing the apartheid government. She sent him all around the country taking depositions. It was a violent summer in South Africa. Paul attended the big demonstrations, some of which started

continues

Box 2.2   Continued

as big funerals for killed activists. He was chased by police. Navi Pillay eventually became the first South African judge on the International Human Rights Court.

Some of these travels took him to KwaZulu-Natal, where he saw grinding poverty. "The day-to-day thing people were worried about in KwaZulu-Natal was, 'Can I get water?'" It reminded him of Tobago, though much worse. The experience steered him toward a different course: "I went to South Africa thinking I wanted to be a human rights lawyer. I had this great internship in the prime human rights case in the world. And I left thinking I don't want to be a human rights worker. I want to go into development." He worked for four years in law firms to pay off his student loans, and then he joined USAID.

He had written his law school dissertation on land tenure security in Zimbabwe. "And that's how I got into land and agriculture issues. So, that became my entry point into doing technical work." When he joined USAID, he was assigned as a lawyer for the Office of Housing and Urban Development.

Paul was fortunate to live history in South Africa.

Early exposure to different ideas and experience, including news coverage and current events, were the sparks for Dr. Katherine Lee and Ambassador Sylvia Stanfield. But it was their love of language that accelerated their paths and became the key to opening doors in their professional careers (see Box 2.3).

Ambassador Gina Abercrombie-Winstanley was similarly attracted to different languages. While in high school she decided she wanted to learn something completely new and different: Hebrew. She later learned Arabic as a Peace Corps volunteer in Oman.

▶ At ten years old, visiting Rio de Janeiro, I knew that my life and career would be bigger than what I had come to know and love back in Chicago. As a tenth birthday present, my mother took me on a two-week vacation to Brazil. We traveled throughout the country, learning about the history of Afro-Brazilians and their many contributions to the Brazilian culture. That trip was so important for me. Beyond the fact that it was a pretty cool way to spend my tenth birthday, I was able to visualize a life outside the South Side of Chicago and see how I could make my impact on the world. I was energized by the culture, the food, and the people. It also gave me an opportunity to see the world differently and ask questions I would never even think to ask had I not left my small world in Chicago.

**Box 2.3   Katherine Lee and Sylvia Stanfield:
Love of Language as the Door and the Key**

Katherine Lee

Dr. Katherine Lee grew up on the campus of Alabama A&M University. She was in the audience there when Ralph Bunche came to talk about the United Nations, when Marian Anderson, the great opera singer, performed, and when the poet Langston Hughes lectured. She and her sister helped their two brothers on their paper routes by delivering newspapers in the women's dorms. "The headlines sometimes made me stop in my tracks, such as when they reported the Supreme Court had outlawed segregation in public schools or the USSR had launched Sputnik."

Her entrée into international affairs started with her fascination with language. She thought she would study math and that German would be a good foreign language for that. Between her freshman and sophomore years at Fisk University, she had the opportunity to spend six weeks in Scandinavia with the Scandinavian International Institute. In an effort to diversify their program, they heavily subsidized the opportunity for the top-ranking male and female in the freshman class. "One day, the two of us and about four or five students from other countries were on a bicycle trip out in the farm areas, and a thunderstorm came. We were under a tree and the farmer's wife came out and invited us in. None of us spoke a Scandinavian language and none of them spoke English. The common language was my little one year of German that I had taken. And I thought, 'Oh, what a wonderful experience. We are communicating, and it's because of me.'"

When she returned to Fisk, she changed her major to German. She went on to pursue a PhD in German and eventually joined the US Information Agency.

Sylvia Stanfield

Ambassador Sylvia Stanfield grew up during the Korean War. She was fascinated by the news reports of fighting "the red Chinese." "I was always curious about why are they red Chinese? Why are they communists? There was very little about this in our classes." She was also fascinated with the Chinese culture and the musical language, the tones. "What do these little symbols mean? Where can I learn them? I'd like to learn how to decipher all of this." She focused class assignments on international- and China-related topics whenever she could. She chose a college with an international focus, Western College for Women, and fortunately for her, she had a professor who was American but had been born and raised in China.

continues

Box 2.3   Continued

When she finished college, she applied for a fellowship with the East-West Center, a program set up under Lyndon Johnson's presidency to increase understanding and cultural exchanges between the peoples of Asia and the United States. The program funded her master's in Asian studies at the University of Hawaii. Through the program, she did more Chinese-language study at the University of Hong Kong's School of Oriental Studies and Linguistics, then traveled with her housemates throughout Asia. Upon her return, she was convinced she wanted to join the State Department. "I was certainly a little oddity, right? I was Black, female and spoke an Asian language." Her language skills opened the door to her first overseas assignments as a vice consul with our then embassy in Taiwan and later as a political officer with the US consulate general in Hong Kong and the US embassy in Beijing.

Twenty years later, I am still asking those questions in pursuit of making a difference in the world, as my ten-year-old self sought out to do.

Comparative Advantages of a Historically Black College or University

Once the interest is there, even if it hasn't fully developed yet, the next step is education: Where should you go to college to develop these interests and lay the groundwork for a related career? We want to pause in the telling of our giants' journeys to address a question that may be on your mind if you haven't yet decided where to go for college: Should you go to a historically Black college or university or select from primarily white institutions? Ten of the giants we interviewed opted to attend an HBCU (Fisk, Howard, Southern, Spellman, and Texas Southern). Many of the giants shared perspectives on the comparative advantages and potential disadvantages of attending an HBCU. As they collectively demonstrate, there is no one path or right answer, but we thought you would benefit from considering these varied perspectives.

Some of our giants, like Ambassador Rea Brazeal, were deeply immersed in the HBCU experience their whole lives. As Brazeal describes in Box 2.4, for her, the choice was clear.

Box 2.4   Rea Brazeal: HBCUs All the Way

Ambassador Rea Brazeal is a second-generation graduate of Spelman. Her mother started there in elementary school and completed college there. After obtaining her master's, she taught at Spelman and was director of alumni affairs for the rest of her life. Brazeal's father, who was the second or third Black to get a PhD in economics (Columbia University), graduated from Morehouse College and became its dean. Her parents met while they were undergraduates at Spelman and Morehouse.

In her oral history Rea encouraged young people to go to an HBCU as she did. Beyond her family ties, she shared, "it seemed to me that I was going to be part of a [B]lack community for my life, so I chose to go to a [B]lack school. . . . Moreover, in an HBCU you are not seen as a stereotype, you can be yourself, with the chance to grow or make mistakes but as an individual, not a part of a race. . . . Because you can find that confidence in yourself without the distractions of having to deal with the structural inequities built into the larger system, you can explore and make mistakes and fail without being seen as a permanent failure of the race, of the class, of the group, of the gender, of the whatever. You have more of a chance, I think, for growth and hopefully for beginning to be a thinking individual."

She added, "Another strength of education at HBCUs is the fact that people can learn about their own culture that you don't get—at least, certainly, when I came through college—from the national textbooks that were being used—knowledge about the contributions Black people have made and a sense of your own history and your place in it. And you do make your friends for life in college, frequently. And so to me that was important."

For others the choice was not so clear. Lauri Fitz-Pegado's parents met and married while at Howard University, but she opted to go to Vassar College. Some were advised by close mentors to attend an HBCU, others to attend a primarily white institution (PWI). Verone Bernard grew up in Mattapan, a predominantly Black neighborhood in Boston, and attended a charter school on the Northeastern University campus. She observed her sister's experience at Boston College. She recalled telling her counselor, "'I do not want to go to an HBCU. I love my people. I've been around them forever. I want to go to a PWI because my sister's getting invited to these yacht parties and I want to go to one of them.' I was young and was convinced that the Black experience was monolithic. What could I get from an HBCU that I couldn't get from Mattapan?" But with the strong support of her mentor, she "made the leap to come to Howard, to come to DC, and it was the best decision that I could have ever made."

Ambassador Johnnie Carson recognized Howard as "a great institution that has produced some stellar people," but he was advised to go to a PWI. He developed a mentoring relationship with his boss when he worked summers at the Chicago Public Library. His mentor advised him, "Don't go to a really big place." And "don't go to an all-Black school because things are changing." His mentor had gone to the University of Iowa and pointed out it was close, but too big. Johnnie ended up at Drake University, a midsized liberal arts university in Des Moines, Iowa. "I was far enough away from home to say I had left, but close enough to home to run back if I encountered any difficulties." Similarly, Ambassador Harry K. Thomas Jr. knew he needed a small college. Both his parents had gone to HBCUs. His mother wanted him to go to Howard. His father wanted to him to go to a PWI. He visited College of the Holy Cross in Worcester, Massachusetts, and really liked it. So that was that. Sanola A. Daley's parents told her not to apply to Howard. Her mother advised, "You are leaving Jamaica to go to college. You grew up with Black people. You don't need to go to a Black school. Go somewhere else, meet other people, and then you can always go to Howard if you want to go to grad school." She opted for New York University because it was the closest university to the United Nations, where she thought she wanted to work one day.

Taylor initially thought she didn't like Howard and would go somewhere else. ▶ My love affair with Howard was one that came in time. My mother wanted me to go to Howard, but I wanted to explore my options. My summer as a congressional page for Congressman Bobby Rush sealed the deal that DC would be my new home post high school. Chicago is a global city for many reasons, but I had never had the opportunity to explore my interests in foreign policy and see what a life in that career looked like until I came to DC. I didn't get into my first-choice school, and Howard became my home.

Howard, for so many, is a safe haven. In the beginning it was like reverse culture shock. For the first time in my life, I was around so many different Black people. It was exciting and overwhelming all at once. My years at Howard allowed me to grow—to make mistakes, fall down, get back up, and do it all over again under the supervision of some of the most brilliant teachers and students. Iron sharpens iron, and there were many days where I would leave class with my ego bruised because I had been outdebated by a classmate. Sitting on the sidelines was not an option. Everyone had an opinion, and it would be heard. Interactions such as these empowered me to go after opportunities that some may have thought were out of reach. If nothing else, Howard gave me the confidence to be bold and unapologetic and take my place in the world because I mattered.

At Howard we are taught to be proud of ourselves and honor the differences that make us who we are. I am so grateful for the countless professors and administrators who took an interest in me. It's one of the few places in my world that I have never had to tone down my Blackness. We were expected to be 100 percent authentically who we are, and we were constantly celebrated for it. When you come to an HBCU, you are forever changed by a culture that is uniquely our own and transformed by people representing the beauty of the diaspora. This was definitely C. D. Glin's experience, as described in Box 2.5.

Box 2.5   C. D. Glin: Activating an African Identity

C. D. Glin's father was in the air force. He was born in upstate New York, and from ages four to eighteen he lived mostly at US military bases in western Europe: Italy, England, and the Azores (Portugal). But his European living experience was all in the bubble of the US military, on air force bases. He longed for integration in local cultures. He shared, "I always felt like I missed something, even though I loved the international exposure and it gave me the travel bug." In Europe, the locals assumed he was from Africa, inspiring in him a connection to a larger African experience. It was a positive experience for him, to be seen as different, in the sense of being unique, special.

At the same time, it inspired a deep craving to understand the Black experience in America. Howard University provided the ideal context, with all the diversity of the Black experience represented. Howard gave him the opportunity to, as he puts it, "demonstrate my interest." He believes people should do more than just state an interest, for example, in international work: "There has to be something that you've actioned, if you were really serious about it."

C. D. studied political science with a minor in African studies. "I started really seeing the linkage of being Black in America with being Black in the world and what that really meant and how important it was to have this connection." In his sophomore year, he interned at TransAfrica, an advocacy organization focusing on US policy toward Africa, the Caribbean, and the African diaspora more broadly. "There's a fifty-year span in America of separate but equal, *Plessy v. Ferguson* to

continues

Box 2.5   Continued

Brown v. Board of Education. I looked at this almost fifty-year span of apartheid to antiapartheid, and I was like, there's this connection with American foreign policy in Africa." A year later, he interned at the Democratic Leadership Council.

"I always wanted to demonstrate this interest. Howard really nurtured that, really said, 'You're allowed to be you, who you are and your panoply, your diversity of who you are. Be all of those C. D. Glins. Howard gave me that ability to sort of be intellectually radical, but to wear a suit and tie and to be able to almost infiltrate environments, to talk about these ideas in ways that I otherwise wouldn't have been able to."

The Howard commencement speaker the year C. D. graduated was Richard (Dick) Parsons, of AOL-Time Warner. Twenty or so years later, C. D. Glin joined the Rockefeller Foundation, when Dick Parsons was the chair of its board.

So what will best prepare you to work in the predominately white spaces that still make up US foreign policy? Maybe you need the smaller university setting and a more personal touch, HBCU or otherwise, like Harry K. Thomas Jr. and Johnnie Carson. Maybe funding will entice you to step out of your comfort zone, like Ed Grier, who received a full ride from Duquesne University because it was trying to diversify its student body. Maybe you need to build your confidence in total embrace of your Black identity before immersing yourself as an only in a particular professional setting. Maybe you are plenty confident already but recognize the uniqueness of an HBCU experience, and you want that before you live and work in a more mixed society. It is true that the HBCU experience is a bubble of Blackness that is rare in American society. ▶ Admittedly, after graduating from Howard, stepping out of that safe haven and going into a world that really doesn't care about what I think and my perspective shocked me a little bit.

One theme across all of these experiences, as well as your own to be sure, is that challenges make us stronger, whether that means adjusting to a mixed and possibly hostile environment at the outset or at the end of an identity-affirming safe bubble when you start your professional career. Ambassador Linda Thomas-Greenfield opted for the former in the extreme. And it paid off (see Box 2.6).

Box 2.6   Linda Thomas-Greenfield: Forging Her Own Path

Ambassador Linda Thomas-Greenfield had other reasons not to attend an HBCU. Southern University was only four miles from her home, and everyone expected her to go there, as almost all of her classmates did. "I just wanted to get away from the people that I was with every day. I wanted to move in a different direction." She decided to attend the fairly recently integrated Louisiana State University (LSU) instead. From the early 1960s to 1970, LSU had only admitted a handful of Blacks. Ambassador Thomas-Greenfield was among several hundred Blacks admitted in 1970 as a result of a lawsuit. Black students were still intentionally isolated, rooming together, with only one shared room on each dormitory floor.

"My goal was to finish because there were a lot of naysayers. There were the naysayers at LSU who felt that: I shouldn't be there; I wasn't capable; and just give her a chance and she'll flunk out. That's what they felt about all of us. Then there were the naysayers in my community like, 'Who does she think she is?' Then I had my family members kind of sitting on the edges of their chairs, hoping that I would succeed and not embarrass them."

One of her professors used the N-word in class. She and two classmates complained and were laughed at. Then she received an F on a philosophy test. "I don't think I'd ever even made a C before. And so I was devastated by the F. And I was stupid enough to believe that I had not done something that would get me a better grade. So I went to see the professor to find out what I needed to do to improve my grade. And he said, 'You can't improve this grade. You don't belong here.' And so if I had bowed to that, I probably would have dropped out. But I went on and changed my major."

The major she was pushed into, because it did not require the philosophy course, was political science. "I think that was the decision that eventually launched me into international relations, because I met a professor from the University of Wisconsin who was teaching at LSU. She was an amazing woman. And she encouraged me to apply to graduate school at the University of Wisconsin."

The rest, as they say, is history. Ambassador Thomas-Greenfield completed her master's in public administration at the University of Wisconsin, and with the encouragement of a professor, Africa expert Crawford Young, she began a PhD program. She traveled to Liberia for dissertation research and met people who worked at the US embassy, including her future husband. She soon discovered she really did not enjoy teaching, so she entered the Foreign Service.

Accessing Study Abroad, Internship, and Preparatory Opportunities

Translating the initial spark of interest into a career is not necessarily easy. Gaining professionally relevant experience early is challenging but important. Everyone will tell you that if you want a career in international affairs, you need to seek overseas experiences, like study abroad, as early and often as you can. And nowadays, for any career, you need to make sure you are amassing some professional experience through internships before you graduate from college. Some of our giants managed this through internship and fellowship programs concurrent with their college study. Others accessed the necessary experience after college, through programs like the Peace Corps and Operation Crossroads Africa. Some of our giants did all of the above.

Some internships and fellowships are very specific and may represent unique opportunities. Paul Weisenfeld's internship with Navi Pillay was unique to its time and place. The Scandinavian International Institute offered funding for Katherine Lee's overseas experience, targeting top students from Fisk. Other opportunities may be specific to a university, such as the East-West Center at the University of Hawaii. The Merrill Scholarship for overseas study, which Ambassador Ruth A. Davis received, is still available to students from Morehouse and Spelman. Your university should be able to provide information on other study-abroad opportunities. More immersive experiences are still accessible, including short-term opportunities like the Encampment for Citizenship and Operation Crossroads Africa and longer commitments like the Peace Corps.

Internships

There are lots of factors to consider when looking at internship options. Of course, paid internship programs are the most appealing, but these can be competitive and place based. Attending a university in a large city provides greater potential for finding an internship with a professionally relevant organization—paid or otherwise. Sanola A. Daley benefited from a short-term consultancy at the Organization of American States (OAS), just across the street from the Elliott School of International Affairs at George Washington University, where she was a graduate student. It was initially for three months, but she ended up staying a year and a half and amassing significant experience and important mentors.

But these opportunities are not the exclusive domain of Washington, DC, or New York City. Some cities may offer fewer opportunities, but opportunities nonetheless. Virtual internships were already on the rise before the early 2020s pandemic. These can be beneficial and are better than no internships at all, but they do not provide the same advantage of more complete immersion in an organization with opportunities for hallway conversations and informal networking. Internships focused on local public service are also very valuable, especially if they help you to develop and demonstrate management and leadership ability.

You can overcome geographic limitations by pursuing summer internships in other places. The most advantageous ones are those in headquarters cities like Washington, DC, or, better yet, overseas. Both the State Department and USAID provide short-term internships, as do many US-based international development NGOs and other government contractors. Following his military service, Ambassador Ed Perkins had an internship with USAID before he joined the Foreign Service in the State Department.

Any internship, whether paid or not, should be worth the investment of your time and the other opportunities you forgo to take it. You should be wary of internships that are short on professional experience and skill building. There is still something to be said for learning an organization and its work from the ground up. But if you end up working in isolation and only doing photocopying, you might miss other opportunities that would have been more beneficial. All internships involve some grunt work. The key is to outweigh the grunt work with other experiences, including leveraging where you are to build professional contacts. And you should ask what you can do to help rather than just waiting to be told what to do. You can look for needs you can fill and volunteer to work extra hours on things you are particularly interested in.

Gaining professional experience becomes particularly important when you are in graduate school. Employers will expect you to be career ready when you graduate, even for entry-level positions. Many graduate programs offer a practicum experience as part of the curriculum. Taylor experienced this through the international development studies master's program at the Elliott School of International Affairs. Her capstone experience included a consultancy for the US-ASEAN (Association of Southeast Asian Nations) Business Council and related travel to Vietnam and Thailand.

But let's face it, many of these internships are not for pay. And some of you may need to be working just to get through school. While important as an investment in your future self and career, they may still be out of reach.

▶ I got my acceptance letter from Howard on Christmas Eve, and they gave me a full ride. But I sat on it for months. Too long. I lost the full ride. Honestly, having to work through college prepared me to take on anything and everything that was thrown at me. I never knew what it meant to truly hustle until I got to college. I was able to piece together grants and small scholarships to cover about 50 percent of my tuition. The rest was up to me. Every year, I had to sing for my supper, in a sense, to secure my financial future at the university. Every scholarship or grant I received was a small win. It showed me a no can turn into a yes, and I am in control of my journey. Every internship and on-campus job I had throughout college in some way got me to where I am today. While I would have loved to just be a student and immerse myself in the full student experience, I gained a level of self-reliance and fearlessness to make things happen by any means necessary.

Paul Weisenfeld recognized his advantages: "My family wasn't poor, but I couldn't have taken an unpaid internship when I was in college. The internship I had in South Africa was compensated. It was funded by the law school. So getting into Harvard was my ticket. At the time I got into Harvard, they told me I was the first student ever from Queens College to get into Harvard Law School. If you have the right pedigree schools, and like me, I think because I spent the summer in South Africa doing interesting work, that made me look interesting on paper. If you come from a disadvantaged background, it's harder to get those extracurricular activities that make your resume stand out."

Peace Corps and Other Overseas Service Opportunities

Overseas professional experiences are the golden ticket—the longer, more immersive, and more work related the better. Fortunately, some of them, like the Peace Corps, support you during your service and may even provide a stipend and other benefits afterward. Like a lot of our giants, Ambassador Johnnie Carson had a formative college experience, but he did not have the resources to study abroad as other students did. His answer was to teach himself as much as possible. As he shares in Box 2.7, eventually the Peace Corps was his ticket to an international career.

Box 2.7 Johnnie Carson: Self-Study and the Peace Corps

Ambassador Johnnie Carson's international interest kicked in with the inauguration of John F. Kennedy as president and the establishment of the Peace Corps. He reports, "I'm still moved by Kennedy's charge to all Americans, but especially young Americans. 'Ask not what your country can do for you, but what you can do for your country.' I was caught up in the notion that we should all go forth and do something good and active and positive. And so that was a driving force."

Ambassador Carson confessed that he had "a little bit of jealousy. I saw people going for a year of overseas study or six months of overseas study. That was totally beyond anything that I could ever do. I was barely surviving financially in college." And so he read voraciously, particularly about changes in Africa and the Middle East. His reading included the dispatches of Smith Hempstone, who was then a foreign correspondent for the *Chicago Daily News* and later ambassador to Kenya (1989–1993). Carson would follow him as ambassador to Kenya in 1999.

Ultimately, he determined to join the Peace Corps. "I thought this could fulfill a number of my goals. Here's an opportunity to travel overseas, an opportunity to expand my knowledge of a part of the world which I was interested in, Africa, and an opportunity to learn a language and to develop some strong historical and cultural understanding and knowledge of the continent. I thought I would also, when I came back from that, either be in a stronger position to go into a graduate program in history, politics, or economics or to go on to law school. And also, people said this would be an opportunity to really enhance my credentials." He graduated in May 1965, and by June 2 he was in a Peace Corps training program en route to Tanzania. He taught English, history, and science in a very remote village.

During his three years of service, he traveled around and talked to a lot of people, including Foreign Service officers. He recalled it was "maybe in conversations with people over beers, when they said, 'Look, you should go into the Foreign Service. This is what you should do. You should find a way to stay in Africa, to do something on the ground here.'" He heard this from several people in the embassy, in Dar es Salaam, some of whom were only five to eight years older. But "they could see the level of interest. And so there was a really strong push."

By 1969, Johnnie Carson was entering the Foreign Service. He would later serve as ambassador to Uganda, Zimbabwe, and Kenya and as assistant secretary of state for African affairs.

Johnnie Carson was not the only one of our giants who got started through the Peace Corps. Others include Gina Abercrombie-Winstanley (Oman), Valerie Dickson-Horton (Sierra Leone and Liberia), Alonzo Fulgham (Haiti), and C. D. Glin (South Africa). Of course, Aaron (Dominican Republic) and Taylor (Senegal) both got their starts in the Peace Corps too. ▶ As for so many of our giants, the Peace Corps was the beginning of my journey in this industry. I am proud to be able to continue that legacy and increase the visibility of Black Peace Corps volunteers. The motto that this will be the toughest job you will ever love is still true to this day. I gained so much insight into international development but also gained a different understanding about my place in the world as a Black woman.

■ *As a US government agency, the Peace Corps has sometimes been criticized as being part of American imperialism. I strongly disagree with this view, and I believe that the beauty and inherent value of the Peace Corps is that it provides a different approach to American overseas engagement. Volunteers live in local communities, speak the national and local languages, and have great respect for the culture of the country. Working at the grassroots level for two or more years, Peace Corps volunteers have a unique platform for acquiring cultural agility. They have the opportunity to build relationships, to understand the priorities of the communities and organizations that they work with, and to play a role in assisting these communities to reach their goals. This special connection to the people they serve is the essence of Peace Corps service, where mutual learning and understanding occurs and the volunteer gains the ability to actually be engaged in the hands-on development process.*

▶ The Peace Corps experience that Aaron speaks of is one that I and many other Black volunteers have lived, but it was not without its challenges. As a Black female volunteer in a northern rural village in Senegal, I was constantly questioned about my nationality and the complexion of my parents' skin, devalued by my counterparts, and seen as inferior to my white colleagues. This experience is quite common for Black volunteers, especially those serving in African nations. The resources provided to me during my service lacked the depth and specificity needed to address my concerns as a young Black American woman living in Africa. Though I faced obstacles that could have been prevented, I am hopeful for the future due to the resources that the agency is putting toward the retention of Black volunteers, specifically around safety and security.

■ *Serving as a Peace Corps volunteer is often difficult, complicated, and self-revealing. Clearly challenges do exist, especially for minority volunteers whose authenticity as "real Americans" is often questioned. However, this gauntlet of sometimes complex situations is part of the transformative experience that can become a building block for the future in terms of one's career. Through this crucible you will be tested, and it can provide you with a newfound resilience, enhanced self-*

awareness, and contextual expertise that rarely can be obtained if one merely had work experience in the United States. If your career goal is to become a global citizen, then this is precisely the type of experience that will challenge you and provide a pathway to professional success and the ability to thrive in this global community.

If the Peace Corps is a longer-term commitment than you are interested in, or if you want to start with something a bit shorter, other opportunities may be available, for example, through your church or other organizations, like the Jesuit Volunteer Corps. Many Black Americans have benefited enormously from participating in Operation Crossroads Africa—both gaining international exposure and also exploring their African roots. Ambassador James Joseph's first overseas opportunity was leading a Crossroads trip to Ghana in 1965. It expanded his interest in Africa beyond South Africa. He began to engage with the NGO Africare and focus attention continent-wide. For Dr. Helene Gayle, Operation Crossroads Africa was a formative experience (see Box 2.8).

Box 2.8 Helene Gayle: Operation Crossroads Africa and a Public Health Career

"When I was in college, there was the Black Student Union, and there were African diaspora organizations as well. So I got very involved with the Caribbean students and the African students, and that was also very important to me in terms of starting to have an experience with African peoples from all parts of the world. And so, my year between finishing my studies for premed and medical school, I went to Crossroads Africa. It was my first international trip other than Canada." Dr. Gayle went to Togo in 1977.

"There are so many memories from that experience. It was great. It piqued for me a real interest. Part of my interest in medicine all along was to be able to have a career that would allow me to also be international and to be able to have something very tangible that would translate into something I could do in the US but also something I could do internationally."

After finishing her training in pediatrics, when she joined the Centers for Disease Control and Prevention (CDC), she opted to join the nutrition division, knowing they did a lot of global health work. In her first year, she traveled to Burkina Faso to do a nutrition assessment during a drought in the Sahel. "We were sent there to do a nutrition assessment so that USAID could figure out how much food they needed to send to

continues

Box 2.8   Continued

different countries." She next served in CDC's international health program office, working on a USAID-funded Child Survival Program, which included travel to several African countries. Despite the politics at the time, she then chose to work on HIV/AIDS, believing it would provide an opportunity to contribute both internationally and domestically. She rose to the helm of CDC's International AIDS Program and then got recruited to USAID as its AIDS coordinator and chief of the HIV/AIDS Division. She subsequently returned to CDC to lead a new center created to focus on HIV/AIDS and related infectious diseases, making her the first Black American to lead a center at CDC.

Specialized Recruitment Programs/Fellowships

There are several fellowship programs specifically for recruitment into public service, some of which are specific to international affairs and some targeted to minorities and the disadvantaged. The broadest is perhaps the Presidential Management Fellows (PMF) program, a leadership development program for recruiting master's graduates into the federal government. Sundaa Bridgett-Jones entered USAID through this program in 1995, and Stacy D. Williams similarly started his career at the State Department in the 1997 cohort. You are only eligible to apply to the PMF Program within two years of completing your master's degree.

The most generous packages cover undergraduate or graduate tuition and offer summer internships and other training en route to federal government service. Lauri Fitz-Pegado benefited from the Federal Junior Fellows Program, which targeted promising minorities. It provided paid summer internships and training for a possible position after college graduation. Through the program, she got her feet wet in public service, completing internships at the Department of Health, Education, and Welfare (now Health and Human Services) and the US Information Agency (USIA), working for Voice of America. People she met there encouraged her to take the Foreign Service exam. While awaiting the start of her junior officer class, she worked in USIA's Foreign Service personnel and training offices.

Some of these programs have ended, and some have been renewed in different forms. Today's prominent Foreign Service recruitment programs offering graduate school assistance, paid internships and special trainings, and a guaranteed job for qualified participants are the Thomas R. Pickering Foreign Affairs Fellowship Program, the Charles B. Rangel International Affairs Program for the State Department, and the USAID Donald M. Payne International Development Graduate Fellowship Program. Ambassadors Rea Brazeal and Ruth A. Davis benefited from Pickering's predecessor, the Foreign Affairs Fellows Program, then funded by the Ford Foundation. The program helped to fund Rea Brazeal's master's degree at Columbia University. Valerie Dickson-Horton benefited from an earlier version of the Payne fellowship, then called the International Development Internship Program. These programs survive as the Pickering, Rangel, and Payne fellowships, thanks to the hard work of Ambassadors Ed Perkins, Ruth A. Davis, and Harry K. Thomas Jr. during their service as directors general of the State Department, as well as a broader support network of other Black Foreign Service officers, including members of the Thursday Luncheon Group (TLG), an affinity support group aimed at increasing the participation of African Americans and other minorities in US foreign policy, and the Black Caucus.

Bringing Opportunities Together

So, you see, there are many professional development opportunities. And they are not mutually exclusive. They can be strategically combined in sequence to provide an ever-deepening immersion into the professional field of international affairs. In Box 2.9, Ambassador Ruth A. Davis and Stacy D. Williams demonstrate this pathway.

**Box 2.9   Ruth A. Davis and Stacy D. Williams:
Seizing Fellowships to Access the World**

Ruth A. Davis

Ambassador Ruth A. Davis's parents expected her to go to Spelman, and so she did. She became a Merrill Scholar, which provided $3,000 to travel and study abroad, enough to support her for one summer and one academic year. She had always wanted to go to Europe, so she chose to go to Dijon, France. While there, she "met students from Cameroon and from other African countries. And while in the United States we were talking about the civil rights movement, these guys were talking about

continues

Box 2.9   Continued

---

going home and actually taking over their countries! They were talking about nation building, and that, for me, was so exciting. I thought, 'Boy, I really, really want to go to Africa. I really want to see this whole process of nation building.' So I went back home, and of course I talked about it, and everybody sort of laughed at me and thought, 'Wow.'"

As she was finishing up at Spelman in 1966, some recruiters came to campus and told her about the Ford Foundation's Foreign Affairs Fellows Program. It enabled her to pursue graduate study at the University of California, Berkeley, and then enter the Foreign Service.

Stacy D. Williams

Stacy D. Williams took advantage of every opportunity he could. He was fortunate to have a lot of support and advising along the way, both to inform him of the opportunities and encourage him to apply. His first experience at the State Department was through an internship program jointly sponsored by the TLG and the American Foreign Service Association. TLG members introduced him to Washington and encouraged him to apply for a summer internship at an embassy. So the next summer he worked at the US embassy in Lusaka, Zambia. Following graduate school, he secured a placement in the State Department through what is now the Presidential Management Fellows Program.

You've Finished Your Undergraduate Studies: Now What?

College graduation is a wonderful achievement. It can also be scary if you don't know what's next. Some of you may be fortunate enough—after a lot of hard work—to access one of the competitive fellowships inclusive of graduate school tuition, described above, such as the Pickering and Payne fellowships. Or you might go on and excel in graduate school and then secure prestigious entry-level leadership fellowships, like the PMF Program. Still others of you may decide that undergraduate studies are the first step and then you need to invest in gaining that intensive overseas experience, perhaps with the Peace Corps. And that investment may make you more competitive for graduate school admission, a fellowship, and eventually a job.

In the next chapter we turn to how to build your confidence once you've started on your path to an international affairs career (Chapter

3). In Chapter 4, we'll address mentoring and networking and how these can support you in your postgraduate transition. In Chapter 5, we will talk about navigating your career more broadly. Ideally, you will not end up graduating from college without having developed a few mentoring relationships and collecting some internships and other preparatory experiences. But even with all of these things, you may still find you don't have an immediate direction after graduation. And that is where mentors, flexibility, and a little luck come into play, as they did for C. D. Glin. He shares his experience in Box 2.10.

Family Support

As our giants' experience suggests, these are unconventional paths that sometimes require some sacrifices and always entail a lot of hard work. And yet this is public service, so your pot of gold at the end of this rainbow is not a gazillion dollars but, as Ruth A. Davis put it, knowing

---

Box 2.10   C. D. Glin: Hard Work, Mentors, and a Little Kismet

---

"I had a ton of jobs when I was in DC. I worked in restaurants, banks . . . I did everything. And I worked at Safeway. I was a cashier at the grocery store. And, literally, right as I was entering the summer of my graduation year, one of my professors came in my line. Doctor Lorenzo Morris, a political science professor at Howard, came in my line, and was like, 'Hey, C. D. . . . this and that. . . What have you been up to? What are you doing this summer?' I'm like, 'Well, I'm looking at this. Looking at that.' He said, 'Something just came through from the State Department, and there will be an opportunity to spend the summer in Africa.' And I had never been to Africa, but I studied Africa. I knew a lot about US foreign policy in Africa. He said, 'You know, I have been sitting on this. I didn't have anyone to recommend because I know so-and-so is doing this, this summer. And so-and-so is doing that. And then luck would have it, I get in your line tonight and you're smiling in my face.' And he said, 'Tomorrow morning . . . by 11:59, I need this application. I need this because we're going to make this happen.' And I was just like, 'What?' Literally stayed up all night, did this application.

"Two months later, I was a Foreign Service intern in Ghana with USIA, the United States Information Agency, which is now part of the State Department."

you've made "a contribution to the betterment of [hu]mankind" and, according to Elijah Cummings, "food for your soul." Still, that can be a hard sell to your parents, who expect you to become a doctor or a lawyer.

One of our students wanted us to explore this question: "We want more people in international affairs, but how do you make ends meet? What's the strategy for just having to stick through that and explaining that to your family, making that investment in your education?" Another student, who shared she was not from a wealthy family, added, "Especially for Black Americans, that's a huge barrier. My family is like, how am I going to pay my bills? How am I going to help my family?"

Some of our giants certainly experienced this. Katherine Lee always had the support of her family in her choice of school, major, or profession. But when she told her parents she wanted to leave academia to join the Foreign Service, her academic father was skeptical: "'Do you really want to leave academia?' He considered that a safe area. I was talking about going into the Foreign Service, and he didn't know how long I could have that job." On the other hand, Ambassador Johnny Young's family had no understanding of the Foreign Service but, thinking it was a good government job, were supportive: "All my family were very supportive. They didn't even have a clue where Madagascar was. And at one point, I remember my grandmother saying, 'Well, you say you are in the Foreign Service, but I've never seen your uniform.' They just knew it was a good job. I think they heard the word *service* and they thought that this was a part of the military service. They learned later on that it was not."

C. D. Glin noted that a good, steady job may still be seen as the holy grail to some. "We really were taught that. Get somewhere. Be happy that you're there. And stay for as long as possible. This get-a-good-government-job joke is a real thing." But, he adds, "that is not the workforce of the future. So, if we're going to go forward and have more people in international affairs, then we need to be talking to each other and teaching each other about what's called 'diversifying your personal portfolio.' Having a lot of different opportunities and being okay with change."

And how do you respond to the common refrain "Why do you have to go over there to do something that you can already do here?" Or as Sundaa Bridgett-Jones eloquently put it, "Why are you putting your talent, time, and treasure into supporting international affairs or supporting people elsewhere?" More than one of our giants heard from their parents, as Ed Grier's said to him, "Do you really want to go away? Don't you want to stay close to home?"

▶ That was the question my grandmother asked me. Peace Corps was always a mission of mine. I didn't have a lot of international-related internships. I feel like every Black volunteer faces this question from their family: "Why do you have to go all the way there to do what you could do here?" It wasn't until they saw the impact that it had on me and the things that I was doing that they knew that I couldn't stay in my little box here, and they started to open their eyes and accept that this would be a part of my journey.

We hope our discussion in the introduction has already begun to explain that service here and service abroad are not unrelated. The two can complement and reinforce each other. And, ultimately, they are part of the same struggle for the betterment of human lives.

Several of our giants had similar experiences, with their families initially confused and resistant but ultimately sharing pride in their accomplishments and experiencing the joy of sharing the world with them. When Ruth A. Davis told her parents she wanted to work in Africa, they didn't believe she would actually do it. She eventually invited them to visit her in Nairobi. "When they came and got off the plane, I laughed at them and said, 'Look who's in Africa!'" They visited her every year she was in Spain and came to Washington for her swearing in as ambassador to Benin. Katherine Lee's family members visited her at different posts. She wants to tell you, "That's something [you] can tell your families: 'Look, if I go abroad, you can come visit me.'" Ambassador Rea Brazeal even brought her mother to live with her in Kenya, as we will discuss in Chapter 7 when we address nurturing your life beyond work.

Ambassador Johnnie Carson experienced more resistance than disbelief initially. He tells the story in Box 2.11.

Box 2.11   Johnnie Carson: Breaking the News to Family—from Devastation to Pride

Upon learning he was going to the Peace Corps, Ambassador Johnnie Carson's parents were "heartbroken" and "devastated." After his college graduation, halfway home on the five-hour drive from Des Moines back to Chicago, "after about the tenth time of being asked by my mother, 'What was I going to do?' I finally broke the news." As he described the moment, "I could feel my father's foot let up off the gas. Jerk. Jerk. And then after that, 'What is that? Where are you going? How long do you have to be away? Are you sure you want to do this?'"

continues

Box 2.11   Continued

He gave his parents about a week to get used to the idea. But they eventually came around. "My mother and father were both alive when I received my first ambassadorial job." It all paid off. His parents came to Washington for all of his ambassadorial swearing-in ceremonies until they passed away (they both missed the third one). "Let me just say, they were proud in multiple spades. I had a great mother and father, really wonderful people, churchgoing people, and people who loved their community. And so, every time I was back in Chicago, they insisted I had to go to church with them. It was a source of pride. It was like, 'We've got something to show you. Here's our Johnnie.' Right? They got over it."

When Ambassador Gina Abercrombie-Winstanley told her parents she wanted to join the Peace Corps, her mother understood she was curious by nature, and it made sense. Her father, on the other hand, said, "'What the hell are you doing? Why would you get a college education at a good school and go off. . . . What? Are you going off to learn how to be poor or something?' So that was a little harder. He wasn't down with that program, but he was down with the results." ■ *Well, of course, once they see what the experience can do for you, the transformation, and the success you've seen—they would have to be supportive.*

Some of our giants benefited from love and trust that seemed to overcome their parents' and family members' fears. Ambassador Sylvia Stanfield's parents even supported her interest in studying Chinese—very unconventional for the time and even now. This was also true for Victoria Cooper and Dominique Harris. Their stories are described in Box 2.12.

Box 2.12   Victoria Cooper and Dominique Harris: Love and Trust

---

Victoria Cooper

Victoria Cooper's gateway to international affairs was the love a man. She and her Liberian husband met in college. She traveled to Liberia with a group of students over the winter break during college. She stayed for a month and decided it was somewhere she could actually live. That

continues

Box 2.12   Continued

was when her relationship became more serious. Marrying an African and moving to Africa was a new idea for what she described as her very traditional Black American family: "The only people in my family who were involved in any international travel, of course, were the men who were military." She had earned her family's trust. "What they've known about me is that I've never been impulsive. I've always thought things through, made very sound decisions. And I had traveled to Liberia as an undergrad before we considered even getting married. . . . My mom said, 'Vicki, you always make pretty sound decisions. We've met this young man. He seems nice enough. You've been there. What are you going to do? How will we stay in touch with you?' And things like that. And then she gave us her blessing. My dad was fine with it because his conclusion was, 'You know what? If anything happens, I'm going to come and get you, so don't worry.' So I was ready to go. There were others who said, 'Oh, they're going to cut your head off and boil you with oil, all of these things.' And I said, 'Okay, but I'm going.'

"My family respected that decision. Many of them said, 'You can do this. We are here to support you, but we're not coming, sweetie.' But it worked. Yeah. It worked out."

Dominique Harris

"I would say my parents know me really well, and whenever I'm like, 'Hey, I want to try this,' their response is typically, 'Okay.' But honestly, when I was in South Africa, I said, 'I think I want to stay over here longer.' And they said, 'Nope, you're coming back.' I was okay with that. People often ask me, 'What has been super influential?' And it really is the support of my parents to just go out and explore. Growing up, my father would tell me, 'The sky is not the limit. It's the floor. We expect great things of you.' And so, having such a supportive home base allowed me to be curious and explore and know that Chicago is always a bit of my North Star. If all else fails in the world, I can always go home to Chicago. And I know that."

▶ Dominique and I have that in common: being from the South Side, and where we come from. Neither of us is at home right now, but we always know that it is a place that we can go when we are in need of community and a break from the daily grind.

Once you're in the job, it can still be tough to feel the support of your family and friends, regardless of your successes. Alonzo Fulgham speaks frankly of this in Box 2.13.

Box 2.13   Alonzo Fulgham: It's Still Different and They Won't Always Get It

"I am not going to sit here and tell you that it's kind of like being a lawyer, or a doctor, or an accountant. Yes, my profession was totally out of the mainstream. I think of my friends—and this is disappointing to say . . . You start to grow apart from them because you are spending more and more time overseas, in a different world, managing totally different problems and issues. So the first year you're back from overseas, everybody's happy to see you. Initially, they're talking about their lives and problems, and then you talk about yours. All of a sudden, after about an hour and a half later, the conversation starts to go quiet. So you go in hard and start to share your stories, and they'll go, 'Oh, that's nice.' So you love your family, you love your friends, but the more and more you steep yourself in the discipline and what you're doing, your life starts to become that. And you have to work really hard at maintaining the support of your friends and your family, because it's foreign to them."

The prospects are exciting, and the pathways are varied. Now that you have embarked on this journey, it's time to explore what happens when you arrive. You will need to build your confidence. The giants continue to offer you their support in Chapter 3.

3

Building Confidence

If you're always trying to be normal you will never know how amazing you can be.

—Maya Angelou

You've worked really hard, and you've finally arrived. While it's really exciting, you now face a different set of challenges, including "being the only" and imposter syndrome. The giants have some advice for you. When they dove into professional experiences, as Aaron described in Chapter 1, they often found themselves to be the only people who looked like them. What was it like to always be the only? Perhaps you already have some experience with that. Our giants will share their own experiences and how they managed. Unfortunately, being the only often comes with the dreaded imposter syndrome. Not all of our giants were familiar with the term, but they certainly had experienced the phenomenon at one time or another. Every one of them knows what it feels like to be told from an early age that they had to be twice as good—even Ambassador James Joseph (born in 1935).

Being the Only

It's tough to walk into a room, look around, and find that you are the only person there who looks like you. It's also a lot of pressure to be the only. As one of our students commented, "If it's just me, I need to present myself accordingly so that I don't mess it up for the next person behind me." Michelle Obama wrote candidly of this feeling, when she became the first Black First Lady of the United States: "Not for one second did I think I'd be sliding into some glamourous, easy role. Nobody who has the words 'first' and '[B]lack' attached to them ever would. I stood at the foot of the mountain, knowing I'd need to climb my way into favor" (Obama 2018, 327).

Our giants have felt that way too. Lauri Fitz-Pegado worked for fifteen years at a client advocacy and public affairs firm where, as a partner, she was the only in multiple ways: the only female, the youngest, the only single and divorced, and the only Black American (or, more broadly, person of color). It is something one must learn to adapt to, and it takes confidence. When Dr. Helene Gayle began working at the Centers for Disease Control and Prevention, she wasn't just the only Black person. She was largely in a man's world. In her early work in Africa, she was usually the only woman on a team. Ed Grier was the only person of color on the Disney Paris marketing team.

The pressure of being the only can be intense. When assigned to the China Desk in Washington, DC, Ambassador Sylvia Stanfield really felt it: "Not only are you responsible because that's your job, you're also in the spotlight—as a Black person in a place that nobody expects you to be, and managing very difficult, complicated political situations. That puts a lot of pressure on you. No doubt about it." This is just a reality, and it requires us to support each other. As Chris Richardson advised, "There aren't a lot of us, and there aren't enough of us. I think that that's always going to be an issue. We have to be able to manage this fact, as Black people, and support one another." Sometimes your only option is to try to ignore it, as Ambassador Stanfield did: "Usually I was the only Black woman in any situation. And some of my colleagues were quite, as I could say, full of themselves. You just sort of ignore them; it's their problem."

Sadly, because you are unexpected and the only, people may bet against you. This literally happened to Bob Burgess when he arrived in the Caribbean for his first international business assignment (see Box 3.1).

Dealing with Imposter Syndrome

The topic of imposter syndrome came up a lot when we were speaking with our focus groups. ▶ It's something that I've had many conversations about with other peers because of our experiences of not being validated because

Box 3.1   Bob Burgess: They Bet Against Him and Lost

Bob Burgess started his international business career with GTE Sylvania in Trinidad and Tobago. GTE had won the government contract to rebuild the telecommunications system following civil unrest on the road to independence in 1961. The company beat its competitors based on a promise to bring jobs to the newly independent country by establishing a light manufacturing plant. And that was Bob Burgess's responsibility.

The chamber of commerce there in 1964 and 1965 comprised mostly expatriate businessmen, many of them from England and the United States. "And we came in and went to a meeting. These two Black guys walk in and say, 'We're from the United States and we're here to set up an operation for the Sylvania division of GTE. We're going to make television sets for the Eastern Caribbean territories.' Guys met us, and they were polite and nice. But between themselves, we found out that there were a couple of guys who were willing to wager that these two Black guys could not run a plant: 'There's just no way that these guys can run a plant. And we bet that that plant is closed by the end of the year, period.' So that's basically what we found out from a white member of the chamber from GTE.

We made it not only run; we made it very successful. And we wrote off all the startup costs in the first year. We showed them we could run an operation at a profit and write off all the start-up costs in less than twelve months. And we grew the business annually."

of who we are, our age, our sex, our race. When I first mentioned this to Aaron, he was like, what is this? The first instance of imposter syndrome was studied in 1979. I think my generation is more familiar with the term. I had to break it down for some of our giants. Sometimes I don't feel like I belong because I'm given a shot I don't think I'm ready for or I'm punching above my weight. I explained, "You all have paved the way for us to have impostor syndrome." It's a blessing. And it's a struggle. Taylor worries there is a generational issue here. ▶ I saw across our interviews that the giants had an enormous amount of confidence. And they were the first. How have we gotten so far away from that confidence?

What exactly is imposter syndrome? Like Taylor, our focus group members understood it well from their direct experience and conversations with peers. It's basically chronic self-doubt and an internalized fear of being exposed as a fraud, even when, to others, you may appear to be succeeding. But let's take care and not cast everything under this label. Everyone experiences self-doubt. It's part of human nature. And, let's face it, it can keep us humble. It's true, some of our giants refused to doubt themselves, or perhaps it simply did not occur to them to question their right to occupy the spaces they were in. They worked so hard to get there, and they needed the determination that they had a right to be there in order to succeed. Once they understood what we were talking about, other giants shared their experience with self-doubt. And they offered advice. Let's start with those who reported not having experienced imposter syndrome. Their experience is important to note so that you know that imposter syndrome is (1) not inevitable and (2) not the same thing as self-doubt.

Imposter What?

Perhaps we sometimes mislabel as imposter syndrome the feelings and stress of being the only or the cringing pain of not having the full support of others you thought you could count on. Ambassador Johnnie Carson's response is noteworthy—literally. Write this down somewhere or commit it to memory so you can ask yourself when that self-doubt creeps in, is it just . . . ?

> I've never had imposter syndrome. What I have felt is the impact of being the only Black person in the room, where there are twenty or twenty-five others. I've felt outnumbered, but I haven't felt as though I've not belonged there.

A relentlessly strategic thinker, he adds, "It's not a question of should I be here or shouldn't I be here. The question is whether or not you have the influence and numbers to push the agenda you want to push."

As the ambassador to South Africa, newly appointed by Republican president Ronald Reagan, Ed Perkins walked into a political land mine that was further complicated by his color and the biased perspectives of both Black (due to politics) and white audiences. He reported, "Jesse Jackson and Randall Robinson were among those who said, 'He won't know when to talk back to the administration.' When the press ferreted out a former professor of mine at USC and asked his opinion, he replied, 'They will eat him alive.'" Nevertheless, Ambassador Perkins maintained stalwart confidence: "Despite such public doubts, it never dawned on me that I would not be successful. I approached South Africa as a problem that needed to be solved" (Perkins 2006, 261).

If you are very technically qualified in a subject matter, especially if you hold an expertise that is not very common, perhaps you can avoid feeling like an imposter. This was certainly the case for both Johnnie Carson and Ed Perkins. And that rare technical expertise served Ambassador Sylvia Stanfield. She reported feeling "quite comfortable" as a minority within a minority. She and her colleagues, regardless of race, shared the experience and challenge of Chinese language and culture study. She shared, "My classmates were, I think, very liberal Foreign Service officers. It was more like the China club and a family."

Where Does Imposter Syndrome Come From?

This is not to say that imposter syndrome and its less extreme relation, self-doubt, are not real. They are. So let's get a better understanding of them. What creates and compounds imposter syndrome and self-doubt?

The pressure to be twice as good. All of our giants understood well the charge to be twice as good—a biography of Condoleezza Rice is even titled *Twice as Good*. It sounds harmless enough, preparing young people to compete when the scales are weighted against them. Chris Richardson, in Box 3.2, reminds us of the downside, the potential lasting impact of this instruction.

Box 3.2   Chris Richardson: The Downside of Being Told to Be Twice as Good

"My stepdad was white. My mom met my stepdad when I was about five to six years old. He has two white children. I grew up in this Brady Bunch world, in that way. I remember, as a kid, my mom would sit up until 1:00 or 2:00 at night, after she got home from work, and she and I would do homework. If I drew a little bit outside the line, my mom would crumple up the paper and throw it away.

"My stepdad would come up some nights, and he'd be like, 'Why are you doing this to this boy? Why are you making this boy stay up until 2:00 at night doing work?' My mom would say, 'Look. Your two white kids can sleep and go to bed in the comfort of being white. My son is always going to have to be twice as good, and twice as smart, and work twice as hard to survive in this country.'

"That always struck me, because that comes into very much a part of what . . . I understand what my mom was trying to do, and largely, I think she was successful at it. But that adds to your imposter syndrome, as well. That's what creates it, is that we're taught, as Black people, that we have to be twice as good. When we're not twice as good, we get a sense that, 'Oh my god, I shouldn't be here,' right? That, 'Oh my god.' I look around the room, and deep down, 'Am I the one that should be making these calls? Am I the one that should be in here, doing these things?'"

Others questioning your worth. If we don't already have some self-doubt, others may doubt our worthiness—as Bob Burgess's experience illustrates. And when that external doubt is made public, it really smarts. It is not uncommon to have the experience Dr. Jacob Gayle and Ambassador Rea Brazeal had: you're great . . . for a Black person. When Dr. Gayle received his tenure as a professor at Kent State University, he reported, "My dean so proudly introduced me to the crowd as undoubtedly the best Black professor she had ever worked with. I took a moment to say, 'While I'm very appreciative of that, I hope someday you'll be able to say that I'm probably the best professor you've ever worked with.'" When Ambassador Brazeal started her post as deputy assistant secretary for the East Asian and Pacific Affairs Bureau—an unusual post for Black Foreign Service members—at her first staff meeting, the assistant secretary "said I was the best person being brought into the Bureau, although I was Black. There seemed to be some little angle there that just deflated my internal ego, because I'd thought, well, this is 1996 and I had not expected to hear that kind of reasoning" (Brazeal 2007, 96).

The back side of affirmative action. Whether others say or think it or you do, there may be a nagging doubt about why, exactly, you find yourself in a particular professional context. Dominique Harris described this: "Particularly when you're a person of color, there's always thoughts in your head, and in others': 'Did I get this role because I am the best? Did I get this role because people are trying to fill a quota? Did I get this role because I bring diversity to the table?'" (Our giants would say, if you are there, just make the most of it. More of their advice follows.) Dr. Helene Gayle spoke candidly of her experience, noting imposter syndrome can be multiplied "if you are African American or a person of color, because you're always filtering out what you think people think of you. And then you have it if you're a woman, and you're also filtering that out."

The "wrong" pedigree or credentials. And maybe you feel you don't have the right pedigree. Your credentials and background just are not as shiny as those of most others in the room. Linda Thomas-Greenfield had that experience. It caused her to doubt that she would pass the oral part of the Foreign Service exam: "You're always questioning that you're not good enough. So I'm meeting people who went to Harvard and to Yale and came from private schools. I'm like, I'm from Louisiana. And I went to LSU, I'm not going to pass this exam." She had been told that people take the oral exam multiple times before passing. To her disbelief, she passed the first time.

But even the right credentials may not prevent imposter syndrome and self-doubt. Paul Weisenfeld wasn't familiar with the term. He and his brother had coined a different term to describe the experience. "Was it Kafka who wrote the book where the guy turns into a cockroach? *Metamorphosis*. I thought of it as metamorphosis syndrome, that I'm going to wake up one day and everybody's going to say, 'Hey, actually, you're not a lawyer. You're a cockroach.'" This, from a Harvard Law School graduate.

New challenges. Self-doubt is a normal response to any new situation or challenge. Almost all of our giants described this in one way or another, whether it was Dr. Helene Gayle describing entering onto the boards of multinational corporations or public speaking or Alonzo Fulgham confronting the greatest challenge of his career (see Box 3.3).

We think it's important to recognize that there may be some gender differences at play when it comes to experiencing imposter syndrome, even if only among those from previous generations. Much depends on your own makeup, to be sure. Lauri Fitz-Pegado was just

---

Box 3.3   Alonzo Fulgham: What Have I Done?

Sometimes you can have a lot of confidence, backed by training and experience, and still wince with self-doubt when confronted with a new challenge that feels larger than life. Alonzo Fulgham experienced that when he arrived in Afghanistan to become the USAID mission director, responsible for the largest USAID program in the world at that time (approximately $2 billion): "The gravity of what I had just taken on didn't hit me until I walked in and saw my name on the door. And I said to myself, 'What have you done, Fulgham?' I was scared, because up until my arrival in Kabul, it was all ceremonial and, 'Oh yeah, this is great!' But walking through that door and seeing your name on the door, that's when I realized, this is going to be the assignment of a lifetime!"

■ *When you're in a position like that, you're now a player, and you have the most important job in the AID world. People on a daily basis come in and give you advice. They write memos to you. They call you. They chat you up. But then you close that office door, and you're in that room all alone.*

Alonzo Fulgham heartily agreed: "You know that old expression, 'It's lonely at the top'? You now know exactly what that statement means."

as confident in asserting her right to place as Johnnie Carson was. As Dr. Helene Gayle described, being a woman adds another layer, on top of being Black, that leads to questioning how others think of you and if you belong.

Coping Mechanisms

None of us is entirely immune to imposter syndrome and self-doubt. Since it may be inevitable, how can we cope with it? First, we need to get out of our own heads and see others more realistically: they probably experience self-doubt too (or if they don't, they should), and they are not that smart.

They're not that smart. Yeah, they think you are not as smart as they are . . . and sometimes you think that too. We have all experienced it at one time or another. ■ *I was introduced to the work of Søren Kierkegaard early on in my university life. He said, "There are two ways to be fooled: One is to believe what isn't true. The other is to refuse to believe what is true."* The truth is, you deserve to be there as much as anybody else, and you are probably just as capable, if not more capable than anyone else in the room.

Take it from Michelle Obama: "I have been at just about every table of power, corporate boards, non-profits, the UN. The secret is . . . they are not that smart! There are plenty of hardworking and talented people, but their ideas are no more exciting. They need our voices at the table to fix things" (quoted in Hirsch 2018). Chris Richardson experienced this in country team meetings, when the heads of sections got together at an embassy to talk about what was going on. Most often, he was the only Black person in the room. "You'd look around the table, and you'd be like, 'Man, how did you get this far?' For a lot of them, it was just being a mediocre white man that'll get them ahead in life. Once you break through into these so-called elite circles, you find out that everybody there is really not that good. . . . As I got older, I'd spend a lot more time with these people. I was like, the question isn't why am I here; the question is, why are a lot of you here?" Ambassador Gina Abercrombie-Winstanley wants to make this specific case with women: "I've told women, 'Speak up in meetings. The guys don't know any more than you do. It doesn't have to be excellent. It doesn't have to be perfect. But you have to be in your space. You have to expand in your space. You have to be present."

Taylor has already witnessed these dynamics. ▶ My general advice for students who want to know the key to success? There isn't one. The one thing that

I've learned in my work so far is that nobody knows what they're doing! You're always a student. You're always learning.

Learn to live with it. Everyone is on a learning curve no matter where they are in their career. It may be particularly daunting in the early years. In describing her imposter syndrome, Verone Bernard said, "I don't think that's going away anytime soon, because I do recognize that I have dues to pay, you know?" Aaron responded, ■ *I think that the fact that you see it in that context is very helpful. That you feel like you've got to pay your dues. Everybody has to do that.* Verone has already made great progress in her career, moving from one competitor to another and advancing up the line of responsibility.

Ambassador Ertharin Cousin described imposter syndrome as a reality that is "part of not just survival but the ability to achieve outside your experience." She observed that it's a normal part of any career, but it may diminish as you attain higher levels of authority and a title that engenders respect. She looked to her role model and mentor, Ruth A. Davis: "Have you ever seen Ruth Davis come into a room? She walks into the room and by her very presence and stature she looks like a person and a woman one must highly regard."

■ *Self-doubt is something that we all face. I mean, anybody that says they don't, I think they're not telling the truth. It's there. I've worked in business, government, and the nonprofit world, just as Dr. Helene Gayle and others of our giants have. And whenever you take a new job, whenever you take on a new responsibility, you're always going to face self-doubt to some degree.*

If you are strategically managing your career, the subject of Chapter 5, then, as Dominique Harris describes, every job you enter should be a "stretch role." And then you "just work really hard to be the best in the room." As you make progress, that nagging self-doubt should diminish. Again, it was Johnnie Carson's, Ed Perkins's, and Sylvia Stanfield's expertise and experience that enabled them to assert their right to place and avoid feeling like imposters. But, Dominique Harris cautions, "if you're the best in the room for too long, then you need to go find another room." In short, if you are not experiencing some tension between what you are confident in and what you need to learn, if you are all confidence and no doubt, it's time to move on.

Just say no. Sometimes imposter syndrome and self-doubt are not just part of the standard progression along a career trajectory, as we observed above. Sometimes the best coping mechanism is flat-out refusal to own it. That refusal can be based on your expertise and experience. And it can be a stubborn assertion of self to protect your psychological well-being. Just don't play along. This was Ambassador Rea Brazeal's approach. Like Johnnie Carson's opening quotation above, this one is worth noting down and remembering:

> Early in my working life, I decided I would never know why I got support or didn't get support, or my position wasn't adopted, or I wasn't promoted, or whatever was happening. I would never know whether it was because I was Black, because I was a woman, because I was young, because I was tall, because I was fat. And that way lay madness. If I took all that on and had to try to figure that out, I would go crazy. So I realized it was the other person's problem, whatever happened, not mine. And so I just continued on my merry way.

Don't misread this. She still sometimes encountered the pain of imposter syndrome. She added, "In my young adulthood, back in the 1960s, there was a song called 'Don't Let the Sun Catch You Crying,' or something like that. And that was my motto. I could cry in the evenings if I needed to, but when the sun came up, I was all about doing my business and getting accomplished what I wanted to accomplish."

Gaining Confidence: Advice from the Giants

Besides these basic coping mechanisms, what advice do the giants have for you for fighting imposter syndrome and self-doubt? What can you do to gain confidence?

Attitude

Let's start with attitude. The best advice one of our students had received was "Don't apologize for the space that you walk upon. Occupy and know that you are worthy of being in that space and you do have a contributing factor to it. That's what got you here." It's helped her already to get through graduate school. Yes. Remind yourself what got you here. When asked what led to his success, Ed Perkins responded, "By God, I had to also accept one thing. One has to love oneself. If you don't, you're never going to succeed." ■ *That's right. You really have to be secure in who you are and respect who you are to get over the many challenges one faces in life.* The women who profile their experiences in *For Colored Girls Who Have Considered Politics* offer this advice: "You must know your own worth, because there are days when you're the only one who will trumpet your own horn" (Brazile et al. 2018, 305). From his experience, Aaron adds, ■ *You have to be confident to be successful in your career. You have to have a realistic level of confidence about who you are, what you can do, etc. That's important, especially during the hard times.*

But that may be easier said than done. How can you build that self-confidence?

Behavior

For starters, you can build up that confidence through your own behavior. Sundaa Bridgett-Jones has a formula she shares with a lot of young people. "Authenticity and courage are two things I keep telling them: They belong here. They are enough; and they belong here." In Box 3.4, she shares three things to be mindful of.

Ambassador Ertharin Cousin stresses the importance of listening. She cautions that it's easier to recognize that others in the room are not as smart as you if you are listening more than talking: "If you stop to listen, and particularly early on in your career, you realize, I do belong here, because I understand the substance of the conversation as well as, if not better than, everyone else in the room. This thinking helps build your self-confidence by recognizing your own talent in comparison to others around the table. You begin to understand and realize what is your value add." She stresses that you need to give yourself this opportunity to learn.

Box 3.4   Sundaa Bridgett-Jones: Visibility, Proximity, Perception

"Visibility is so important. We need to be sitting at the table. And we need to raise our hands and say, 'Yeah I can do that.' I do like the word *determined*. And showing the leadership qualities we have.

"Proximity is another one. How close are you to where the action is happening? Because if you are over there doing the analysis but not getting to the center where decisionmaking is made, and the power is over here. . . .

"How people perceive you is another really important thing. I've always been one to be very much protective of my own reputation, often because I would be the only African American or woman in the room."

Focus on Purpose

Dr. Helene Gayle manages self-doubt by focusing on purpose. She tells herself, "This is not about me. This is about the mission that I'm trying to accomplish." She explains, "I've got to get myself off of me, and onto what I'm trying to accomplish. It minimizes my own sense of self-doubt."

■ *I've had the same feelings myself many times. And it comes with being a person of color in this society. It comes with the territory, and you have to overcome it. The point about having a sense of purpose and determination makes a big difference.*

Have Your Script Ready

Sanola A. Daley is no stranger to imposter syndrome. She has developed a script to get her through those difficult moments of self-doubt, which she describes in Box 3.5.

Amanda Gorman, National Youth Poet Laureate and the youngest ever inaugural poet, has her own script. She calls it a mantra: "I am the daughter of Black writers. We are descended from freedom fighters who broke their chains and changed the world. They call me" (quoted in Saad 2021).

■ *Scripts are about having in your tool kit approaches to help you deal with the moment and move on and build on that. Everybody has that. I have it. Winston*

Box 3.5   Sanola A. Daley: Have Your Script Ready

"When I started at Inter-American Development Bank, I had moments of panic about changing the course of how we were doing business. I was working on gender in the private sector. This was a new direction for the department. And I was new to the institution. I was bringing it to the organization, to my department, based on the work I had done previously. So, when I started getting challenged, I had to remember, 'You've done this before.' When I started feeling insecure about my recommendations, I remembered, 'You've done this before, and you've seen the results. Stick to what you've done and what you've seen.'

"And so that's what I started focusing on. And I realized that the more I started focusing on that, then the imposter syndrome started to go away. And so I've been able, over the years, to just always attack it with 'You've done this before. You know what you're doing. You have the results. It's proven.'"

Churchill used to stop all meetings and leave the room and go get a new cigar, just because he couldn't handle the pressure of that particular moment. Everybody I know who's been a leader, whom I've read about, whom I've met and worked with, they all have their techniques and approach. You have to have it in your tool kit. That's really important. It is realistic to recognize that and be prepared to use it, whatever it is.

I'll share with you something that I do. I've given hundreds of speeches in my life, and everybody thinks that you just walk out there and do it. Well, first of all, any speech you give requires preparation. But before I start my speech, I will go on my tiptoes when I'm just about to walk out on stage. I will rise up on my tiptoes and squeeze my feet as hard as I possibly can, just to have a diversion from what I'm about to do. I learned that many years ago, and I do it all the time. I find it relaxes me for that moment. And even though I'm not really nervous about giving the speech, there's always a little tension. We all have our little devices.

Trusting That Others Believe in You

Remember the advice one of our students got: remind yourself of what got you here. No one gets to where they are alone. No one. You arrive at these places of responsibility because others believe in your potential. To the extent you have been mentored to get to where you are, then you really know someone believes in you. And if you were sponsored—if someone suggested you for the job and praised your capabilities for it— well, then you are golden. Trust that. People believe in you.

As Sundaa Bridgett-Jones puts it, "If they are willing to sponsor you and lead the way and let you know that you have the skill sets and competencies to do it, it just boosts your confidence." Like Sundaa Bridgett-Jones, Alonzo Fulgham took solace in the support he had received from those who went before him: "I had guys like Aaron, John Hicks, Irv Coker, Al Harding, and a few other guys, who had taught me that if you weren't able to take on that responsibility, it wouldn't have been bestowed on you. And so I knew that there was something in me that said I could be successful. But I had to pull from everything I had learned from my previous experience and from outstanding mission directors over the fifteen years before I assumed that Afghanistan assignment to be successful." Ed Grier adds that you can also trust that others can help you if you need it: "Did someone push me in the right direction? Yes. Did someone give me a safety net at times? Yes. People are willing to help you. If you take the attitude, I can do this, it's very likely someone will come along if you need help."

Look to Others for Their Example

You can save yourself a lot of heartache and also learn a lot just by talking with others about how they deal with these challenges. This is a core component of mentoring (which we'll talk more about in Chapter 4). Dominique Harris's experience pulls together a lot of the advice we discussed: attitude, behavior, learning from others, and being helped by others (see Box 3.6).

Box 3.6   Dominique Harris: Support, Hard Work, and the Right Attitude

"I've been very fortunate to have really great relationships with older women who speak and advise from their lived experience. They've shared, 'Yeah, this imposter syndrome is real. I had to take on this big role, and I'm trying to figure it out.' I've had very candid, very open discussions and talked to people who are ten, fifteen, or twenty years older than me who say, 'Hey, I experienced that too. This has been my approach.' Those conversations have been incredibly fruitful.

"Yes, we have it, but the real question is, What do you do about it? For some people, it fuels them. For me, it fuels me. And for some people, yeah, it can get into your head, and you're constantly thinking about it. But for me, it's simple. You have been given this opportunity. Imposter syndrome or not, whether you're the best or not, whether you belong— you have been given this opportunity and it's a question of what you do with the opportunity. And I am such an optimist. I may have a few bad moments, but I don't stay there. There is always good to discover in every opportunity.

"For me it's, how bad do you want it? Or how hard are you willing to work for it? What are you willing to sacrifice in order to be the best in the room? And then, once you're there, what do you do to bring people behind you? Imposter syndrome becomes part of the process. But it's something that . . . either it fuels you or it burdens you. And you have a choice in that.

"I started my job when my boss was eight months pregnant. So, after a month, I was on my own. One of the first meetings I went to, I was out of my league. I'm just there trying to figure it out. And there was a lady whom I met once. I was waiting in line to talk to an ambassador. She came and put me on the side of these two men who were hogging up the ambassador's time. And she was like, 'I'm going to take care of you while your boss is gone.' A Black woman, who met me once. But in a space where there isn't a lot of representation, she was like, 'I got you.' Now

continues

Box 3.6   Continued

she's a very close friend of mine. But you just need some of these small acts of kindness to really break in, for you to be like, 'All right, this is a space I can see myself in.'

"I want others to know my work so that they know that I didn't get this opportunity because of the color of my skin or my gender, but I got this because I'm willing to put in the work. So, when you meet me, when you see how hard I grind, it then becomes really difficult to say, 'Oh, she's not qualified for this role.' Or 'she got it because she's a Black woman.' It's a bit of, 'Hey, I'm going to do the things that other people aren't willing to do so that you know that I'm committed.'"

Dominique—and all of our giants—remind us of the importance of mentors. We probe this more deeply in Chapter 4.

4

Seeking the Support of Others

A mentor is someone who allows you to see the hope inside yourself.
—Oprah Winfrey

I'm here because I stand on many, many shoulders, and that's true of every [B]lack person I know who has achieved."
—Vernon Jordan

All of the giants had (and still have) extensive networks that enabled them to advance their careers. These networks have been especially important in helping them navigate the unknowns and unpredictability that are especially challenging when you work in a complex global organization and when that organization is predominately white. But the power of these relationships is not just in building a network. It is about sustaining that network and deepening the relationships within it.

The best preservice support programs move beyond providing financial assistance (e.g., graduate tuition) and even professional experience, such as internships, however impactful. The best preservice programs ensure that, when you are ready, the door will be open for you. Whether it is through a formal program like the Payne, Pickering, and Rangel fellowships or through your own networking with professors, peers, and their contacts, networks are essential to ensuring someone will be there to open the first door for you. And the next one. And the next one. And it is the mentors within those networks who will ensure that you are prepared. And, yes, they may even push you through that door whether you think you are ready or not.

This chapter reviews the many facets of mentoring. Mentors come in all shapes, sizes, and colors. They operate in a variety of ways to support you, whether you are aware of their efforts or not. And with their help, you become known to sponsors. These may be mentors who know, or others who trust your mentors to know, that you are ready for an opportunity and recommend you for it. The best mentors exercise tough love. They may rain on your roses to ensure that those roses will endure and bloom bigger and brighter. And all of these gifts come when you take your responsibilities in a mentoring relationship seriously.

In the following we introduce some networking basics. We affirm the importance of role models. And we discuss the many faces and colors of mentors and the varied roles they can play in your professional and personal development. We'll share our giants' experiences to show how you can find and accept mentors. And we'll introduce and provide examples of the difference between mentorship and sponsorship. A fundamental theme throughout this chapter is the importance of building and sustaining authentic relationships. Our giants benefited from tough love and also took responsibility in their mentoring relationships. We'll discuss that too.

Networking

Networks seem tough. Networks seem inaccessible. Networks seem to be for others but not for you. Wrong. ▶ I was participating on a panel at the Elliott School about unconscious bias in international development, and another panelist argued, "We need to get rid of networks"! In the Black community, your network is your net worth. We need to figure out how to retool these networks and make them work for everyone, make them more inclusive. Because we know the power of networks. Historically, if you look at some of these spaces, and at race relations in the US generally, we're already operating from a disadvantage. Our white counterparts have networks with deep histories across all industries. If you go to some of these networks, there are just not enough people to get you where you ultimately want to go or not enough people with the political capital to spend on you to advance you where you want to go. We need networks. And not everyone will look like us in those networks.

Throughout their careers, the giants had people who knew them, the quality of their work, and were in key positions to make a difference. ■ *First, you need to be good at what you're doing. Second, you need to build a network of people in the organization where you work. Third, you need to have a network of people external to the organization where you work so that you can have an objective point of reference and mentors who can help you think through any particular challenge that you might encounter. And you have to be purposeful in your approach to that task. Some people might think that this is trying to curry favor with your superiors or not being your authentic self. But the fact of the matter, as I have observed, is that every successful leader has an approach to developing a network, and it's understood and seen as integral to career advancement. It's part of a professional culture. And there's a way to accomplish this in a very skillful fashion.*

Just getting in the door. That's the first challenge—and one that networks are essential for overcoming. As Victoria Cooper put it, "Creating an opportunity for yourself is a challenge. Because if you don't have the exposure to do that, if you don't know what they're looking for, how to maneuver it any way, shape, or form, you're outside again. Where do I even start? Getting in the door, by knowing how to shake the lock, is the challenge. Part of it is identifying a network."

Networking is not a once-and-done endeavor. You may have amassed the largest LinkedIn network on record, but if you don't actually know any of these people, it's meaningless. And if you met them once and never followed up, well, that's not very meaningful either. Some of our focus group participants already understood that well. One of them reported having stayed in touch with teachers even from elementary school. She reported that she had taken pretty much every step in her education and career so far because someone in her network said, "You might be interested in this." Ambassador Ed Perkins provides a strong example of sustaining those support networks. For his swearing-in ceremony as ambassador to South Africa, he invited his high school counselor, Carmen Walker, as well as two of his teachers. He reports that visiting Portland throughout his career kept him "grounded": "I keep in touch not out of courtesy, but because their friendship and counsel are important to me. . . . I rely on them to speak candidly and knowledgeably. . . . They have been my true north, the place I return for replenishment" (Perkins 2006, 71).

Peer Networks

Often we think of networking as a means to connect to giants in the field, or at least those who have already arrived in the places we see ourselves going. It might surprise you to know that your peers may make up the most important network you have throughout your career and lifetime. It's talked about all the time in business schools: you don't go for the degree; you go for the network. Your peer network is critical in this very small field of US foreign policy because you're always cycling through with the same people; you will come across them again. Peer networks are the easiest to develop, though they still require effort. Those efforts might entail joining formal organizations, such as one of the Divine Nine (Black Greek letter organizations) or other young-professional organizations. The friendships and even acquaintances you forge in school contribute to your peer network, especially if you make efforts to stay in touch and follow what each individual is doing. LinkedIn and Facebook are great resources for that. Your peers may not be super helpful in connecting you to new opportunities at the beginning, but as each of you finds a place, you can be in positions to make introductions and referrals for each other.

Gateways

But how can you extend your network beyond this more immediate circle? If you are lucky, even while you are still in school you may meet people who can become gateways to broader networks. Sanola A. Daley benefited from having a career advisor at the Elliott School of International Affairs at George Washington University. As she was new to Washington, DC, it was particularly important that she develop a network fast. And given her Jamaican origin and her interest in Latin America, her advisor thought a recent graduate from Guyana might help. Ironically, Sanola never even met him in person, but he opened his network to her, and the rest is history. She met with the people he suggested, one of whom worked at the Organization of American States. Sanola shared her interests and aspirations over lunch, and the woman offered, "There's an opportunity coming up in my department. You should apply." Sanola did so and got the position. It was a short-term consultancy that was supposed to last three months, but she ended up working there for a year and a half.

Dominique Harris's gateway was a professor at George Washington University, senior executive in residence Joan Dudik-Gayoso, who had worked in international development with postings across many agencies throughout her career, including the State Department. "I needed somebody to take a chance on me, and I needed somebody to sit down and talk through what are the options. Joan was great. She said, 'I think I can do something with that. I think I have just the person that you should meet with.'" Dominique ended up interning for Teresa Hobgood, who subsequently also became a longtime mentor. "I saw this Black woman leading congressional affairs at a State Department office. It was that one introduction, starting at the State Department, that opened my eyes. Now, I'm like, 'Okay, maybe I can make a career out of this. Maybe this is a space that I belong. Maybe this is a space where I can thrive, because I've seen all these people that are doing incredible work.'"

Chance Encounters

Networks can evolve from unexpected places. And this is sometimes what makes networks less inclusive or more challenging for Black Americans. Ambassador Sylvia Stanfield observed this when she stayed with a friend during a visit back to Washington: "African Americans in Washington tended to live in certain areas. I was riding home with a friend and I noticed this was a carpool. There was only one African American member of the carpool. I realized this was a part of an informal network that we generally don't have. They can share information about job opportunities coming up. And if you don't live near them or in their same social circle, you aren't going to hear about it. You aren't the next-door neighbor who's going to share things over drinks or riding home in the same carpool."

■ *That's the unseen network and support system that white society has, that we do not have access to. I was in a carpool for a long time. And it's amazing the amount of information you can pick up from the other members of your carpool. I was the only Black in the carpool for five years. The people in the carpool turned up in different parts of my career in extraordinary places. It's really an important part of that informal network, and it's hard to replicate.* You never know. So it's important not to burn bridges and to keep conversations open. On the other hand, ■ *your casual conversation in the carpool can end up in different parts of your agency or in different offices. You never know where that conversation is going to go. So listen. And be circumspect.*

Sometimes your identity can be the spark that lights a chance encounter, igniting a relationship that can extend your network in career-changing ways. That was Lauri Fitz-Pegado's experience. When she was at a party with her boyfriend, she met a Black attorney, Florence Prioleau, who worked at Patton Boggs and Blow, a law firm that did lobbying. After talking with Lauri at this party, Florence Prioleau went to Ron Brown, who was a partner in the firm, and told him he should meet this woman. "At the time, Ron Brown was in conversations with the Haitian government to represent Haiti in the United States on various bilateral issues, and on some legal issues as well, that were important to the Haitians and to the US-Haiti relationship. So I met Ron, and he immediately wanted me to work with him on this client."

Much later in her career, Lauri Fitz-Pegado worked for then commerce secretary Ron Brown as the first Black American assistant secretary and director general of the US and Foreign Commercial Service.

Finding Common Ground

Lauri Fitz-Pegado's experience illustrates the benefits of finding common ground in each new encounter. In her case with Florence Prioleau, that common ground was their affinity as Black women and the fact both were working for organizations concerned with international public affairs (at the time Lauri Fitz-Pegado worked for Gray and Company, a cutting-edge public affairs company). It is precisely in less formal conversations that you may discover you have a seed of connection with others who otherwise may seem inaccessible or just unknown. That seed can quickly grow into a sense of empathy and goodwill, sometimes faster than you might imagine.

It turns out there is quite an unspoken understanding and connection among those who are from the South Side of Chicago. Johnnie Carson and Aaron went to the same high school. ■ *Johnnie was four or five years ahead of me. We never knew that. I was visiting him when he was ambassador in Kenya, having dinner with him one night, and I said, "I know you're from Chicago, but where'd you go to high school?" He says, "Tilden."* When Jennifer first introduced Aaron and Taylor, she figured they would get along just fine the moment they discovered they were both from the South Side of Chicago. Dominique Harris is a sorority sister to Taylor, but they also immediately bonded over their South Side origins.

Some affinities are formalized precisely for the purpose of networking. That is certainly the case with the Divine Nine. Dominique Harris gives back through her sorority, for example, mentoring others like Taylor, but she also has used it to build her confidence and assist in her sometimes dramatic career transitions, like when she moved from Washington, DC, to Kansas for Cargill. "Honestly, I've lived all over the country. When I moved from DC to Wichita, Kansas, I was like, 'If there is a Delta network, I'll be fine.' You can send me anywhere. And it really is that notion of, 'Hey, I don't know you from Adam, but you're a Delta, I'm a Delta. We're sisters, I got you.'"

Volunteering

One more point on how you can build external networks: C. D. Glin reminds us of the importance of volunteering. "Volunteering has been really, really important to me to mitigate challenges of entering the space. Whether it's Society for International Development, BPIA [Black Professionals in International Affairs], later on the Council on Foreign Relations. . . . Once you do the research and know who they are, volunteer to be a part of these important organizations. I was able to enter into spaces that I otherwise wouldn't have gotten into. . . . I was also very clear on visibility—not in a peacock way but being visible in the sense that this guy wants more, wants to do more, or to be able to be more. Volunteering and being visible made it easy for people to help me or want to help me."

Internal Networks

As important as these external networks are to get you where you want to be, it's essential not to forget that, once you are there, you need to continue those efforts inside your organization and subfield. Wherever you are in US foreign policy, it can be very competitive. So as Ambassador Harry K. Thomas Jr. put it, "You have to find a way to be the best 24/7. And that's not just at work. You have to socialize with your colleagues. . . . You can't be the person who doesn't socialize with your colleagues, because we have such an informal system, especially as you go up the ranks. If you're known as that outsider, it's going to be tough."

Building your internal network is not always easy or fun. Alonzo Fulgham warns it's much more than just "going out to lunch with people other than the fun people you like." He adds, "Here's what you have to do if you want to compete. When they go out for beers, you go out for beers. Even if you don't drink beer. Order a club soda with lime, or a sarsaparilla. I don't know, but you have to be a part of the conversation. And create your own narrative about who you are. You want people to leave the event saying, 'Oh, so-and-so is a really nice person. I have to find a way to work with her because I like the way she thinks, and I like her disposition.' It's about creating an opportunity for folks to be comfortable with you."

■ *It's important to understand the symbiotic nature of your workplace and the environment that you inhabit for most of your daily life. Clearly one cannot expect to become friends with all of one's colleagues. But forming a network of like-minded coworkers is essential to one's professional success. I would encourage you to engage in learning about the duties and responsibilities of your colleagues across the entire organization. Strive to learn and understand what the technical or staff offices do and how the individuals in each area view their respective roles and relationship to the rest of the organization. Such an understanding will pay off as you ascend to positions of more authority and responsibility and, in the process, provide you with the capacity to build your own cadre of teams.*

Role Models

If we are lucky, our networks encompass people we would consider role models. Sometimes we benefit from just knowing these individuals exist. And perhaps later we will have opportunities to actually meet them and count them as part of our networks. Maybe one day they may even become mentors. But these relationships may initially start from an awareness and recognition that these individuals model what is possible and what to emulate. Dominique Harris reminds us, "If you don't see people who look like you moving up through the ranks, who can serve as a bit of the model, it's tough. It's really tough."

Stacy D. Williams did his homework. He researched the Black leaders in the State Department who went before him. He learned all about Terence Todman, the first Black career ambassador. And he got to meet some of these greats, like Ambassadors Ed Perkins and Ruth A. Davis. "Their first message to me was, 'We expect great things from you.'" Later on, he worked in General Colin Powell's State Department. He could observe and experience Powell's leadership style and example. To this day, he is influenced by Secretary Powell's theme: "Taking care of the troops—one team, one mission." "We could see him walking the hallways, and not just on the Sunday morning talk shows. He was in the halls going to the credit union and the cafeteria. . . . He would be among us where we felt like we know our leader, we see our leader, and he's taking care of us. . . . It was like a holiday every day that we had somebody of this caliber leading us."

Everyone, no matter how accomplished they eventually become, needs role models. Ambassador Ruth A. Davis's role models, not surprisingly, were Ambassador Terence Todman, in terms of career achievement, and Ambassador Ed Perkins, in terms of institutional impact (Davis 2016). She reports, "[Terence Todman] was always my polestar. He taught me to strive for the best and to be conscious of my responsibility to make the Foreign Service more inclusive of the American population." Beyond his pathbreaking work in South Africa, she reports, Ed Perkins, as the first Black director general, "instituted the Pickering Fellowship program that is essential to the department's diversity efforts. He taught me, above all, that one person can have a lasting institutional impact" (Davis 2016). Ambassador Harry K. Thomas Jr. also praises Terence Todman, who "wasn't an easy man, but he showed you how to act."

Just like mentors (discussed below), not all role models have to be Black. Early in his career, Ambassador Johnny Young benefited greatly from working for, observing, and experiencing what he called "an extraordinary ambassador," Albert Sherer Jr. "I'll never forget him. Because I never dreamed that I would ever become an ambassador, but he was the model that remained in my mind as what a good ambassador does. We went through a really tough time in Conakry, Guinea. . . . He looked after his people. He was concerned. He was caring."

As you see, everyone needs role models. Our giants found role models in giants who went before them, before they became role models themselves. C. D. Glin brought that home for Aaron. "I want to give Aaron real credit because we have to see success leading to success—that you can be a Foreign Service officer and then be an NGO leader and then be a government senior executive and then be on corporate boards or what have you. It's one thing to be successful in one area. To see an Aaron Williams do it again. And then do it again. And do it again. That tells you it's really possible for me—I'm getting goosebumps—that's when you really see talent and people being able to make it. As Black people, we can't necessarily say, 'I'm going to be here and only do this, and then this way and make it up here,' because maybe there is a ceiling there, or maybe it's not the place where you're going to grow. So don't be afraid to go somewhere else and do it again."

Our giants became role models for many, and you can too. When assigned to his final ambassadorship, to Slovenia, Ambassador Johnny Young opted to hold his swearing-in ceremony at his vocational technical high school in Philadelphia. "It was a school that catered to underprivileged kids in the inner city, and I wanted to do it there as a symbol of what is possible for kids coming from that kind of school, not that they could all aspire to be ambassador or what have you, but to offer them a symbol and some encouragement. . . . There was one thing that made me feel particularly good about the whole thing. I was talking to a young girl who was graduating from this high school and she said, 'I wasn't sure that I wanted to go to college until today. Now I know I want to go'" (Young 2013, 221–222). As they say, seeing is believing.

Mentoring

We have networks. We have role models. But what matters most is relationships. What matters most is mentors. They may come in unexpected packaging. They may come to us, or we may seek them out. They support us in many significant ways—we'll focus on a few key contributions. Some mentors—and others—may become your sponsors. All of this is possible only if you build the authentic relationships we introduced at the opening of this chapter. And that means you have responsibilities in that relationship too.

Who Are Our Mentors?

■ *As you get higher and higher up in this game, you're going to have fewer and fewer chances to have Black mentors because there aren't that many of us out there. What's really important is that you have authentic mentors: people who really care about you and want to nurture your career; they see in you the right stuff to be a leader in the organization, to make a difference. I've had plenty of those. I didn't have many Black mentors, because there were few Black or Brown senior leaders at that stage of our social and professional trajectory in this country. I was fortunate to have both white and Black mentors, really outstanding mentors, and together they made all the difference in my career.*

General Barrye Price was very clear about his most influential mentor, who happened to be someone who didn't look anything like him. He describes his mentor in Box 4.1.

Ambassador James Joseph had a similar experience of someone who was a mentor not just in terms of his career but who also embodied the ethics and vision that he aspired to: J. Irwin Miller, the CEO of Cummins Engine Company, a pioneer of corporate social responsibility. "He sort of took an interest in me from the outset and made sure I had all these international experiences, plus many other experiences that led me to the positions that I had later. He was an unbelievable person, and he shared my vision of excellence."

■ *You have to be open-minded to be able to receive willingly and in a positive way when assistance is being provided. If you have any kind of negative concerns about someone's identity or presumed experience, you're not going to accept it. And that would be a terrible mistake.*

General Price was fortunate to find so much varied support all in one person. Most of us will have a range of mentors, each of whom may have very different things to offer. Ambassador Ertharin Cousin was President Bill Clinton's White House liaison to the State Department. She was, in many respects, a fish out of water in that she had not intended originally to engage in issues related to international affairs, she did not come up through the State Department bureaucracy, and she was one of very few Black Americans at her level of appointment. She

---

Box 4.1   Barrye Price: Andrew Bacevich, a True Mentor

"There were many mentors, who taught me a lot of different things. I remain connected to them up until this day. But the most pronounced and the one who had the greatest impact on my life was Skip Bacevich, A. J. Bacevich. Mentorship is a deep, invested interest in the life of your mentee. The mentor imparts vision where there's only sight. They allow you to see over the horizon based on their experience."

A. J. Bacevich was General Price's regimental commander. Bacevich was the one who suggested General Price should pursue a PhD in history from Texas A&M University—becoming the first Black American to ever do so. But that was not all.

"I didn't know what a White House fellow was or a congressional fellow or an OSD fellow [Office of the Assistant Secretary of Defense for Sustainment Fellows Program]. He told me about those things. And all of these things from getting this PhD to becoming a White House fellow to becoming a general officer, he really laid it out for me. His investment in me is really what changed my trajectory."

There were other mentors, and, like Bacevich, "They were all Caucasian. They didn't look like me because there was nobody up there that I could look to and say, 'Ooh, I'd like to grow up to be like that guy.' I got to know General Powell when I was a White House fellow. I was a major. He became a role model of excellence for me, but he wasn't a mentor. I believe that the best fit is one when you see somebody who has the knowledge, skills, and attributes that you aspire to have. If I were waiting on somebody who looked like me, I wouldn't have a mentor. This guy Bacevich was everything I wanted to be as a husband, a father, a Christian, as an academic, a soldier, as a man. I got it all in one person. Now, there have been people who have been sponsors. There've been people who've given me advice. There've been people who have opened doors for me. But I don't see them in the same way as I see Bacevich."

---

struck mentoring gold through the combination of two very different mentors (see Box 4.2).

Whether Black, white, or purple, people are people. People can disappoint. We can expect too little of white people or too much of Black people. After gaining more experience, Alonzo Fulgham was better able to make sense of some of his early experiences looking for Black mentors. Chris Richardson also puts these experiences into a broader context of need. They describe their perspectives in Box 4.3.

Box 4.2   Ertharin Cousin: Different Mentors and Their Varied Support

"Pat Kennedy [a white male] taught me the system—the department versus the agency and knowing how they all work together and how they don't. Pat's also from Chicago. He served in the highest level of our government for both Republican and Democratic presidents, bringing all of his talents. But more importantly, he identified people like me, regardless of our race, and helped ensure that we could navigate the system effectively and appropriately.

"On a more personal basis, Ruth A. Davis was one of those people who took this young person and kind of 'shined me up.' Ruth would invite me to her house for dinner. She shared a meal and stories of her Foreign Service experiences, all the while teaching me, through her actions as well as her shared exploits, the behavioral and communication nuances required to ensure a then unpolished and unsophisticated yet talented young Black woman could successfully climb the diplomatic ladder. Her tutelage heightened my self-confidence and raised my comfort level when maneuvering unfamiliar settings, right down to the little things like 'crunchy on the left, liquid on the right.' She never said it, but learning those things—learning how to eat from forks from the outside in when you have six pieces of cutlery on both sides of the plate, hearing her stories about how she greeted heads of state or worked a room in a foreign country—those little things and more molded me into someone who was not just intellectually capable of leading in the foreign affairs community but who had the necessary social skill set, which my personal background did not provide—skills normally developed through privileged experience by my peers who don't look like me or didn't grow up on Chicago's West Side.

"Those who are second- or third-generation foreign policy operators have the benefits of conversation and relationships with those who've been in and out of the system over the years. Someone like me, who came in as an appointee, not having trained as a Foreign Service officer and from the political side of the house, those are the kinds of people who, regardless of color, don't usually make it in the department. Too often, people of color don't even usually get into the Foreign Service or become political appointees. But to get in, serve well, survive, and grow . . . I found the career Foreign Service leaders willing to give me opportunities and assignments outside my job description because I learned how to ask, how to participate and function in the system. People like Ruth and Pat helped shape me into a colleague who could add value and flourish when given opportunities, even at a young age."

Box 4.3   Alonzo Fulgham and Chris Richardson: Why Black People May Disappoint as Mentors—Power, Reach, and Time

Alonzo Fulgham: Power

"I sometimes felt that there were people of color who didn't help me when I was coming up through AID. And one of the things I learned is that a lot of them simply didn't have the power I thought they had. And that's something you must acknowledge early in your career. What's more, rather than tell you they don't have the power, they pretend. And that's where you have to acquire the skills to peel the onion back a little bit more and ask, 'Why isn't she or why isn't he really helping me?' Also, it's imperative that you cross-reference assertions when people tell you they're trying to help you. A fun fact, when I was desperate to join the agency, one person of color told me they were influential in the process and that they were going to write a letter on my behalf to increase my chance of being recruited. This never happened. And the way I was able to learn about the missing letter was that someone of color in personnel called and informed me that I needed another good recommendation to put me over the top. I told them about the person who was supposed to write a glowing reference. He said, 'That is why I am calling you off the record.' The person never wrote the letter. 'What?' I was crushed.

"So sometimes people who say they're about you, ain't about you. You can't take it personally. A lot of them don't have the power. You can't expect people you call for help to always be invested in you. You know the old expression 'Just because they're of us, doesn't mean they're about us'? Or perhaps they don't feel comfortable helping you. Maybe they don't like you! Maybe he didn't like me! I don't know. But you can't let that be an impediment to you pursuing what you want in a career."

Alonzo Fulgham: Reach

"Doris Mason Martin [then senior advisor to the Africa Bureau at USAID] said, 'Hey, Alonzo, you need to really start working on your career. I'm going to bring you in to meet John Hicks [assistant administrator for Africa] and Nate Fields [deputy assistant administrator for Africa].' So I walked into Hicks's office, and he sits me down, and Doris says, 'Okay, Alonzo,' and runs out. So here are these two extremely intimidating African American men with stature, grace, and power. And John Hicks immediately said, 'Look, I can't directly help you. I know Doris wants me to do something for you, but I can't help you. Let me tell you why. It's not that I don't want to. I would love to. But you're an FS-4. The reach is too far'—meaning that he's at the career minister level,

continues

Box 4.3   Continued

and I'm at the mid-level. Simply put, there's not much he can do to maneuver me around the internal process, because my personnel grade is not high enough to assign me to anything significant. I understood and appreciated the moment later, much more than at the time of the conversation.

"Most people would have been offended. The imagination runs away with you when you're young and insecure. 'Oh, the guy is up there in the suite, and he doesn't want to help me.' But he continued the meeting and asked me what I've been doing and what were my interests long term." John Hicks ended up giving Alonzo Fulgham some really important career advice that we will introduce later in the chapter.

Chris Richardson: Time

"The hard thing about mentorship is that the higher you get as a Black person at the State Department or a person of color—the people that I would turn to also were trying to mentor ten or twelve other African American officers. Even when I got to my mid-level positions, I was mentoring three or four African Americans below me, and those people just don't have time to deal with all of these needs. As time goes on, that just becomes really hard, because not only do you have to deal with all these intersectionalities and all these issues, not only do you have to mentor ten or twelve people, but you also have your own job as well."

So Black mentors may not be where you need them. They may disappoint for various reasons. Perhaps they can't give you the personal time you really need, or they—or you—are not in the right position for them to help. Other individuals may have everything you seem to need. That's great. But let's be clear. Sometimes having a Black mentor is exactly what you need. Sometimes only someone like you can understand and know from direct experience how to best navigate certain situations—because others don't understand your experience, and, yes, they may have their own biases. No matter how well-intentioned, they may steer you wrong.

Chris Richardson shared, "I do think that white mentors don't necessarily understand all the rivers that you have to cross and all the means that you need to use to cross them, because the rivers that they crossed are very, very different than the ones you did. They'll say, 'Just go to Nigeria' or 'That's not a problem. You'll always get ahead,' not realizing that what it takes for a white officer to get ahead isn't the same thing as what it takes for a Black officer, or a person of color, or a woman to get ahead."

No matter the mentor, you need to be confident in who you are, especially when you encounter potentially well-intentioned but ill-advised mentors, as Verone Bernard reports in Box 4.4.

Verone added, "I'd say I've had more peer mentors in this industry than actual folks who have reached back to pull forward. I don't think it's because folks don't want to; I've just never been in the room with many of them."

How Do We Find Them?

So how can you find good mentors? As with networking, sometimes it's just luck—some would say destiny: a chance encounter, being in the same place and finding some common ground, or crossing paths with

---

Box 4.4   Verone Bernard: The Limits of Non-Black Mentors

"I had mentors who didn't get it. I had a supervisor once who had an issue with how I communicated. She would say things to me like 'Use your mouth, not your hands.' And 'Can you try scaling it back a bit?' I didn't have the vocabulary back then, but I now know that I was constantly dealing with microaggressions. As a young professional, who desired to be known as someone who was coachable and eager to learn, I clung to every piece of feedback I received. This was different though. This was feedback I knew I did not want to internalize. I struggled with this because our industry requires you to learn, acknowledge, and respect the different cultures that we work with. Yet that simple courtesy could not be extended to me and my expressive way of telling stories? I finally decided to push back on her commentary. When she asked me whether I could tone it down, I said, 'I can't, and I won't. Does it truly distract from what I'm trying to tell you?' She said, 'Well, I think it's unprofessional.'

"I remember going to one of my mentors at the time who was a white woman. I recapped the many events and shared my most recent response, hoping that she would affirm me or share words of wisdom to help me navigate this relationship with my supervisor. After I told her the stories, she sort of stared at me and finally said, 'Is that a thing? I don't get it.' I had to explain, 'She's trying to paint me as this angry Black woman.' I was like, 'Oh my goodness. You can't help me. How am I supposed to navigate through this workspace?'"

peers from the past. Sometimes it's through introductions, including through formal mentoring programs. It rarely happens without your actions, including keeping an open mind about what appropriate mentors look like, but also more specific actions. We share some experience and advice below. First, let's hear from Aaron and Taylor about what you should be looking for.

■ *It's popular in our current culture to say, "Go and find a mentor," as if this person is going to be your personal coach. But it's hard to find a person who's going to give you that kind of attention and time, especially in big, complex, high-pressure environments. So you need to take pieces from everybody who can be helpful to you and create a composite mentor. And maybe some of them will step up out of the crowd and be that kind of direct one-on-one that you want. But you just can't pick a mentor. Even in these so-called formal constructs that companies and organizations create nowadays—I mean, it's okay. There's nothing wrong with it. But I just don't see it working that effectively because it's artificial.* ▶ It's like having a board of advisors. That was something one of my mentors pressed upon me. You may have somebody who's warm and fuzzy or somebody who's directly straight to the point. You're not going to get everything from one person. ■ *You have to have more than one person to go to.*

Formal mentorship programs. Formal programs still have their place. Several of our giants benefited from and now contribute to them. In fact, some of these programs were created by the first generations of giants who knew what they needed and likely did not have that or had difficulty acquiring it. Ambassador Ed Perkins and John Gravely, along with seven or eight other Black officers from USAID, USIA, and State, helped to create the Thursday Luncheon Group (TLG) in 1973, "dedicated to advancing the cause of [B]lacks in the Foreign Service." Ambassador Perkins was TLG's first executive secretary. As he reported, "Not only were [B]lack Foreign Service officers scarce—numbering only about twenty-five—but traditionally [B]lacks did not fare well in promotions or assignments. European assignments were rare; [B]lack officers were typically assigned to Africa. The Thursday Luncheon Group would lead the charge to make a dramatic change for [B]lacks. We wanted to open the Foreign Service to accepting and promoting more minorities" (Perkins 2006, 155). The TLG made significant progress in opening doors for Blacks and other minorities through continuing advocacy and watchdog efforts. Today it also provides internships and mentoring for Black officers. It provides quarterly luncheons and other events to facilitate networking and lesson sharing among its members. Stacy D. Williams took on the mantle of the TLG, which was instrumental to his starting out, as reported in Chapter 2. The Rangel, Pickering, and Payne fellowship programs also have mentoring components.

Sometimes your mentors will be the ones to tell you about these formal programs. Sundaa Bridgett-Jones learned about the International Career Advancement Program (ICAP) through her early mentors. ICAP is a mid-career professional development and leadership program. It "provides a support network, career advising, mentors, policy and research background and other assistance in order to help professionals from underrepresented groups and those who are strong advocates of diversity and inclusion have a more effective voice, achieve their potential and assume leadership positions in international affairs in the United States, in both the public and the private sectors" (ICAP n.d.).

Such programs can be instrumental in terms of providing networks, the possibility of developing mentor relationships, and access to professional development and coaching. Like Aaron, Ambassador Ruth A. Davis believes such programs cannot substitute for authentic mentors. "I believe that the most effective mentors are those who are developed through situational connections without a formal structure" (Davis 2016). This is why we started the chapter with networks. They provide an opportunity to more naturally identify and develop common interests, resonance, and relationships.

Proaction. Finding and developing such common interests and resonance requires effort on your part. Ambassador Linda Thomas-Greenfield offers an example of why we dearly need mentors, especially early in our careers (see Box 4.5).

Ambassador Thomas-Greenfield worked hard and was very effective in her work. *And* she was very lucky. Without Ambassador Perkins's intervention, who knows what might have happened.

So how can you better ensure that you get that kind of talent recognition, opportunity, and support? Being proactive means that you will likely need to push beyond your comfort zone. Dr. Jacob Gayle realized that late in his career: "I can remember early in my career feeling like I had no mentor, that I didn't have anybody necessarily to turn to. And later in life I realized that could be true because I haven't turned to anyone. Sometimes the ones who are needing of the mentoring need to take that first step and offer the first handshake." You will need to learn to advocate for yourself, assert your needs, and ask for help.

It's hard when you're just starting out. One of our focus group members shared, "When we're new, we're just trying to figure out what is expected of us. What our roles are. How we're going to fit into the

**Box 4.5   Linda Thomas-Greenfield:
The Importance of Mentors**

"In my first post, I learned that I didn't have the kind of mentors that I needed. And so I struggled. I remember my boss asking me, when he did my first EER [employee evaluation report], what were my major short-comings and my major weaknesses. And I told him, and he put it in my EER. And I didn't get tenured two times around. And every time it was those things that I, myself, had identified as my weaknesses. I don't know that he would have identified these, but I thought this was an honest process. Nobody told me otherwise. [We will say more about performance evaluation in Chapter 5].

"I kind of thought at the time that success in the Foreign Service was to make it to an 01 level, to not be involuntarily retired at an 02, which had happened to a lot of African Americans. I knew quite a few. And a friend said, 'Linda, we just got to make it to an 01. It's respectable. We make it to an 01 and we can be retired at a respectable grade.' So that was my goal. My goal was not to be an ambassador or get into the senior Foreign Service.

"I wasn't proactive in seeking mentors. I came with the idea that people were supposed to embrace me. And I wasn't embraced." ∎ *Did you think they should embrace you, that "If I do a good job and show how good I am, then people are going to recognize it and try to help me?"* "Yes. And eventually, that's what happened. And it was Ambassador Perkins [who was then the director general]. I had met him when I was in Lagos and I was his control officer. I heard from his people that he said, 'We're creating this new staff assistant position. I met this young woman in Lagos and she did a great job. See what she's doing and see if you can get her to come and work for me.'

"And that changed my whole career. At that point I started thinking, 'Maybe I can get past an 01,' because I started seeing how the system worked. I still felt that doing a great job was the way forward. So I always took seriously the jobs that I took."

larger picture. But at the same time, that doesn't mean that I just have to accept what is given to me or what's assigned to me from the organization. It's important to say what you need. It doesn't have to be hostile, but it does have to be said."

▶ I've already seen, the people who get the right coaching, mentorship, and exposure are the ones who ask for it. A lot of times, managers don't get the proper training that they need. So they don't know how to manage and develop their supervisees. Sometimes they don't think, "Oh, this would be a great opportunity.

This is a learning moment. This is what you're doing well. This is what you need to be doing better."

Stacy D. Williams's mindset at the beginning was "I know nothing about international affairs. I want to meet all the people who can help me. . . . It was kind of like you're putting yourself out there where people who want to see talent can attract that talent and recruit that talent. I always had the elevator speech before I knew what an elevator speech was. I knew within one minute I had to persuade this person to get to know me, invite me to the office, and have a larger conversation. You have to be comfortable, articulate yourself very well, and indicate that you're willing to contribute or you have the skills to contribute to the mission."

Finally, don't be afraid to ask, especially if you have something specific in mind. Aaron counts among his mentors Harris Wofford. But Aaron never worked with Harris Wofford. There was no particular reason they would have even met. ■ *He was a civil rights advisor to President Kennedy. Then he was a senior advisor to Sargent Shriver, was instrumental in the formation of the Peace Corps, and became the first director of the Peace Corps in Ethiopia, president of Bryn Mawr College, and senator of the state of Pennsylvania. He became a mentor. And he introduced me at my confirmation hearing in the Senate. When my name came up for the nomination of Peace Corps director, I reached out to him because I wanted to get his advice and counsel as part of this process. And that's how we became friends.*

What Can They Do for You?

Mentors can contribute many different things during your career. Beyond being role models, they can open their networks to you (as we discussed above), provide you with exposure and learning opportunities, explain how things work, coach you on your career choices and professional development, believe in you, push you beyond what you think you are ready for or even want, and, by extension, exercise tough love. They can also become your North Star, the people you call in a crisis.

Learning and exposure. The backbench may seem like an undesirable place to be. Yet it can provide the footstool for learning. And the backbench, too, requires an open door. Ambassador Ertharin Cousin was fortunate that Strobe Talbott, through his then special assistant Victoria Nuland, opened that door for her when she arrived at the State Department. "Then deputy secretary Strobe Talbott would hold early morning meetings where all of the assistant secretaries participated, check-in meetings. A group of backbenchers sat along the wall. Backbenchers didn't ever talk; you were just fully present. The experience gave me the opportunity, as a thirty-something, to sit against the wall and hear all of the issues of the day. I tell people I earned a PhD in international affairs after two and a half years sitting along that wall five days a week. Strobe and Victoria gave me that opportunity."

When they think you are ready, your mentors may not only introduce you to important people but also push you to speak to and represent them to these individuals. Ambassador Harry K. Thomas Jr. had that opportunity working for then national security advisor Condoleezza Rice. "She gave all of us opportunities. At first, she'd take you in and say, 'Mr. President, you remember Harry.' And then she left us. Boy, you know, you're briefing the president! And she's gone. So you always wanted to do your best for her."

Explaining how things work. We already learned from Ertharin Cousin (Box 4.2) how important mentors are in explaining everything from organizational systems to social etiquette. A huge component of how things work includes the unspoken rules. Sometimes these concern what you might expect in terms of biases in a particular context. Sometimes it's just how anyone might get ahead in that organization.

Sanola A. Daley gained an early understanding of the challenges of being an Afro-Caribbean working in Latin American regional organizations. "When I was at the OAS, I had a mix of supervisors from the Caribbean. They told me about how regional organizations worked, about some of their own challenges and some of their own opportunities." As a consequence, Sanola understood how important it was for her to perfect her Spanish-language skills and to live and work in mainland Latin America.

Dr. Jacob Gayle confirms how mentors helped him "see the unwritten rules. Every institution has a handbook of rules that are unwritten, unspoken, and the only time you ever know if you in some way infringed upon them is when something goes wrong. Something as simple as—James Dallas, who was executive vice president at Medtronic when I started there, he said, 'Listen. When you go out to dinner with any of the C-suite, any of the senior leaders, remember, one drink is fine. Two drinks, maybe, but be very cautious. But if you take that third drink, start looking for a smaller office, because you're bound to do something wrong.' That's funny for me, who's barely a drinker. But those kinds of things were very helpful advice."

Career coaching. Remember General Barrye Price's description that a mentor provides vision? That vision concerns your potential and what you can make of it. Even the great leaders benefit from others providing some of that vision and coaching them to realize it. We don't know what may be possible without having observed and experienced it. Ambassador Ed Perkins, for example, listened to USAID mission director Howard Parsons when he was working in Bangkok. "'You are having a great time here as an USAID officer,' he said, 'but you have the potential to make a difference in the shaping of foreign policy. You will not be able to do it, however, unless you become a commissioned Foreign Service officer'" (Perkins 2006, 145).

Part of career coaching is providing guidance about career options. This is how Sanola A. Daley determined she needed to leave the OAS to take up an opportunity to live and work in Costa Rica. Ambassador Johnny Young benefited from such support: "As you begin to move up in the service, you need people to tell you, 'Oh, don't take that assignment, take this assignment. I want you to consider this. I want you to consider that. You're having a problem here. Let me hear about it. Here's my suggestion about what you do.' And on and on and on. Those people, those mentors are extremely helpful." Ambassador Young's career counselor, Mary Ryan, provided him such assistance. Qatar had been a challenging assignment, and she was determined to find him a post in Europe. Later, when she became deputy assistant secretary of state for European affairs, she supported him for a post as counselor for administration in The Hague. Still later, when he was offered a position as deputy chief of mission in Cameroon, "Mary Ryan said, 'Johnny, don't take it. Don't go." Fortunately, he followed that advice and waited. His next assignment was his first ambassadorship, to Sierra Leone.

Believing in you. If we are very lucky, we experience others' belief in us at a very early age. That's important not just once you start your career but at every step toward it. Ambassador Perkins was blessed to have a counselor at the local recreational center in Portland, Oregon, Carmen Parrish Walker. "'I don't believe in boundaries,' Carmen said. 'If you set your mind to it, you can do it. Don't let doors be closed to you'. . . . Some [B]lack youth were like runners to the blocks waiting for the gun. 'You only said the word and they were ready to go,' she said. I was one of those, in Carmen's opinion, and she became my steadfast booster. . . . Almost forty years later, when Secretary of State George Shultz called Carmen to ask about my nomination for ambassador to South Africa and my ability to make a change in the entrenched

Apartheid system, she did not hesitate with her answer. 'I have no doubt that he could be the person to take that leadership,' she said. 'If anyone can do it, Ed can do it'" (Perkins 2006, 68).

Once you're in the workplace, among the most consequential people who need to believe in you are your supervisors. ■ *The most important things other people did for me were, first of all, they gave me a chance to work on important and interesting assignments. Second, they trusted my judgment, gave me a chance to voice my opinion and have a say in final decisions. And also—very important—when things went wrong, they supported me. They didn't say, "Well, I guess that didn't work out for you. Too bad." They said, "Here's where we think this didn't go right, and here's what we want to do to help you correct it."*

Ambassador Johnnie Carson had similar experiences. Some of his bosses, he said, "helped to give my career an enormous boost, turbo charged it at a very early period. I think they did it in large measure because they were confident that I could do it. Because, in fact, my failure would have been their failure. My failure would have been a judgment on their capacity to determine good officers from bad. And so I don't think they did it just for the love of doing it. They did it because they also said, 'Johnnie Carson can do this. Johnnie Carson can take on tough assignments. He can do Mozambique. He can do Uganda. He can do Kenya after the bombing. He can manage the postbombing trauma. He can rebuild embassy morale and a building. He can run things.' And I think that's the basis on which it happens."

Sometimes people believe in you, and the context simply requires that you have the opportunity to stretch and do things differently. Katherine Lee experienced that early on (see Box 4.6).

Pushing you. As implied above, sometimes believing in you means that mentors (and supervisors) push you to do things you may not necessarily feel ready for or may not think you want but that are actually in your best interest. The latter requires some trust on your part (which is why an authentic relationship is so important in mentoring). Alonzo Fulgham didn't think he wanted to go to the War College. Yet doing so completely changed the trajectory of his career, eventually leading him to run the USAID programming in Afghanistan and, later, to become the first Black acting administrator of USAID. He explained, "Ken Yallowitz, the American ambassador to Georgia, was the instigator and mentor who recommended me to the EE [Europe and Eurasia] Bureau for the War College. It was his insistence and Don Presley's acquiescence that allowed for my ascendency. The administrator opportunity would not have been possible

---

Box 4.6   Katherine Lee:
Entrusted to Act Outside the Box

Katherine Lee went to Nicaragua when they were rebuilding the post there after the Sandinistas had taken over in 1980. She was charged with developing a cultural program. "I initially came up with recommendations for future cultural and educational programming, but I wasn't completely satisfied. I felt limited by our programming budget and by having, I thought, to rely on our usual USIA resources typically available. . . . I wanted to offer more and different suggestions, but as a still-new officer I felt I needed to stay within our budget and the usual programming choices while somehow trying to incorporate as much as possible suggestions made by Nicaraguan officials. I presented my draft recommendations to the Ambassador, all the while thinking, 'This isn't really completely right for the conditions in Nicaragua, but what can I do?' Ambassador [Lawrence] Pezzullo agreed. I was not surprised when he said, 'This is not what we need. Forget the usual Washington guidelines, forget about the budget. Do whatever you want, recommend whatever you want.' That was music to my ears!! With his blessings I went back to the drawing board, excited about the opportunity to really think and act outside the box" (Lee 2005).

---

without the trust that Andrew Natsios bestowed upon me in making me the USAID mission director in Afghanistan, as I had never been a director or deputy before being asked to run the largest bilateral development program in the world. The magnitude of the assignment and the risk that Andrew accepted left an indelible mark on my life and career. Simply put, he would have been fired if I had not been successful."

Linda Thomas-Greenfield (Box 4.5) originally didn't aspire to an ambassadorship; she didn't think it was possible. She was taking a conservative approach to her career, thinking she wasn't ready for promotion. A mentor told her, "'Linda, you need to open your window.' And I said, 'I can't open my window. I'm not ready. . . . I'm going to wait until six years, and then I'll open my window, and if I don't get promoted, I'll retire at a respectable 01 level. And he goes back down to his office, he drafts the cable, comes back, puts it in front of me, and says, 'Sign this. You're ready to be promoted.' And so, I said to my husband, 'This means my career could be over in six years.' And he said, 'Yeah, go for it.' And I got promoted that one first time. From that moment on, I sailed forward. I also realized that I was better than making it to an

01 and that there was a future career trajectory. And I owned it at that point, but it was only at that point that I owned it."

Ed Grier describes how his mentor at Disney, Judson Green, "kind of put his arm around me and, for whatever reason, just helped me along. He'd take the time to give me very direct and specific feedback, especially on my writing of audit reports. He would say, 'That's not a very good report. Let's rework it, and here's how.' Honestly, he would sit down with me, give me some tips and direction, and I'd work hard to meet his expectations. I always felt very satisfied when he finally said, 'That's a very good report.' He gave me opportunities, and he let me know that he had confidence in me. I can still hear his voice saying, 'Trust me. I think you can do this.' He was probably the first person to support me in that way. It gave me a whole lot of confidence."

Seemingly undesirable jobs. Sometimes being pushed means being pushed into jobs that seem very unappealing. Remember Alonzo Fulgham's encounter with John Hicks (Box 4.3)? He describes the advice he got in Box 4.7.

Box 4.7   Alonzo Fulgham: Advice for Getting Noticed

"John Hicks said, 'Look, I'm going to give you points that I need you to remember for the rest of your career.' He said, 'If you're going to be successful in this business, Alonzo, the first thing you must remember is go somewhere where everybody else isn't working. Personally, I don't want you to come into the Africa Bureau. There are plenty of us here. Okay? I want you to go to another bureau and find a job and make a difference there. And, by the way, do well.' He said, 'The second thing you can never let happen is you can never let your supervisor define who you are.'

"And those lessons played a major role in how I defined my career going forward, because he was telling me that because of the competition, all of the places that you would like to go and enjoy, you're never going to get the experience that you need to be successful and distinguish yourself. He said, 'Alonzo, you have to distinguish yourself. And I think you need to think about the following . . .' And he started naming off places. I was like, 'Yuck.' It was all the places nobody else wanted to go at the time. 'Most importantly, please do a good job. Because that's how you're going to get noticed.'"

Ambassador Johnny Young took on those tough assignments nobody wanted. Guinea Conakry was one of them. After that, opening up the first US embassy in Qatar probably seemed a breeze. Like most of our giants, he frequently advised others on their career paths in this field. He reported, "I tried to impress on these young people the importance of keeping your eyes open and doing the kind of work that's going to bring you to the attention of people that you're dependable, reliable, you do excellent work, etc., etc."

■ *Raise your hand; take on a tough assignment; volunteer for the opportunities that nobody else wants to do.*

Tough love. Part of this pushing is tough love. But mentoring tough love can be even tougher. Ed Grier described the criticism he would get for his writing. He, rightly, recognized that as mentoring and coaching. He was not defensive but grateful. Ambassador Harry K. Thomas Jr. couldn't agree more: "I try to tell some of these Black kids who haven't been criticized by their white supervisors, 'That's patronizing. People are being patronizing. They think you can't take it or you're not good enough, so they leave you alone.'" ■ *Yeah, they let you wallow in your mediocrity, and that's a disservice to you. Being challenged is critical for career advancement.*

▶ Being on the receiving end of tough love is not always easy. It is rare to find someone who will take the time to give you that piece of advice and sometimes criticism that could mean the difference between you excelling or regressing. As a young Black professional in a white world, it's easy to feel that every negative comment is racially based, because more times than not it is. However, if you are fortunate enough to have someone talk straight with you, see it as an opportunity to learn and grow. Ideally, we all need to find someone who tells us, "I'm going to tell it to you how it is. I'm not about to sugar coat it. When I see you slipping, I'm going to call you out." And in the best of all worlds, they will also say, "I'm going to go to bat for you when no one else is. I'm not going to play politics with you."

It's not always easy being the one providing that tough love. ■ *I think it's important that a young person coming up has the ability to listen and take good advice from people who really have their best interest at heart. But sometimes it can be tough. I've had those conversations with people about how they thought they were ready to take the next steps. I said, "You're not ready yet. You need to do a and b before you go to c."*

Calling in a crisis. We all face challenges at one point or another in our careers. Sometimes they rise to the level of crises. It's important to know whom you can call in those circumstances and for what. Dominique Harris reports, "I can pick up the phone and call a litany of people and say,

'I'm having a hard time. Here's what I'm dealing with. Here's what I'm working through.' . . . I have people in their thirties and in their forties, and in their fifties, sixties, and seventies, who are kind of part of my life board of directors, and I go to different people for different things."

When still at USAID, Ed Perkins had a mentor he could turn to help him "think about avenues [he] should take." "And when I had to fight battles, he'd help me characterize—well he would characterize what the battle entailed and how to go about it." Ambassador Ertharin Cousin reported, "I was in the middle of something crazy, a really thorny diplomatic issue. I knew I had to find and talk with then assistant secretary for Africa Linda Thomas-Greenfield. She was out for a run, and her office tracked her down. She talked me through the situation. I served more effectively as World Food Programme executive director knowing that I had a relationship and access to Linda's keen experience through the phone in my pocket, that I could call her up and she would answer. She gave me much more bandwidth than I possessed operating alone." These networks are helpful not just in helping you personally but also in supporting and achieving your professional agenda. Ertharin Cousin said, "I can't overstate the importance that your network provides toward building your value add and political leverage. I could call up an ambassador or foreign government official and say, 'Well, I was able to talk to [then former national security adviser] Susan Rice, and she suggested x, y, and z.'"

What Are Sponsors?

We've already seen some great examples of sponsorship in the examples above. It's different from mentoring. Sponsorship is when people recommend you to others, like Mary Ryan supporting Ambassador Johnny Young's bid to become counselor for administration in the Netherlands. Dr. Jacob Gayle summed it up nicely: "A sponsor is almost like a secret Santa. You don't even know sometimes who your sponsor is. The sponsor sees your potential, believes in you, and is willing to put her or his reputation on the line to step up and make sure that you have opportunities for growth and development. That's something you don't ask somebody, like, 'Hey, would you be my sponsor?' It's something that I think you merit. You develop a relationship, and you demonstrate your ability and your worthiness and readiness to be sponsored."

A sponsor relationship does not necessarily have to be a personal mentoring relationship. Sponsors, in fact, could be people who have not mentored you per se but still see your potential and believe you can do the job they recommend you for. Effective sponsors have to have the power and influence to actually help you get the position they put you up for. Not every mentor will have this kind of credibility and clout for a particular context or post. ▶ Aaron gave me a good piece of advice. Sometimes your sponsor can't be Black. Sometimes you need someone else to legitimize you, but you can have others on the sidelines waiting for you, giving you that advice to help you navigate these rocky waters.

■ *Sponsorship should be viewed in the same context as mentoring, and one should practice broad engagement. Become well known throughout your agency, department, or firm and within your industry or sector. My advice has always been to cast your net widely and attempt to gain the attention and support of key decisionmakers across the organization.*

It's a Relationship

■ *From my experience, I can see there's a hunger and a thirst for mentoring out there, but it's also become kind of a formulaic mentality. Young people will come to me and say, "I want you to be my mentor." Well, what does that mean? And often an organization will create a corps of mentors to serve in this role, but in my view, this is an artificial relationship. Although one must recognize that in some cases this can be a useful approach, I find that often it fails to provide one with the type of concerned engagement that really counts.* Dr. Helene Gayle has had the same experience. "Mentoring develops naturally because of a relationship, not because of a forced mentorship." And there is no secret formula. Dr. Gayle continues, "Young people come expecting that there's a prescribed path. People ask, 'What course should I take in undergraduate to do what you're doing today?' There is no such course. So I do think that this whole notion of mentorship has become a check-the-box obligatory thing versus how do you actually develop authentic relationships with people?"

▶ So much of today's success is measured by one's accomplishments, affiliations with prestigious institutions, and what you can fit into a 140-character tweet that gets however many "likes." The value of soft and interpersonal skills has become somewhat diminished. A mentor is more than a source for upward mobility in one's career. Being genuinely interested in someone's well-being leads to the strongest relationships. People remember when you take the time to ask how they are doing or how their family is or to recall a unique detail of their lives. The mentors in our lives have enormous responsibilities and may lack the time we might need from them. But making "the ask" is so much easier when you have established the foundation for a genuine relationship. Mentorship is not a transactional relationship. It takes two people to make it work.

Sanola A. Daley learned this. When coached that she needed to do better at networking, she knew she had to do it in a way that was true to herself. She calls it "authentic networking": "I needed to be aggressive about networking, in the sense that I shared what I was doing with others without tooting my own horn, but just trying to understand where others were, what they were doing, what opportunities were in the organization. Just be really intentional about it. And so I learned the value of networking, but I say 'authentic networking,' because I can't do fake. I try to connect with people. I try to understand what people are about, and so that has served me very well."

Dominique Harris is very assertive when it comes to seeking mentors. She has made a career of making mentors lifelong friends, as she describes in Box 4.8.

Box 4.8   Dominique Harris: From Mentors to Friends

"I'm such a people person. There is something about genuine friendships, genuine mentorships, genuine sponsorships that makes them worthwhile. Everybody has twenty-four hours in a day, and I tell people all the time, 'I don't spend time with people I don't want to spend my time with.' A lot of my mentors have become really influential people in my life and really good friends. And that is the highest point of pride when you can say, 'This person started out as my mentor, and now they're my sponsor. And now we're friends.'

"I think people really enjoy folks who are like, 'Tell me about your career, tell me about your journey.' And I think, our generation, we don't do that enough. We always go into it thinking, 'What can they do for me? How can they help me find a job? How can they connect me with their network?' versus saying, 'Tell me about your journey.' Young folks need to invest their time and learn and hear about the history. And at some point down the line that will be reciprocated.

"I met a lady at Cargill whom I just liked. I met her for ten or fifteen minutes. I thought, 'I like her.' And every time I came to Minneapolis, I would put time on her calendar. I was in DC. She was in Minneapolis. We had very different roles within our company. And then, two or two and a half years down the road, she said, 'Hey, I have this awesome job. I think you'll be great for it. You should apply.' And that was when I made the decision to move from DC to Wichita, Kansas. The opportunity to work for her, to learn from her, was a game changer for me, from a professional-development and personal perspective.

"So this notion of instant gratification when you're talking about networks and mentors and things like that, I think that's something that we probably need to get beyond. We really need to think holistically about what this person can add to your life and what you can add to theirs."

■ *As experienced professionals, I think, we have to be available for young people. When I was coming up, people were always available for me. And I have always tried to be respectful and grateful for the assistance they gave me. One of the things that irritates me, and one of the things I've always tried to avoid my entire career, is what I call the "I-only-contact-you-when-I-need-you-syndrome." I believe in building relationships with my mentors. I don't just call somebody when I need them. I try to stay in touch with them over a lifetime. The guy who was my first boss in Honduras? We are still the very best friends. I touch base with Tony three or four times a year. And I always tell him how much he meant to me as I was coming through the system—because I know people appreciate that and because it's true.*

Your Responsibility in a Mentoring Relationship

Being genuine and building authentic relationships is the most important responsibility you have in a mentoring relationship. Too often young people can overlook that. Whether consciously or not, they may be thinking that mentoring is just part of the giants' job; it's expected of them, so they should do it. Mentors mentor, and mentees receive. Period, full stop. Or perhaps they think, "Why would that giant want to take more of an interest in me than what I am already asking for? I'll just leave them alone." In fact, a mentoring relationship can bring a lot to both sides, including deep friendship, as Dominique Harris and Aaron suggest. And it's just obvious that when you bring your whole self to a relationship, the potential for a deeper, more mutually beneficial relationship is that much greater.

There are other responsibilities as well. You need to demonstrate that you are worthy of your mentors' investment. That doesn't mean you won't make mistakes, but it does mean that you will work and try hard, as they expect. Ambassador Reuben Brigety counts Aaron as a mentor, who, among other things, taught him, "If you have a mentor, you should never make that mentor embarrassed to be your mentor. I've been burned that way a couple times, and I'm sure I've made decisions that have disappointed some other people that have mentored me."

You also have a responsibility to listen to and follow up on your mentors' advice, or at least to provide a good reason why you did not. As Stacy D. Williams explains, "A mentor would say, 'Stacy, I want you to go talk to x,' and they would give you a certain amount of time to go talk to x. They would then come back and say, 'Well have you talked to the person I asked you to speak to?' So I took to heart whenever I was given a directive to immediately go do it, and people paid attention to that. That word would carry to others, so you're going to get more help."

Sometimes great advice or even opportunities are not the right fit, at least not at that time. Taylor had an early experience turning down an offer from a potential mentor. ■ *I saw Taylor handle that challenge, and I thought she handled it extraordinarily well. That was the right decision, because she was in a position where she was gaining valuable experience. To leave her current organization would have been a mistake. And she stayed in this leader's good graces. She didn't burn any bridges.* There is an art to that, and it starts with appreciation and respect.

C. D. Glin has thought a lot about what he can and should do in a mentoring relationship. He has focused on trying to make it as easy as possible for people to see and appreciate him, then help him. We already talked about how he recommends volunteering as a way to become visible. This is also a way to demonstrate interest, "because if it's something that you've actioned, you demonstrate you are really serious about it." In asking, "How do I make it easy for people to want to support me?" he answers with three things: demonstrate your interest, do your research, and "if you're going for an ask, go with an offer as well. . . . I want to shape everything around being a giver. 'How could I be helpful to you?'" Finally, he has been very intentional about taking advantage of every opportunity. "The biggest challenge is the pressure of not squandering that opportunity, of living up to the expectations."

You Can't Do It Alone

Mentoring is a lifelong endeavor. It takes a lifetime to identify and assemble a network of people who genuinely care about you and want to see you succeed. While it seems daunting at first, it's important to look at the long game. ▶ What I initially lacked in mentorship and counsel, I have now. I'm accessing more circles and getting the ability to talk to more people. Mentorship is a long game. At first, I felt like, "I'm just kind of flailing in the wind." But now I feel a little bit more grounded. I have people I can go to. As Ambassador Johnny Young put it, "You can't do it alone, I don't care how brilliant you may be." Everybody who is successful in this world has to have a network of supporters and mentors.

In the next chapter, we'll look more broadly at how to navigate your career. We've already touched some on that here, because it cannot be done effectively without support, mentoring, and sponsors.

5

Navigating
Your Career

*For me, becoming isn't about arriving somewhere or achieving a
certain aim. I see it instead as forward motion, a means of evolving,
a way to reach continuously toward a better self. The journey
doesn't end.*

—Michelle Obama, *Becoming*, 419

A career is not a passive thing. It requires action. It's a process that you
navigate. This chapter takes you through that process, from how to
think about your first job to creating and seizing opportunities, making strategic choices, and making the most out of lucky breaks . . . and
disappointments. We'll tackle some hard issues, like how racism can
impact the opportunities available to you. And we will demystify the
formal process by which you advance in organizations: performance
review. Our giants provide important guidance on how you can take
the reins at every step in your career to ensure you get to where you
want to go.

This chapter will become more relevant as you embark on and
begin to move along your career path. We hope you will return to it
when you are at career decision points and every time you prepare for
a performance review. We want to start with where you may be now.

I'm Just Starting Out:
How Should I Be Thinking About My Career?

We want to make three important points for you to focus on as you think about the start of your career: (1) don't focus too much on the far beyond; (2) know what entry level means, get in the door, and know when to move on; and (3) assert your talent. Aaron has advised a lot of people on these points. He shares his guidance with you below.

First, when we think about a career, we often start with where we want to go and what we ultimately want to become. That's great. Having a vision is crucial, as we'll discuss below. ■ *You should be thinking, but not worrying, about the long game. At the beginning, you just need to make sure you are taking the necessary steps to excel at your current job, position yourself for the next steps, and so on. Besides, you can't tell what the long game is anyway, because by the time you get there, it's going to be very different. So have a sense of direction, be flexible, and make sure that you are always working toward amassing that next skill set you need for excellence.* Dominique Harris got similar advice from her mentor, Joan Dudik-Gayoso, who said, "Life happens while you're busy planning, so don't be so stuck on that pathway that you miss some other great opportunities that will develop you or shape you in ways that you don't expect."

Second, we understand you want to move fast. We understand that younger generations put a premium on their experience, whatever it may be, and believe themselves ready for anything. A lot of entry-level jobs seem heavy on the clerical and administrative, and you just want to move straight to the substance. We get it. Our giants commented on their admiration for these characteristics and the confidence and energy they represent. But everyone has to put in some time and do some learning to get beyond entry level.

It's not enough that you have experience in x, if the job calls for y. And you may believe you have done x. Perhaps you had a related project in school or even gained experience with it in the workplace. But if you haven't done x in this particular organization, you may not be ready for that next step. Let's take proposal writing as an example.

■ *The cold-blooded reality is, if they hire you and put you into a higher-level job, would you be ready on day one to write a proposal to USAID on behalf of this organization? If not, then you're not ready to take a mid-level job. A mid-level job means you should not expect training before hitting the ground running. You might get some minimal organization orientation, like, "This is our computer system. This is our cost-analysis package. Here are the people who are working with you on this proposal." But you shouldn't expect training on "Here is how we do this." If you're going to be at the mid-level and get that salary, you better be able to perform when you walk in the door. So are you ready?*

Now, if you take the entry-level job, we don't expect that. Because we're going to train you. You may be a good writer, who now needs to be trained to do this organization's style of proposal. And we're going to give you a chance to fail, which you're going to do extensively in the first year. But you'll also get mentored by other people and learn the ropes in a safe environment. Also, we're not putting your name on anything that counts against our bottom line. And yes, you will be at a lower salary. It's more than paying your dues. You will be learning and getting supported.

You should never be worried about starting at the entry level. And what you might call entry level, we might not necessarily characterize as that. If you're good, you're going to rise up. Everybody wants talented people. Smart organizations recognize and reward talent. And if your talent is not recognized and rewarded, Aaron has more advice for you. ■ *I've seen this happen. I recommended someone for a new job in my organization, but over time, I observed that he didn't receive the promotion opportunities that I thought he merited. He didn't work for me. He worked for another group. He came to me and said, "I've got this other opportunity." I said, "You need to leave and go work there, because they obviously want to give you a chance, and the person you work for here doesn't see it that way." So that's a reality. And that might happen in your first couple of jobs. That's okay. You will gain experience, and your talent will grow and will ultimately be recognized. This environment is so competitive, you've got to get in the door. So don't turn down something at the right place because you think it's not at the right level. Because if you get in and you do well, it's going to be fine.*

Third, now that you have that first job and are maybe in your dream organization, don't rest on your laurels. Alonzo Fulgham learned that early: "When I got that first job, I didn't think about, 'Will that first job get me the next job?' I thought, 'I'm happy to be here.' And that's the pitfall that a lot of young officers fall into. Most of your contemporaries took the job because they have their sights set on another job eighteen months from now. . . . So you're happy, but the boy on the outside lane is just lapping you." ■ *One of my first jobs after getting my MBA was at General Mills. One of my fellow associates had a chart up on his wall. Every year they brought in about ten to fifteen new MBAs. He had all of our names up on the wall and had them marked out by category: what brands we were working on and our anticipated future promotions. If you don't understand how the game is being played, you're going to be frustrated by it, as you watch others and ask, "Why are they moving so fast?"*

As you learn the way things are done and you gain confidence in the systems as they are, you also need to assert your talent. ▶ When you're at a junior level, you learn how to do your job in a certain way. And you're going to achieve results. But I'm striving to advance. I'm not trying to be in this position forever. So I know I need to make suggestions and be confident in what I'm saying. And I need to watch for when it's time to move on. The values and the tools and techniques that you learn from big organizations are great. But to exercise your innovation and imagination, you may need to get outside them.

What Does the Trajectory Look Like?

The trajectory of careers in US foreign policy has changed, and continues to change, since the time many of our giants started out. The new pathways are not linear. As C. D. Glin puts it, "It's a zig and a zag. . . . We need to be talking to each other and teaching each other about 'diversifying our personal portfolio': having a lot of different opportunities and being okay with change." C.D. Glin talks about reinventing yourself along the lines of Madonna or Will Smith: "These people reinvent themselves and they are still relevant." You need to be adaptable. You may need to reinvent yourself in order to be relevant in the world today and as the world of your profession evolves.

■ *I think your biggest challenge will be deciding if you want to zigzag or if you want to go straight. There is still a road for people who want to go straight. I think sometimes that straight pathway is disparaged by younger generations. They think, "That's just traditional. It's not creative, not innovative. You've got to be able to move around." Well, maybe, maybe not. There will always be a place for somebody who comes in, let's say to the Foreign Service, at the age of thirty and makes ambassador by the time they're forty.*

▶ You've got to run your own race. Whether mine is straight or all outside the lines, it's going to be mine. I've always been a person who likes a plan. I like to see where I'm going and know my end goal. But now, knowing that I'm not taking the traditional route, I'm not starting out in the Foreign Service, I'm kind of breaking ranks with what I thought I was going to do. My biggest obstacle will be playing it safe. There are so many things that I could do with development. I know I need to continue to dream big and to bet on myself. I can zigzag, I can jump, and I can be a chameleon every time I move to the next thing.

We want you to know there are many roads to success in US foreign policy careers. Many of them are multisectoral, crossing the lines between the government, for-profit, and nonprofit sectors.

Multisectoral Careers

■ *Taylor's generation—your generation—is likely to have multiple career tracks, in multiple organizations, in multiple sectors of our economy. Thus, in my view it will be valuable to gain experience in business, government, or the nonprofit world as your career moves forward. And make sure that every stop along the way is a building block toward opening up an opportunity to go into and to be successful in this next phase of your career. Again, there are always people who will prefer the continuity and security of a particular organization or sector, and I certainly respect that. My point is that planning on a multisectoral career and gaining experience in various sectors will make you a stronger leader. My business experience with International Multifoods and General Mills was golden; both were Fortune 500 companies. It was another version of graduate school, but in the real world. This experience has proven to be invaluable throughout my career. I felt like I was playing on the Yankees. The environment was demanding; I was surrounded by driven individuals pursing common goals, with significant risk and reward.*

Many of our giants worked in different sectors during the course of their careers, sometimes sequentially and sometimes moving back and forth among them. Dr. Jacob Gayle, for example, worked for the US government, in academia, at the United Nations, in the nonprofit and philanthropic sectors, and most recently in the private sector at the world's largest medical technology and solutions company, Medtronic. James Joseph was a civil rights activist, became a minister, worked in academia, led major corporate social responsibility initiatives in the private sector, became a politically appointed undersecretary of the Department of the Interior and then ambassador of South Africa, and then made a major impact in the foundation world, serving as the president of the Council on Foundations and organizing and becoming the founding chair of the Association of Black Foundation Executives.

There are many facets to US foreign policy, well beyond the State Department and USAID. There are also foundations, private-sector consulting firms, and NGOs, for example. Sundaa Bridgett-Jones expressed hope that you would consider and populate all of these types of organizations: "I would like for us to be viewed as a group that is as diverse in its thinking and as diverse in its representation as white foreign policy practitioners are."

The Value and Limits of Private-Sector Experience

Aaron encourages you to get some experience in the private sector in particular. ■ *Because if you want to have a government career, having private-sector experience is magical in government—way beyond what it should be. We give the private sector far too much credit for being this magical place where brilliant people do amazing things. In our society we celebrate the captains of industry: Jack Welch, Steve Jobs, Bill Gates. But in my humble opinion, I don't think that any of those individual leaders would be successful leaders in government. I believe it's infinitely harder to be successful in government than in the private sector. In the business world you control most of the factors that go into your decisionmaking and your business operations, up until the point that you come in contact with the consumer. Obviously, there are a lot of competitors in any business, but you're in control. In government, you're rarely in control.*

Here's an example. Let's say I was the head of AID's Latin American Bureau, and I decided, based on conversations with the president of Ecuador, that we should support his interest in creating a major environmental program in Ecuador, which is also in the US national interest. Then, as a very wise government executive, I go up on the Hill and I brief all of the key committees, subcommittees, etc.; and I would brief other key players at the State Department and the National Security Council, those officials responsible for Latin America. Everybody is on board, and we agree to move forward. We have a handshake agreement with the government of Ecuador. As we're about to launch this project, some staffer on the Hill— who works for a member of Congress, who was not involved in the consultation process whatsoever and has no authority per se over this—could determine that this project should not proceed and bring it to a screeching halt. Bill Gates, Steve Jobs, Jack Welch never faced that. Ever. To be successful in government, you have to be extraordinarily resourceful and a great manager, to handle this wide array of factors and stakeholders. A lot of very successful businesspeople would never have the patience for that.

But because in our society, people believe in this magical place called the private sector, it's infinitely valuable to have that experience. And, don't get me wrong, it is valuable. You learn the discipline of managing financials, the profit and loss or bottom line, and develop the ability to lead people who are very smart and talented in a certain direction. And you have to work really hard, because there are a lot of people just as smart as you are who are often vying to take your job. So you have to be assertive and hardworking.

No matter where you start, have the courage to try it out. Believing you have options creates options. You can walk away if and when you feel you need to, whether because the job isn't a good fit or because you just see something more fulfilling out there. Ambassador Rea Brazeal took this attitude: "I decided to try out the Foreign Service. . . . I say 'trying out' intentionally because I think it's important for people to believe that they have options" (Brazeal 2007, 29–30).

Having a Vision

No matter where you start, it's important to have a vision. What is it you want from your career? What are the passions you want to make sure you play to? What values will drive you? These are the things that give you a sense of direction. They can help you assess when an opportunity is a good fit for you personally, and they can help you to stay on course with what matters most to you.

As we mentioned above, having a vision doesn't mean that you have a very specific idea of what you want to be and how you will get there. It's more about your general aim and values you want to live by. In Box 5.1, Dr. Helene Gayle provides a good example of a guiding vision and its various components.

In this type of work, we don't often get to see the fruits of our labor. And even if we do, it's hard to specify exactly how we contributed.

Box 5.1   Helene Gayle:
A Guiding Vision for a Meaningful Career

Dr. Helene Gayle was interested in medicine. Her experience with Operation Crossroads Africa (see Box 2.8) confirmed her interest in finding a way to work both internationally and domestically. Beyond that, she explained, "I wanted to make a tangible contribution, to find a way of giving back. The notion of equity and social justice has always driven me. And I have moved more and more toward things that I feel get at that crucial issue of inequity. That's why I wanted to do public health as opposed to practicing clinical medicine. I love clinical medicine. It's great. But you take care of one person at a time as opposed to changing systems. That conceptual commitment to creating positive social change has been what has always guided me." Dr. Gayle's vision encompasses a broad category (medicine), some guiding principles (equity and social justice), and, based on those, a selection of a subfield (public health) and a vision for the kind of impact she wants to make (systems change).

Being able to articulate this vision made it easier for others to support her and for her to assess options and opportunities. "I had a vision. And it wasn't myopically focused, where I was the subject matter expert, and I only do 'this.'" It was also sufficiently broad that people could advise her on the various ways to work internationally, such as development and not just diplomacy. But, as she put it, she didn't just tell people, "I want to save the world."

Philip Gary described it this way: "Your failures, you see immediately. Your successes you often never see. And that's something unique about development. It's rare that any single action or program is going to be wholly successful within the timeframe you're participating in it. Conversely, if you get something really wrong it's likely to be there for everyone to see almost immediately. . . . You have to have a long-term goal, commitment, and vision—not just for yourself but whatever you're working on. That has to guide you" (Gary 2017, 84). Understanding these dynamics and having that vision can help you to be more resilient when you encounter inevitable frustrations and enable you to see the bigger picture and long game of what you are contributing to.

It's okay if your vision is not very clear at the outset. It takes some time to know yourself and your interests better and to learn what the options are. ▶ I hear some people say, "I want to be the director general of the Foreign Service or USAID administrator." I'm not going to sit here and say that I want to do that. I just want to lead a life and leave a legacy where I have made an impression on people. Whether it's something super big or really small, I want to continue to be of service to others. I don't care if I get an award, I'm in a magazine, I give a TED Talk. . . . I don't care. I just hope that over the span of my career I can leave pieces of my legacy where people say, "Taylor Jack did something phenomenal." That's it. That's all I really want. I can't tell you what my specific aspirations are because I feel like I'm still learning. We hope that, like Taylor, you will dream big.

Finding a Vision That Fits

The vision you land on doesn't have to be absolutely fixed. As you learn and experience more, you can amend, expand, or specify it. The one aspect that should not waiver is how that vision fits with who you are: your identity, your preferences, and your strengths (which are frequently based on what you most enjoy doing). It's important to start with knowing yourself and your personality, as Philip Gary puts it. "If you want to be in Foreign Service, you've got State, AID, the foreign agricultural service, the foreign commercial service, the labor service, the intelligence agencies, etc. Each one of those appeals to different skill sets and personalities. Make sure you pick the one that's right for you." When Paul Weisenfeld decided he would leave private law practice to work in international development, he investigated the World Bank and the US government to see where his aspirations and personality would fit best. He learned that in the World Bank lawyers mostly do contract work, whereas in USAID and the State Department, there are more opportunities for lawyers "to get involved beyond just the wording on the page."

Dominique Harris wanted to make sure her path was a strong fit with her values. Like many of us drawn to development work, she was worried about what it might mean to work for a for-profit company. As she contemplated an opportunity at Cargill, she discussed these issues with her close mentors. "I had been on Capitol Hill and at the State Department. And this opportunity came, and it was a new space. I didn't know what lobbying was, and I was going to a big corporation." She worried she might be "selling out." Her mentors assured her, "No, you're not. We need good talent everywhere. We need good talent in the nonprofit, government, and private sectors. So, if you think that this is a right road for you and that you can make a difference, take your talent there." It's good to ask these questions. Dominique's example tells us it's also good to discuss these issues with people you trust and who know you. Ultimately you need to decide what the best fit is for you.

Ambassador Rea Brazeal provides an example of knowing and playing to your specific preferences. She knew she wanted to work in international affairs but also wanted to spend time in Washington, especially at the height of the civil rights movement. She opted to become an economic officer. "I could argue for assignments in Washington because economic policy is made in Washington. And if you're going to be part of that, you have to be back here." But economic policy work has other features that may not be a good fit for some. She advises that you consider how tolerant you are of ambiguity. If you are not comfortable with not seeing the resolution of issues you are working on, she suggests you not work on the economic or political sides of diplomacy.

Taking Risks in Support of Your Vision

Knowing yourself and having a vision can help you to know when taking a risk might be worthwhile and also when it's time to walk away from an opportunity. Ambassador Ed Perkins took important risks in his career, some of which didn't appear logical from the outside looking in. Even in a seemingly linear path (the Foreign Service), he zigged, and he zagged. Perkins was a management cone officer waiting for an assignment when a political officer position opened in Ghana. As Ambassador Johnny Young described it, "They couldn't find a political officer. Ed said, 'I'll go.' The job was two grades below his job. And he went out to Ghana, and he made friends with everyone. There was a coup. Jerry Rawlings came to power. He knew everybody. And that was the beginning of great things for him. . . . He demonstrated that he could do exceptional work there, and it made all the difference in the world to his career."

Ambassador Perkins was very clear about and committed to his oath and his values. He took jobs no one wanted because he was asked to do so. When offered the ambassadorship to apartheid South Africa, he reports, "The president asked me matter-of-factly if I would consider this assignment as a risk to my career. 'I imagine it will be, Mr. President, but when I took the oath of office, I didn't take an oath to go where there were only risk-free assignments. That is the way we are taught in the Foreign Service'" (Perkins 2006, 258).

Sometimes it's harder to walk away from something you've worked hard for and earned. Sanola A. Daley took this kind of risk (see Box 5.2).

**Box 5.2   Sanola A. Daley:
Winning and Then Walking Away**

"When people don't know your background and they make assumptions about you, your leadership ability, your education, and your ability to perform, they will cut off opportunities. This happened to me.

"There was a transition in an organization I was working in. It was very competitive. There was a limited number of jobs available, and we were all asked to reapply for positions. What was previously ten people doing ten jobs had become ten people competing for one position. I was selected for that spot. The reorganization occurred. However, there was new management, a new philosophy, and an obsession with getting rid of everything from before.

"I never got a chance to establish who I was or what I could do because assumptions were made about me and my leadership capability— I think, because I was a young Black person, and therefore I could not be taken seriously in the role—even though I was qualified, competed, and beat out other candidates. Several incidents happened and comments were made. Some of them had racial undertones. I eventually decided to walk away rather than stay, because I felt that the environment had become toxic. What really affected me was the inability to feel comfortable enough to perform and to flourish, to do what I was capable of doing.

"The minute I walked away and found leadership that listened, I did so much better. I started doing exactly what I wanted to do. The initiatives that I suggested as ideas to explore, which were previously dismissed, were the things I began working on that continue to be successful. So I have no regrets. I really trusted my gut. It was the right thing for me in terms of growth, and everything worked out in the end. I learned a lot about personal resilience from that experience. It was a very traumatic experience for me, I won't lie to you. But I came out of it stronger, better, more confident, healthier."

▶ I'm so glad Sanola shared her story, because often, when you do get an opportunity in this field, you think it's a golden ticket. And you hold onto it, even though it's toxic, professionally and personally. But we're almost ingrained, as a people, "Know this is your shot; just bear down and get through it." But you have to bet on yourself, know when enough is enough, and know your worth and that something better will come to you. I think that is so important, especially for young people who are getting started, because all of us just want a big moment, and we don't always think about the cost when it's not the right fit. Sanola's is a great example of holding the reins of your career.

Holding the Reins of Your Career

▶ Some people have their mind made up that "one day I'm going to be this." And they ask, "How do I get there? What's going to make me different?" I never try to be the next anyone. I want to be Taylor Jack. ■ *It's not easy. And you also have to be lucky. Never underestimate luck. Timing is a part of luck. But you have to be ready. When luck extends her hand to you, you've got to be able to take her hand and walk through that door.*

We want to make sure you can grab that hand of luck when it is offered to you. We also want to make sure that you are not just waiting on luck and that you do not assume that every opportunity extended to you is your lucky day. You need to stay in charge and maintain responsibility for your career. It starts with having the tenacity to withstand imposter syndrome, as discussed in Chapter 3. Always be at the ready to say no to "can't"—whether you are responding to others or to yourself. Holding on to the reins of your career also means working to not get pigeonholed, even if it's in an area where you excel; knowing when and how to say "I won't accept this"; and learning how to maneuver within the system you find yourself in.

The Africa Circuit

Black people have been, and still are, most commonly assigned and associated with positions in sub-Saharan Africa and, to a lesser extent, the Caribbean. Historian Michael Krenn (1999) refers to the "Negro circuit" of the 1920s to the 1940s. Many Blacks served in Liberia, where they lived out their entire Foreign Service careers. If they enjoyed subsequent appointments, these were largely on a circuit that included Haiti, other African countries, and eventually Portuguese-speaking posts (e.g., the Azores and Portugal) and a few others (such as the Canary Islands, Cuba,

Egypt, and Turkey). By extension, even today, very few Black people serve in Europe through the State Department. Ambassador Harry K. Thomas Jr. called the Africa Bureau the "Affirmative Action Bureau." This geographical bias persists in both the State Department and USAID. Because African posts have not been considered as important as others historically, and because Black officers are most often assigned there as a matter of course, more senior Black officers (and mentors) often advise avoiding African posts. Barbara Mae Watson, then deputy assistant secretary of state for security and consular affairs, so advised Ambassador Rea Brazeal, for example. Ambassador Johnny Young was similarly advised.

There is nothing inherently wrong with being assigned to and working in Africa. Beyond a personal passion and an interest in heritage, Africa is crucial to international affairs. As Ambassador Rea Brazeal put it, Africa is "the continent of the future and it should be where every Foreign Service officer wants to be working over the next 20, 30 years" (Brazeal 2007, 136). Several of our giants made their careers on that continent, as intended. C. D. Glin knew he wanted to work in Africa. He also knew the implication for his reputation: "Are you seen as someone who made Africa a strategic choice, or did you get pigeonholed and are now seen as not able to do anything else?" Glin's passion has always been Africa (Box 2.5).

Ambassador Johnnie Carson's response was to be sure he was always the top expert on Africa in any room. He doubled down on his expertise and work ethic. People have asked him over the years, "Why not serve in other parts of the world?" In fact, he did hold posts in Europe. He also turned some down, including a European ambassadorial post. He realized it would be "a career ender." He had just completed his ambassadorship in Uganda (1991–1994), one of the most difficult postings in Africa at the time, where, he reported, "politics, conflict, and insecurity were all at play. One of Africa's rising leaders. And then go to Malta? Can you name the president of Malta today? Most people can't identify the capital." Ambassador Carson recognized that, in the Africa Bureau, "I have a comparative advantage based on my knowledge, skills, and work ethic." These advantages make his potential for impact in advancing policy greater than they would be anywhere else in the world. For Ambassador Carson, Africa is the strategic choice, both in terms of where the most exciting work is and the potential for impact given his cumulative experience and expertise.

The point is to serve in Africa because you *want* to, not because others see you in a particular way. And you should consider what your strategy is in seeking (or not seeking) a posting in Africa. If it is not part of your self-determined vision, based on passion or expertise, for example, then perhaps you need to ask yourself where else you might serve to have the impact you seek. Ambassador Harry K. Thomas Jr. agrees that "there's nothing wrong with going to Africa," and he enjoyed his posts there. But, he believes, "Europe and Asia are more important these days, than Africa and Latin America." Working in the posts considered important will open doors in your future. Understanding that can help you determine what is most important for you: working in the region of your choice or advancing to the most prestigious positions.

Strategies to Avoid the Pigeonhole

Our giants shared strategies for how to avoid getting pigeonholed where you don't want to be or where you don't see the best prospects for your future. These include seeking assignments no one else wants, developing underrepresented skills and knowledge in another region, and saying no as diplomatically and strategically as you can. Like Aaron in Latin America, Alonzo Fulgham wanted to have an impact in a region other than Africa: the Middle East. He was determined to demonstrate that Black Americans can add value worldwide. He ended up taking on the toughest posts, including Jordan, Georgia, Azerbaijan, Serbia, and Afghanistan. Ambassador Johnny Young's strategy was to take jobs that were not very desirable but "allowed you to establish a reputation in that bureau that you could then use to move on" (Young 2013, 89). He also took on the toughest posts, including in Amman, Jordan, then considered the second most dangerous post in the world after Beirut (1983). He went to Qatar when no one else wanted to go there. And though it was not anticipated, a bloody coup happened during his first ambassadorship to Sierra Leone. He was able to work in three regional bureaus besides Africa: the Middle East, Latin America and the Caribbean, and Europe.

■ *I've always tried to raise my hand for the tough assignments in every organization I've worked in. First, I found that if you took on the tough stuff, it was always very interesting. Second, you could shape the direction of any given initiative or project. You were going to be in the driver's seat or with a group of people in the driver's seat. Third, the boss usually appreciates people willing to step up and take on the difficult stuff. It's hard. You will certainly have to work overtime. But people appreciate that.*

The right specialization can also help you avoid being pigeonholed. Ambassador Sylvia Stanfield was so proficient in Chinese language and culture it would have been crazy to assign her anywhere else, especially as China was becoming of such strategic interest to the United States. And once you have gained some gravitas, don't be afraid to use it to get to where you want to be. When Ambassador Johnny Young was promoted as the second Black career minister in history, he leveraged his position to argue that "it was time once again for the Service to demonstrate that it could assign minority ambassadors to regions other than the traditional places in Africa" (Young 2013, 218). His next and final post was as ambassador to Slovenia.

Saying No

Of course, when you say no, you need to be diplomatic and try not burn any bridges. In Box 5.3, Aaron shares an experience about career management to avoid a promotion that he did not think was in his best interest.

Box 5.3   Aaron Williams: Saying No to Somalia

"I was determined to pursue a career in the Latin America region given my regional experience and language skills. I was successful in achieving that goal, but I had to be vigilant. My first office director position at USAID headquarters was leading the new Latin America and Caribbean private-sector office, and I was becoming more well known in USAID/Washington thanks to that position. Then I got a call from the Africa Bureau. They wanted to talk with me about an important assignment. The mission director in Somalia had tapped me for her deputy director position. This would have been a big promotion for me, especially at my age. At this stage of my career, my goal was to be a mission director in Latin America, where I would be the first Black mission director in the bureau.

"I told senior management in Latin America that I had this opportunity to go to Somalia. They were not happy; I believe that they probably thought that they didn't want to lose a solid officer with potential to move up in the bureau. However, I had to give the Somalia offer serious consideration. So, I said, 'This is a serious opportunity, Somalia. The mission director is a big shot in AID. . . . But I would prefer to stay in the bureau. I really enjoy working on Latin America.' I tried to stall making a decision, but the mission director called and made it clear that this was a great opportunity and that she was really surprised that she was offering it to somebody as green as I was. I told her, 'It's just not the right thing for me to do right now.' A senior Africa Bureau official called me later and said, 'You are making the biggest mistake of your career right now.'

"Six months later I was named a mission director for the Eastern Caribbean. I didn't even know that I was under consideration. And that confirmed that my strategy was the right one. I speak Spanish. I'm in Latin America. Why should I give up my strategic career position just because I receive another offer?"

Aaron's vision had always been to work and lead in Latin America, ever since his days as a Peace Corps volunteer in the Dominican Republic. His treasure—the skills, relationships, expertise, and experience he could bring to any job—was developed in and based on Latin America. His no was based not just on what he didn't want but on where he thought he could have the greatest impact, both for Latin America and as a role model for other Blacks in the Foreign Service, who need to see themselves worldwide.

Sometimes you may need to say no because you can see that your potential impact may be limited and, worse, you may conclude that the position is a setup for failure, whether intentionally or not. This was Victoria Cooper's experience, described in Box 5.4.

Victoria Cooper left the confines of a great corporate situation, with all the trappings, salary compensation, and support systems, to go out on her own. She followed her convictions about what was right for her, what was possible with others (like the people she would have been assigned to support in South Africa), and where she could have the greatest impact.

Both Aaron and Victoria were prepared for the options they took. Some of that preparation stems from knowing how the system works, how best to maneuver within it, and how to get out if there are no further options for maneuvering within it, as Victoria Cooper found. Ambassador Rea Brazeal provides another example. She wasn't convinced she wanted to stay in the Foreign Service. She learned how to maneuver within the system to prepare for better opportunities both inside and outside the Foreign Service. She took a leave of absence without pay to enroll in a management program at Harvard University. "I had learned enough about the system to know that I should line up the job I was going to have when I came out of Harvard and not depend on the system to take care of me. So I did that." She advises, "If you don't learn the system you're in, you don't know how to go around it, over it, or under it." Ambassador Brazeal stayed in the Foreign Service and later served as ambassador to Micronesia, Kenya, and Ethiopia.

■ *You have to seize control of your own career. You are responsible for your career, and you have to figure out how to make it work within the system. You have to know how to investigate, create the proper networks, and make sure you get the right job so you can move forward. Sometimes there will be obstacles, personality conflicts, or things will happen, but a lot of it has to do with how you decide to pay attention to the system and how it operates.*

Box 5.4   Victoria Cooper: Saying No to South Africa

Victoria Cooper was a partner on the consulting side of PriceWaterhouse-Coopers, based in Ghana, when the 2000–2001 Enron scandal hit. There was a big shake-up in the effort to create more distance between the firm's consulting and auditing arms. She was given a choice: move to South Africa or Nigeria.

"I was the only African American and female consulting partner in the Africa firm. I had experienced my partners in South Africa. At a meeting of all of the Africa consulting businesses, a partner in South Africa said to me at a social event, 'Oh, I didn't know we had women partners in the consulting business. They're usually in the kitchen.' That was 2000, before we decided that we needed to separate the consulting business from the auditing business.

"The South Africans were running the consulting practice from there. I was still in Ghana. I had begun to interact with them. And they said, 'We want you to mentor some of our Black and colored consultants through the process, so that they can grow the business.' So I started asking a few key questions. Who's supervising them? Who's giving them assignments? Who's doing their evaluation? In our business, if you're not being placed in the right assignment, you're not going to grow. If you don't grow, you will never become a manager, and you will never become a partner.

"As a manager, if you don't know how to supervise people because they don't look like you, it will restrict your growth. Here's the example I gave one of the partners. Two of my juniors can come into my office, and they can ask me a question. If someone looks more like me, who I'm more familiar with, I might say, 'Why don't you just think about that?' and mention a few things. I don't give them the answer, but I've helped them with things to consider. For the other, I might say, 'Why don't you go back and think through the issue a little more?' and offer no suggestions. I also don't give them the answer, but I haven't helped them either. That's the difference. He looked at me and said, 'Oh, I don't know about that.' I said, 'I know about that.' And that was my conclusion. So South Africa was out for me. I would not do it. They also did not come back to me anymore about mentoring and coaching.

"My life was based in Ghana. I made a decision to withdraw from the partnership to start my own firm. And I did not move back to the United States. I stayed because that's where my clients were. Governments knew me. I knew the presidents of these countries. They knew me, the ministers knew me. This was my client base, so why would I leave my client base?"

Creating and Seizing Opportunities

Ambassador Rea Brazeal provides one example of how you can create your own opportunities. Knowing the system and investing in your skills, knowledge, and credentials are important. How else can you create and seize opportunities? Additional strategies include choosing whom to work for, doing good work and getting noticed, advocating for what you want, and saying yes.

Choose for Whom You Work

Alonzo Fulgham advises, "Research who it is you want to work for and with. What is he or she known for? Are they someone who is going to encourage you, or are they just looking to fill a billet and not give you an opportunity to do *a*, *b*, and *c*?" Researching your potential boss should be a part of your calculus each time you consider a new opportunity. Ambassador Rea Brazeal sought a position in the Office of Development Finance precisely because the director was "someone I wanted to work for, someone who I thought could educate me about particular economic issues as well as about leadership/management skills" (Brazeal 2007, 62). Even as her good work garnered notice and her reputation led to new offers, she reports, "I would, of course, check to see if they were bigots or their corridor reputation, because I wanted to work for people I could learn from and who were not bigots."

Do Good Work and Get Noticed

As you look to create new opportunities and plan your path toward your goals, it's important to always do your best work in the here and now. Many of our giants told stories of doing just that and later finding their work had been noticed and would be rewarded with new opportunities. This is how Ambassador Linda Thomas-Greenfield came to work for then director general Ed Perkins. Early in his career Ambassador Johnny Young secured what he described then as his "dream job" simply by having performed well (Young 2013, 54). A temporary administrative officer in Guinea Conakry noticed his work and sought to bring him to Kenya as her general service officer. It was a stretch role and not a likely option. But she was impressed and was able to make it happen.

■ *From time to time very talented people in USAID and the State Department, or in any part of government, will be able to leapfrog over steps that people normally take in terms of career development because one of their mentors or a supervisor recognizes that they're ready for this next move. But you always need to signal that you're prepared to put in the time to learn and excel in that new position. Because you'll be surrounded by people who put in the twenty years, who are watching to see who's going to leapfrog and not go through all the paces they went through. Good work gets noticed, and the rewards require that you continue to work even better.*

To be noticed as you do work, you also need to participate. General Barrye Price strongly recommends full participation. "You can't self-marginalize and not expect to be marginalized. I attended all the events. From the day that I joined the military to the day I retired, I had every uniform that the army had. I probably was the only second lieutenant in the army who had dress whites, mess whites, dress blues, mess blues—because had I gone to Wall Street. . . . I wouldn't join Wall Street with one suit. If this is what they have, this is what they do, I joined. I was all in."

Advocate for What You Want

Even in an organization as seemingly formal as the State Department, with all its mandated processes and rules for ensuring transparency and fairness, informal networks still operate and can be key to at least getting you on a short list for that next job you so dearly want. To those who are new and less networked in large bureaucracies, this may come as a surprise. Ambassador Harriet Elam-Thomas only learned of this when she participated in the Senior Seminar: "I sat in our conference rooms between sessions. I listened to several officers calling area directors to convince them that their qualifications made them the optimum candidates for positions or assignments. At first I listened in disbelief. Self-promotion seemed so crass. However, that was the accepted practice at State, and officers who were not proactive did not get the career-enhancing assignments" (Elam-Thomas 2017, 118). Ambassador Gina Abercrombie-Winstanley was fortunate to have figured this out early in her career (see Box 5.5).

This early assignment put Ambassador Abercrombie-Winstanley on a path that capitalized on her previous experiences and interests in the Middle East (she had served in the Peace Corps in Oman) and established her related trajectory as one of the few Black American women working in and specializing in the Middle East.

One of the ways you can lobby for that next position is through the performance review process (which we will address in further detail

**Box 5.5   Gina Abercrombie-Winstanley:
Working the Halls to Make the Case**

"Early on, I recognized that I was going to have to advocate for myself, that the easily accessible mentors or sponsors were not going to be mine. I had to be the one to speak about my bona fides—and with confidence. And that's one of the ways that I went from being consular officer number 18 in London to being the head of the consular section in Baghdad. I had to convince the NEA [Near Eastern Affairs Bureau] that I could do that and that I came with the necessary equipment. My husband is English. I was young. And I had joined the Foreign Service for adventure. And London is family. So I didn't want to go to London; it was too easy.

"As soon as I got that assignment, I went back to the department, and I went up and down the hall to every office in NEA, every single one of them. And I said, 'I'm Gina Abercrombie-Winstanley, and I've got two plus in Arabic.' Two plus will get you off of language probation in a hard language. And I said, 'I'm headed to London, but I'm an NEA person, and I want to serve in the Middle East. I'll be looking to you as soon as I get to bid on an assignment, so please keep me in mind.' I went to every office. And maybe a week, if that, went by, and the Iraq Desk called me and said, 'Come and talk to us again. Give us a little more information about yourself, your language, your background.' Then they said, 'Well, we've got an opening in Baghdad to run the consular section.' So who doesn't want to be a big fish in a small pond? Small ponds are fine if you get to be the boss."

below) and, of course, in that first interview. In both instances, Paul Weisenfeld cautions that people often make the mistake of focusing on their past achievements. "What you did in the past is a proxy; it's not a reward. . . . Promotion is a recognition that you can operate at a higher level in the interest of the organization." In other words, talk about what you offer to the organization and this new role, not about what you think the organization may "owe" you in recognition for your achievements to date.

Lauri Fitz-Pegado provides an example of building on your strengths but also advocating for how to take those strengths to the next level and not just get pigeonholed into what you've already done (see Box 5.6).

Box 5.6   Lauri Fitz-Pegado: Advocating to Be a First

Lauri Fitz-Pegado worked for Ron Brown early in her public affairs career and over a long period. When he became the secretary of commerce, he wanted her to work with him.

"Ron wanted me to be his communications director. I had supported him informally in that role and as an advisor on international issues for many years at the 1988 Democratic Convention and when he was chairman of the Democratic National Committee, and he was very confident in my ability to do that. I didn't want to do that anymore. I had done twelve years enhancing others' image and being the public affairs person. My interest and training were in the Foreign Service. I was interested in policy and in change. So I told him I didn't want to be communications director, and I recommended a good friend of mine to be communications director.

"She and I scanned the Plum book, which listed all the positions in the government and the political positions. We found this position that was assistant secretary and director general of the US and Foreign Commercial Service. That was a presidential appointee position, and I told Ron that was the position I wanted. To me, it was a mini State Department within the Department of Commerce. It had a domestic end with ninety offices. It had 130 offices around the world with foreign commercial officers. It was a huge challenge, but it was a worthy one." Lauri Fitz-Pegado was the first Black person to hold this position.

Say Yes

It might seem odd to include a strategy of saying yes. But sometimes, for a variety of reasons, you may not be immediately inclined to do so. There are good reasons not to, as illustrated above. Sometimes you may be tempted to say no for the wrong reasons. Ambassador Ed Perkins provides an example in Box 5.7.

Ambassador Rea Brazeal was advised to say no to an opportunity but took it anyway, because she thought it was the right opportunity for her. Her first ambassadorship was to the Federated States of Micronesia. People told her it was a small country, and she shouldn't take it. "But I learned in my parents' house when opportunity knocks you take it. So I took it. It was a very small embassy. I was the first ambassador actually, although some of the white men who were representatives before me played the ambassador title." It was a rewarding and great learning experience. She went on to serve as ambassador to Kenya and then to Ethiopia.

Box 5.7   Ed Perkins: The First Black Director General of the Foreign Service

Ambassador Ed Perkins was ready to say no to his dream job as the first Black director general of the Foreign Service. The timing, he thought, was all wrong. He was making progress in South Africa with the apartheid government. And resolution of the Namibia conflict, which he had been working to broker, seemed very near. He had nine months left on his tour of duty in South Africa when the call came.

"I still had so many tasks yet to perform there. . . . With all of this in the balance, could I walk away from Namibia and South Africa? It was a wrenching decision. I was surprised, elated, and overwhelmed at the offer before me, but I hesitated. . . . 'When the gods want to break your heart, they grant you your deepest wish.' I told outgoing director general George Vest that I thought I should stay in South Africa another year, being uniquely placed and qualified to finish the job."

Luckily, Ambassador Perkins had great support from Director General George Vest. "'Ed,' he said, 'do you want to be director general of the Foreign Service?' 'Yes,' I replied. 'I have dreamed of having this job.' 'Then take it now. You will only get the offer once in your career. You have done what no one else could have done, and that is to craft the demise of the apartheid system. You must know when it is time to move on to the next challenge. That time is now, and the challenge is being director general. The Service needs you at the top.' Vest thought the time had come to appoint a [B]lack director general, and I was the [B]lack he wanted for the job" (Perkins 2006, 421–422).

Making Strategic Choices

These are great examples of saying yes. We also learned of great examples of saying no. We want to explore further the specifics of how you can make strategic choices while navigating your career. For starters, every new job you seek should be a stretch role. As Dominique Harris shared in Chapter 3, "If you're the best in the room for too long, then you need to go find another room." You should not only watch for when you're not learning anymore but anticipate when that will begin to occur. And that's when you will need to scan for new opportunities that fit with your vision (as above) and begin to make strategic decisions about which options will best meet your ambitions. Ideally, you will already have some ideas in mind. Your strategy should include being intentional about specializing and choosing opportunities with the potential for impact and an ability to measure your success.

Attention to Specialization

One strategy for getting ahead is to anticipate what the needs will be one or even five years down the road and to invest heavily in the skills and knowledge that will be required to address them. For example, there may be a near-future demand for regional or language expertise. Our nation certainly experienced that with respect to Arabic and Middle East studies after September 11, 2001. Ambassador Sylvia Stanfield was fortunate that her passion for Chinese language, culture, and history coincided with important openings in diplomatic relations with China. She had a front-row seat and became a driver in that agenda with seemingly very little attention to the fact that she was so unexpected in that space as a Black woman. As noted in Box 2.3, foreign-language skills can open important doors in a foreign policy career.

Even in areas that seem general, there are opportunities for specialization. Management and administration are considered generalist skills and skills that travel—across functional sectors as well as geography. Some people end up in these areas by default and remain very general in their application of such skills and knowledge. Ambassador Ed Perkins saw it differently. Very early on, he had intensive training through an internship entry program at USAID. Independently, he also studied the administrative law relevant to USAID. He reported, "I read it all, volume after volume. Because of that self-study, when I was assigned to my first post, I happened to be the only person in the mission who knew most of the administrative law governing USAID" (Perkins 2006, 137). Ambassador Johnny Young started out as a budget and fiscal officer, became a general services officer, and developed the skills and expertise necessary to create an embassy from scratch in Doha, where he served as the administrative officer and deputy chief of mission. He went on to serve as ambassador to four countries: Sierra Leone, Togo, Bahrain, and Slovenia.

It's good to be intentional about your areas of specialization. Otherwise, perceptions of your specialization could begin to emerge based simply on patterns across the posts you've held, suggesting that others have determined where your specialization lies, not you. Or maybe your postings are so dissimilar there doesn't seem to be much of a pattern at all, suggesting that you are not deepening your skills in anything in particular. Ambassador Rea Brazeal suggests you consider what your specialization could be, despite the varied geographical posts where you have served. She points out that most people don't take the time to reflect and recognize what they may have learned from their varied assignments and how their cumulative experiences bring them particular knowledge that could be cast as a specialization (Brazeal 2007).

Potential Impact and Measurable Success

Your choices might not be very obvious to others. That's okay, as long as you are clear about why they are the right ones for you. Dominique Harris encountered a lot of raised eyebrows when she announced she was leaving Washington, DC, for Wichita, Kansas. "I'm willing to make those leaps when it doesn't make sense to other people. Because in my mind, I know exactly where I'm trying to go." Dominique's move to Kansas enabled her to shift from public affairs to the more technical and business side of Cargill's operations. After two and a half years she was moving again, this time to Cargill headquarters, where she served as global strategy and business development lead for Cargill Alternative Protein, before transitioning to her new role as strategic account manager.

When Disney asked Ed Grier to go to Japan as executive managing director for Walt Disney Attractions Japan, people thought he was "crazy" to go. "They said, 'You're doing well here in the US, and you want to go literally to an island, away from everything? They're going to forget about you. It's going to be horrible.'" And on top of all of that, Disney was having challenges with its Japanese partners at the time. Yet, he reports, "I went, and it was probably one of the best experiences of my life." As he describes in Box 9.11, he built trusting relationships with his Japanese counterparts, and it was a breakthrough moment for him. His success there led to him becoming president of Disneyland Resort in Anaheim, California.

On the other hand, you may not think an opportunity is the best choice, and your mentors may counsel you differently. When then director general Ed Perkins inquired about Ambassador Linda Thomas-Greenfield becoming his staff assistant (see Box 4.5), she initially thought she wouldn't want the job, questioning, "What does a staff assistant do? And how is that going to help me career wise?" Of course, it turned out to be instrumental in her learning about how the State Department works, meeting key people and stakeholders from across the department and beyond, and setting her on a new trajectory.

Ed Grier had been working in the "glamorous" area of marketing and was then asked to become the finance manager for the entire construction area for Disney World. "I left my nice office, in the middle of everything, and they put me in a trailer in the middle of nowhere." But it turned out to be one of the best jobs he could have had. "I got to see the entire property, I got to learn about construction, I got to learn about project management, got to learn about engineering, work with union folks. It taught me something that I didn't know I needed to know. . . . And it helped me deal with people from all points of view, and all different levels in the company, from the executives to the maintenance person working on a project."

In moving from one job to another, you should always be thinking about that next set of skills and experiences that you need in order to advance to where you want to eventually go. Ambassador Thomas-Greenfield's and Ed Grier's experiences suggest that one set of skills and knowledge to consider is gaining a deeper understanding of the organization you are working in and becoming known within it. Ambassador Johnny Young learned thoroughly about how the State Department operates—the good, the bad, and the ugly—by serving as executive director of the Office of the Inspector General. It was a great opportunity to learn about what did and didn't work well and why. Ambassador Sylvia Stanfield also spent time in the Inspector General's Office. It helped both of them to better understand what makes a good ambassador versus a less effective one. And they learned more about the people who populate the State Department.

Without mentors, it's difficult to learn what the plum jobs are for career advancement and where the hotspots are that can help you advance your career. Among the places that stand out, Ambassador Johnnie Carson served in the Bureau of Intelligence and Research in the State Department, where he began to distinguish himself for his analytic work. And Alonzo Fulgham, among others, attended the War College, giving him the credentials to eventually lead the USAID mission in Afghanistan. Ambassador Harry K. Thomas Jr. learned by observing. He determined he wanted to go to the Operations Center as a senior watch officer "because that's where I saw people having success." He also saw it as a chance to move out of the Africa Bureau. After that, he sought out "a hard language" that would help him stand out. He ended up going to India and studying Hindi, "which was the hardest year of my life." In weighing two opportunities—political chief in Mozambique or political officer in Senegal—Ambassador Johnnie Carson reflected on where the action was. He chose Mozambique. It was an easy choice. It was 1974. There had just been a coup in Portugal, and its colonial empire was starting to unravel.

Certain assignments carry their own gravitas, as Aaron mentioned in starting out at General Mills. Some consider the War College a similar "golden ticket." Hardship posts stand out for, well, the hardship and your willingness to take it on and stick it out. When hardship posts also provide opportunities for major turnarounds, they too can be a golden ticket to career advancement. As already noted, a lot of jobs in US foreign policy don't offer that immediate gratification, where you can see specific outcomes of your skills and efforts. Philip Gary advises that you try, whenever possible, to opt for the types of assignments that afford the opportunity for measurable results.

Race and Job Opportunities

Let's be clear. You can be as strategic as possible and still encounter roadblocks. Those come in different forms, as we'll talk about in Chapter 6. Among the more prevalent forms you will encounter are racism and sexism, whether they reflect unconscious bias or are intentional but veiled to protect the perpetrator. Sometimes your identity as a Black person can also bring opportunities.

We already introduced the Africa circuit as something you should be aware of, even if you aim to focus on Africa. The point, as Philip Gary emphasized, is not to allow anyone else to define you (see Box 5.8).

Box 5.8   Philip Gary: Not Letting Others Define Him

Philip Gary's career at USAID was off to a great start in the Office of Housing. He had most recently worked on Asia and had also developed some expertise in the Middle East before joining USAID. But when it was time for an overseas assignment, the deputy director informed him that he would be assigned to Liberia.

"So I say, 'Excuse me. I know the Middle East. I know Asia. Why are you assigning me to Liberia?' 'Oh, we just think that would be the best place for you.' It had appeared to me that virtually every Black person I knew in AID had been assigned to Africa. So I counted to three and then went to talk to the director. I said, 'It's been a lot of fun working with you, but I'm leaving.' He laughed. And so I laughed. But then I said, 'No really, I'm not going along with this kind of stereotyping. I think Africa is important. I think there are all sorts of things that I would be interested in at some point. But I'm not going to Africa because that's sort of, here's who you are.' And he said, 'Okay.' I ended up going to Sri Lanka. That's an example of not letting somebody else define who you are."

Even after completing the Senior Seminar, Ambassador Johnny Young watched as all of his white classmates got wonderful assignment after wonderful assignment. And he waited. And waited. We all know the story. It's not legal, but it happens. As Chris Richardson reports, "If you had a white officer who had a bad Black officer, they might say, 'Well, I don't want to hire any more Black officers, because one of them had a chip on their shoulder, or one of them had an attitude.' Sadly, that's the price of being Black in America."

You may be the most qualified person for a particular job, as Alonzo Fulgham was, and still have others focus on your identity as a Black person. Alonzo Fulgham had served as a private-sector volunteer with the Peace Corps in Haiti, where he worked for the Office National de l'Artisanat providing microcredit to artisans to create jobs and income in the rural areas. When he returned, he was offered a job at Peace Corps headquarters in the Office of Private Sector Development. As qualified as he was, the supervisor confessed, "We think some of the things you did in Haiti will be very helpful to us. But it's also a great chance to diversify our staff. I'm just going to be really honest with you."

We asked Aaron how it made him feel to always be the first. ■ *The way I look at it is somebody has got to be the first. And after you do it a couple of times, you anticipate what it's going to be like. So you have to approach these opportunities with a couple of things in mind. First, you have a lot of responsibility to do the best possible job you can. Because you're the first, you're going to be the example. You've got to do your homework. You've got to be on your toes. If your performance falters, or you make a series of mistakes, that could result in fewer desirable assignments or a poor annual evaluation. Others may think, "Why should you be there in the first place?" And second, you need to do everything you can to diversify the organization that you're in as much as possible. Because now you may be in a position to have some authority and power to pursue this goal.*

Disappointments That Lead to Opportunities

As the saying goes, you can't always get what you want. Some disappointments can be devastating. While many of our giants have experienced deep disappointments, they also shared how these missed experiences would have closed off opportunities that were even better. How could you know? When this happens at the beginning of your career, it can lead you on a dramatically different path. That's what happened for Ambassador Ertharin Cousin, as she describes in Box 5.9.

**Box 5.9   Ertharin Cousin: From Local Water
Sanitation to Global Food Security**

"When I was twenty-seven years old, I ran for water reclamation district commissioner in Chicago. I got beat quite badly. But, as someone pointed out to me, if I had won, rather than pursuing my diverse career achievements, I would have been a water reclamation district commissioner! An honorable and important position, but a quite different path. My run for office was in the mid-1980s, when many Chicago communities remained very segregated. Our campaign team included mostly young people under thirty or in their early thirties. These volunteer workers came from every community across the city—more diverse campaign talent than the party establishment had ever experienced. As a result, the Democratic Party decided to train me. They taught me how to run a campaign from nuts to bolts, positioning me for state, national, and ultimately international leadership opportunities. Losing the election pivoted my career and moved me forward in a completely unexpected direction.

"After the election loss, I worked hard, learned lessons, and other doors opened. I first came to Washington as the research director for the Democratic National Committee (DNC), and then became the deputy chief of staff for the DNC. When we lost the midterm elections during the Clinton administration, one of my mentors was working in the White House and said, 'We have another plan for you. You studied international law. We need somebody over in the State Department.' Had we not lost the midterms (regrettable as it was at the time), I would not have gone from the DNC to the State Department. Serving in the department put me on track for another set of career opportunities, including service as ambassador to the UN Agencies on Food and Agriculture and executive director of the World Food Programme."

If you are further along in your career, such a disappointment can be really devastating, especially if it concerns what you thought of as your dream job. ■ *I've had things that have happened in my career where I thought, "I cannot come back from this ever," and it opened up a door to something much better. I was offered the presidency of the Inter-America Foundation (IAF). I accepted the position, and then Senator Jesse Helms took it away from me, even before I sat in the chair. He had a preferred candidate and forced the IAF board to accept this person. I had to do a 180-degree turn and returned to my job as the executive secretary at USAID. But that turned out to be the best thing that could have ever happened to me. It set me on the path to South Africa as the USAID mission director during the era of Nelson Mandela and eventually to becoming the Peace Corps director. You never know. I was really distraught and angry and wanted to fight back. But you can't go to war with the chairman of the Senate Foreign Relations Committee, especially Jesse Helms.*

As you face the inevitable disappointments in your career—and they will definitely come—keep in mind that they may leave you open for other opportunities that may be greater than what you could have ever imagined.

Managing Performance Reviews

A lot of the strategies we've discussed for navigating your career concern what you can do beyond formal organizational processes. Those strategies still take place in the context of larger structures that you have to pay attention to. And, as noted above, you have to learn how these systems work and how best to navigate them. This is the subject matter of the unwritten rule book no one will give you unless you have supportive mentors . . . or you learn it from our giants here. First, we want to introduce you to the major challenges inherent in the performance review process: competition, systemic racism and sexism, and unconscious bias. Next, we'll describe how the system works and how you can proactively manage it and not be a passive participant. The latter includes seeing the constructive side of evaluation too and accepting how it can help your professional development.

The Challenging Context

Over several decades, a lot of the racial barriers, discrimination, and exclusionary policies in American organizations have been removed or become less evident. Further, affirmative action efforts, as we saw across our society, led to the recruitment of larger numbers of Black professionals in the foreign affairs arena. However, despite these advances, structural inequality persists, and it's important that we collectively insist on broad-based policies and programs that will promote diversity and social justice.

Competition remains fierce. General Barrye Price warns that you should always see yourself as competing with standards, not with people. This is great advice, both for being comfortable with your own professional ethics and for ensuring you don't make any enemies, perceived or otherwise. Your reputation will follow you. In the State Department it's referred to as your "corridor" reputation. That label signals that it is about not just what you do on the job but also how you do your job and how you treat people along the way. Chris Richardson describes the State Department as a "hypercompetitive environment, where people anticipate and want you to compete against one another." You will hear your coworkers being bad-mouthed in this cut-throat environment, and people may expect you to go along. He wants to emphasize that even as you compete against standards, "you always have to be your brother's keeper. Be courageous enough to tell a white colleague, 'No, I don't believe that,' or, 'No, we shouldn't stand by that.' If your brother or sister is doing things that you think are not right, you have to speak up for that too."

Yes, it is so important to focus on competing against standards, not people. That said, it's also important to understand, as always, that the standards you are competing against are not the same as those for your white and/or male counterparts. Philip Gary learned early in his career that "you don't get to be average. As a Black person, the normal scales don't apply to you. You get an A or an F. You're either a superstar, or you're a disaster." Dominique Harris has observed this in the corporate world too. "In order to be seen as talent as a person of color, you have to be extraordinary. You can't be mediocre. You can't be just okay. You have to be great in all aspects."

When Linda Thomas-Greenfield was director general of the Foreign Service, she saw that different standard firsthand. And she found herself in a position where she had to enforce it. "I had to fire three African American men. It was the hardest thing I did. And one of them said to me, 'But other people do this all the time.' And I said, 'They do, but nobody keeps a record of what they're doing. There's a record here. I can't help you.'"

The systemic discrimination starts with what others expect of you. Ambassador Ruth A. Davis recalled, "What I remember most about my A-100 class was the implied expectations. One speaker told us that only about three of our 30-odd classmates would become ambassadors. It was clear to me that my classmates believed those three would come from among the white males" (Davis 2016). She told us, "I'm happy to tell you that I ended up outranking them all, every one of them." Her experience illustrates that Black women face even greater challenges. As the powerful Black women who wrote *For Colored Girls Who Have Considered Politics* put it, "You need to know that sexism, like its related cousin racism, is part of the DNA of this country" (Brazile et al. 2018, 304).

The clearest indicator of systemic racism and sexism is representation at the top. At the time we interviewed Ambassador Ruth A. Davis (in 2019), there were only three Black ambassadors serving, all of them male. Ambassador Johnnie Carson also lamented that fact. He sees the problem as "worse today than at any time in the last fifty years." He saw it in the State Department, in board rooms in New York City, and at the Office of National Intelligence. "There are no Black faces in the boardrooms and the C-suites. Even the second tier down, very few Black faces."

This is why the performance review process is so important. It is the mechanism that determines who rises, who languishes, and who gets moved out. In up-or-out promotion systems, like in the State Department, they are even more important. These processes are often the place where you may see unconscious bias playing out in devastating ways. As Ambassador Ruth A. Davis observed, "The reports that are written on white male officers are certainly more glowing generally than they are for females and minorities. That's just a fact. And although we do get promoted, we don't get promoted at the same rate that white males get promoted, because they have better efficiency reports. That is a systemic thing, and it comes from unconscious bias."

■ *I remember so many times you would read a review about so-and-so. "He's a brilliant writer. He's a tremendous thinker. He's analytical." And you knew this person was a white male. Then you would see a female or a minority; it would be a different write-up, same writer. At the end of the day, it would sound like this person deserved to be promoted. But it wasn't the same level of narrative, nuance, and detail.* Ambassador Ruth A. Davis recalled reviewing one of her early efficiency reports and thinking, "'This is pretty nice.' Then I read my colleague's report. The adverbs and the adjectives made the thing fly off the page, whereas mine was just on cruise control."

■ *There were several times that I had to remain adamant and be a determined advocate for individuals.* Ambassador Ruth A. Davis underscored the unconscious biases that were often in play: "If you don't expect somebody to do well, and you are the boss, probably you're not going to give them as much attention and care and feeding as you would the person who you expect will do well." So naturally when it comes time to writing their performance review, you might have less to say about them. Because you did not expect them to succeed, you may not have set goals for them. Because you set no goals for them, you don't reflect on whether and how they might have excelled.

Ambassador Ed Perkins corroborated this experience from when he served as director general: "Women and minorities were not always given a good shot at assignments, and [B]lack women had a tougher time than [B]lack men in the Foreign Service." He recognized that his presence might make a difference in checking people on their unconscious bias as they reviewed files. "Sometimes I sat in on the meetings of the assignments panel, which surprised the panel members at first. I made it clear that they were there because as director general I had delegated that authority to them, and that I was reviewing that authority. I wanted to make sure that due process did indeed obtain" (Perkins 2006, 450–451).

How to Proactively Navigate the Process

It's tough to overcome biases. And leaders are not always as dedicated as Ambassador Perkins to combating systemic preconceptions, racism, and sexism. But there are actions you can take. The first step is understanding the process. Remember Ambassador Linda Thomas-Greenfield's early experience with evaluation? She thought she was supposed to authentically identify her weaknesses. Those became easy targets for her evaluation report and did not help her to advance (Box 4.5). So the first step is knowing that in this process you need to sing your own praises, because you cannot assume that anyone else will. You may not be comfortable with that, but it's the way the game is played. And this may be particularly challenging for women. ▶ Women sometimes downplay our actions. Whereas a man? The first thing they're going to do is tell you is, "I've done this. I've done that. And this is how I'm going to continue to give you return on your investment." Women are just not taught to do that. We're supposed to be humble and polite.

It's also important to understand the limits of pleasing your boss in order to get a good review. Early in her career, Ambassador Harriet Elam-Thomas served for four years in Greece without a promotion. She reported, "I did not realize that my boss, the public affairs officer (PAO), might have perceived my actions as threatening to his role in the embassy." Her boss wrote in her performance evaluation that she was "so well received that they thought she was the PAO." "In my naivete, I thought this was a compliment." She was later counseled by others, including the deputy director general of the Foreign Service, that "such comments and other less substantive observations added nothing to my evaluation and, in fact, were detrimental" (Elam-Thomas 2017, 100–101). Sadly, when women and minorities succeed, they can just as easily be resented as praised. It's important to understand your superiors and what drives them and learn to manage up.

When it comes to pleasing a boss, Ambassador Johnny Young learned about limits of another sort. He once reported to a politically appointed ambassador who did not understand the limits of his office. "I said, 'Mr. Ambassador, I cannot do all of these things you want me to do. Because if I do, I'll end up in jail.' He didn't like that at all. So when it came time for performance reviews, I thought I was dead in the water. We had a deputy who thought otherwise and wrote me a glowing report. The report went to the ambassador for a review, and I thought, 'Well this is going to be the nail in the coffin.' And I waited and waited. Finally, the report came back, and it had one sentence: 'I have nothing further to add to this report.' It was exactly what I wanted because any panel could read straight through it." ■ *If you can't win, you want them to say as little as possible.*

Hopefully, you won't encounter such difficult bosses. But when it's review time, all bosses should be reminded of your accomplishments. General Barrye Price said it this way: "You don't just leave it to hope that they remember. You write it. You articulate it very well. If there is dialogue, you reinforce. I wasn't a fire-and-forget-it kind of a guy. I was top of my game for thirty-one years. But it wasn't just because of my deeds and my works; it was because I also had to remind them. And I wasn't afraid of engagement."

■ *The documentation part is something that people really don't understand. You go in and see your supervisor. They say, "So let's see what you've accomplished here." Now, you've got two ways to do this. One is that you can rely on him or her to remember what you did, and some of them really might have a few notes about what you did. However, as I learned as a junior officer, you cannot assume that your supervisor will have detailed notes about your annual performance. They are not in charge of your life. I always went in with a three- or four-page layout: under each goal, this is what I did. Just to remind them. And inevitably, they would say, "Oh yeah, right. I remember that project we worked on. We didn't know which way we were going to go, and you made recommendations." It wasn't discrimination. It wasn't that they didn't want to help you. It's that they didn't know how to go about doing it. You've got to give them the path, the blueprint. Help them to help you. And then when they slip up and don't write it up the way you think it should be, you go back to them and say, "Hey. What about paragraph three? I don't think that accurately describes what I accomplished."*

Performance review processes are also an opportunity for you to know yourself better. Some of that is simply owning and being okay with who you are. General Barrye Price saw his evaluation reports as validating something he already knew about himself and about which he is perfectly comfortable: his candor. All his reports mentioned it. He explains, "I've got to say what needs to be said, and I've learned the way of how and when to say things. I advocate not for myself but for what's right for others and the organization." So candor, for him, was never a dirty word.

On the other hand, you may learn important information through your performance reviews that can help you to learn and grow professionally. You should view evaluation and feedback as a means of not just advancing in terms of assignments but also becoming the best professional you can be. Ambassador Ed Perkins was masterful at strategically seeking feedback. Instead of waiting for the annual evaluation, he requested a meeting with his boss every three months for an informal interview where he would say, "Tell me how I'm doing. Give me some suggestions about how I could do better." He advises, "Don't wait until the end of the year and a rushed evaluation." He practiced that with every supervisor he had and also with the people who reported to him (Perkins 2006, 230). Such periodic feedback not only enables you to make corrections and improve throughout the year but also increases the likelihood that you will not have any unwanted surprises at the end of the year.

Katherine Lee served as a career counselor. She offers advice on how you can engage others to help you grow professionally. She advises that, especially when facing challenges on the job, you "go to your supervisor and ask for help." She adds that your supervisor may appreciate that you are trying to learn. She would sometimes coach people by examining their performance reviews with them—something a career counselor or a mentor can help with. Together, they could identify areas for improvement and/or next steps. She would counsel them, "When you go to your next post, focus on this. Go to your supervisor and let him or her know you would like to work on strengthening this skill or that skill. Most supervisors will appreciate it. . . . I advised them to pay attention to their evaluation reports, to notice the skill or skills a supervisor indicated needed improvement and to ask for help. 'That's the only way you're going to develop or get promoted'" (Lee 2005, 80).

We recognize it's not easy to look at your shortcomings. Ed Grier confessed, "It's kind of tough for me. Feedback can sometimes be stinging. But if you don't get better from it, you'll just go backwards. We all think we're very smart, but I was told, we all have our flat sides. So you need to learn what those are so you don't slide backwards."

Navigating your career is a path of discovery, challenge, and growth. We all have a role to play in helping ourselves and each other to excel and succeed. Part of the process is confronting challenges, seeking help, and knowing when to fight. We'll explore that next.

6

Knowing When to Fight

Get in good trouble, necessary trouble, and help redeem the soul of America.

—John Lewis, Edmund Pettus Bridge,
Selma, Alabama, March 1, 2020

The giants did not become who they are today without struggle. It's not always easy for them to talk about those difficult moments in their careers. They want to inspire you, not focus on the negative. ▶ There is no denying that inspiration is needed. But knowing the sacrifices and hard decisions they made along the way helps to ground the truths of what we do and why we do it. We knew you would benefit most if we could have an honest, real, and raw discussion about the challenges the giants faced, the difficult moments they endured, and how they survived and thrived despite these challenges.

We start this chapter confronting the reality of what you may face in a US foreign policy career and, frankly, in most any workplace in American society: racism and sexism, as well as jerks and bullies. The main thrust of the chapter is what to do about it. ▶ Young professionals in today's workforce have the privilege to lean into our distinct voices and speak truth to power, calling out injustices in society. We must discern when it is time to put it all on the line for the sake of the cause and when to hold back and play the long game. So we asked the giants, how do you know when to fight? They shared their stories of having the good fight: triumphing in their

137

ultimate purpose, even if sometimes they did not attain the broader justice they deserved, and having the courage to do what's right. They
shared their approaches, including placing the affront in the appropriate context, working around it to achieve your goal, and ultimately
remaining strategically focused no matter your approach. Sometimes,
yes, that also means knowing when not to fight, when it is better to take
a deep breath and move on.

This is where the intergenerational dialogue is so important. Some
of our giants had compartmentalized these experiences. Not only is it
not easy to talk about these things, but these experiences could place
them right back into the box that labels them only according to their
race and gender, disregarding their specific identities and many achievements. It was with great gratitude and sensitivity that we pressed them
to share with you what we knew you needed to hear from them. Once
they understood why we needed them to talk about these things, it was
like pushing on an open door. We all want you to succeed and thrive. To
do that, we need to begin with the tough stuff.

Racism and Sexism

Racism is enduring. As Ambassador Ed Perkins described it, "The concept of racial bigotry is one that just does not bear simple explanations
or simple solving. It does not. Because you're dealing with people. And
it's not just people who are there yesterday. It's people who are there
today as well. . . . People don't change just because we say it's right to
change." ■ *It was no surprise that all the people we interviewed had a common
experience of having to deal with racists and systemic racism in every step of their
career. No matter what they attained, no matter how high they went, there was
always a situation where they had to, once again, reestablish themselves as people who deserved and had earned their positions.*

Ambassador Reuben Brigety reported feeling like he had to work
twice as hard "every day"—"because there is always the underlying
assumption that either you are inherently not as smart, not as good, or
you got there because of somebody else's affirmative action program.
You never walk into anybody's presence with a blank slate, with a
neutral assumption of who you are." Presumptions led Sanola A.
Daley to walk away from an opportunity she had competed for and
earned (see Box 5.2).

It's a familiar story. Philip Gary had been working somewhat independently of the rest of the USAID bureaucracy, at a separately funded

and located Office of Housing. He experienced a rude awakening attending broader USAID meetings: "I would make an intervention and, depending on who it was, be told, 'Well, that's not quite how these things work.' Then somebody else would say the same thing twenty minutes later, and I would hear, 'Well that's a good point.' While I had gotten all sorts of microaggressions, until that point, nobody had been bold enough to say to my face, in terms of professional work, 'We really don't care what you think.'" Sadly, this is a common experience.

Racism may not always be as visible as it once was. Ambassador Johnnie Carson was taking up a new assignment working on Angola and Mozambique in 1971 and had to transit through South Africa. The embassy in Pretoria, led by a political appointee, refused to obtain or demand a South African visa. The deputy chief of mission in Lagos, Nigeria, where he had been stationed, fought hard, confirming this was outrageous. In the end, Ambassador Carson only received a laissez-passer, allowing him to stay at an airport hotel to wait for his connecting flight. It was the first time he had experienced the notion that "we're willing to tolerate handing out second-class treatment to our own people if it will accommodate somebody else's bad governance."

Ambassador Carson's experience in South Africa illustrates how complex racism can be. It is many layered, with perpetrators of different backgrounds and agendas (including foreign nationals) and a hierarchical classification regarding who is more or less worthy and knowledgeable, for example, among people from less developed countries, generations of Americans, and American minorities. Verone Bernard recounted observing how two foreign PhDs were treated very differently. "I was working with two subject matter experts on a proposal; one was South Asian and the other was West African." She observed the assumption that "for some reason the South Asian must be an expert on what the water security issues are in Ghana." She attributed the attitude and behavior as a more universal "anti-Blackness." One of our focus group participants noted that as a first-generation American from Ghana, she is treated differently from her multigenerational peers. When people learn her parents are from Ghana, they respond with a different attitude: "Oh, you're not really from here." Paul Weisenfeld tells the story of a Jewish colleague learning that his father was Jewish: "He remarked it must be why I'm so smart. . . . When I insisted that my mother was also smart, he started stammering and the conversation became so awkward that we let it drop" (Weisenfeld 2020b).

An important component of the hierarchy of discrimination concerns gender. Ambassador Harriet Elam-Thomas described it as facing *two* glass ceilings. She reported observing how her older, more senior colleagues were "subtly unsupportive of any initiative I suggested, no matter how valid." She attributed these challenges more to her being a woman than to her being Black (Elam-Thomas 2017, 62). Even with a PhD in hand, Katherine Lee was seriously underestimated as a Black woman. Having read a report she wrote, her office director pronounced it very good and asked her what her background was. "I explained I had a BA from Fisk University, a PhD from Stanford University, and had taught German at the university level. He seemed very surprised. Having grown up in the segregated south had prepared me for such reactions, so I took it all in stride; I was used to having to prove myself to gain respect" (Lee n.d.). Ambassador Gina Abercrombie-Winstanley reported, "You don't walk in the room with people saying, 'Oh yes, of course.' My mother was always saying, 'Yes, you're great, you're great. But Baby, it's a man's world.'" If these intersectionalities are not challenging enough, Verone Bernard faced the added challenge of being a *young* Black woman. She confirms her biggest challenge has been feeling her experience is not valued only because she is a young Black woman. ■ *That's right, especially early in your career. When you walk in that room, you're not expected to excel. There's no expectation you're going to be a key player on a given topic.*

Organizations are microcosms of our society. That means tokenism and microaggression occur in this field as they do anywhere. Paul Weisenfeld reported being called to accompany the then USAID administrator at the last minute for a meeting on the Hill. "So, I assume it's something about food security. So I get in the car, and he says we're meeting with the Congressional Black Caucus because they want to complain about the lack of diversity amongst senior people in the agency." Ambassador Johnny Young reported working for a "wonderful ambassador" who always confused him with the only other Black man working in the embassy at the time.

And then there is the diversity work within organizations. You become the focal point. You are expected to do the work. Sanola A. Daley has championed a lot of this work, both as a member of affinity groups and as diversity advisor at the Inter-American Development Bank. It's exhausting. She poses an important question: "How do you take feelings of anger and frustration and do something with them that's not window dressing?" Because she saw authentic commitment from leadership, she is now working on a task force at the World Bank. Dominique Harris has had similar experiences. She generated a list of twenty things her organization could be doing if it was really serious and committed to improving diversity and inclusion. The list has become her litmus test for whether or not she will engage: "If we're not talking about any of these twenty, I have nothing to say." She stresses, "Time is my most valuable asset."

Paul Weisenfeld has called for all of us to engage more in difficult conversations, especially in the international development industry: "We are drawn to international development because of our passion to address human challenges. Let's use this passion to be at the forefront of change, modeling uncomfortable conversations that lead to racial justice and diversity within our own organizations and in society" (Weisenfeld 2020b). ▶ Now is not the time to relinquish our seat at the table. In this moment in history, Black professionals across industries have the unique opportunity to be a part of the solution and craft policy at the highest levels that impacts our communities. Taylor is a founding member of the Black employee resource group at Chemonics International.

Jerks and Bullies

While racism and sexism are endemic to our organizations and society, sometimes the challenge before you is more individualized. Sometimes people are just jerks. ▶ I received advice from a former boss about microaggressions and gaslighting. He said to be slow to anger and look for patterns. You have to know the difference between when someone is tone deaf and willing to receive constructive feedback and when they are simply a jerk and their behavior is well documented. Knowing the difference is critical and can shape how you are viewed in response to difficult situations in the workplace.

Ambassador Johnnie Carson shared that he learned a lot working with a difficult deputy chief of mission (DCM): "I learned that he was a bad manager. That he picked favorites. He probably didn't particularly care for people like me. But I also learned that you have to be the best at what you do." Every year Ambassador Carson wrote a report on the state of politics in Portugal. After two years, the DCM tried to shift that responsibility to someone else. The following year, he had it back. The ambassador recognized his good work and, despite the DCM, Ambassador Carson received two promotions during this assignment. He viewed the DCM as someone who felt threatened by his knowledge and potential influence. He concluded, "That's inferiority. My notion is to push beyond people like this. See them for their weaknesses and overwhelm them with your knowledge, ability, and hard work." In the corporate world, Bob Burgess benefited from being the boss in the country where he operated. He reported, "Every once in a while, you'll get a manager or a boss that is a jerk. Or you realize that you're a lot smarter than he is. But since he's the boss and you are in a foreign country and you control your own environment, you just let him fly in and spout his [expletive] and then let him leave."

Katherine Lee had to deal with a bully. When she was filling in for someone on sick leave, the DCM immediately directed her to fire three of the staff people. She later learned he was used to bullying people to get his way. He said to her, "If you want to get a 'C' you'll do it your way; if you want to get an 'A' you'll do it my way." She calmly replied, "With all due respect, Sir, I didn't come to make a grade; I came to help out during a difficult staffing period." Before leaving that post, she recommended some of the staff for training. By then, the DCM thought it was a great idea. She reported, "If you're on firm ground, you stand up for yourself." She added, "By the way, I got the equivalent of an 'A' from both the Ambassador and DCM" (Lee 2005).

Alonzo Fulgham shared a very difficult experience with a jerk of another sort. It started with others perceiving he did not deserve the post he held. It got ugly. He tells the story in Box 6.1.

Box 6.1   Alonzo Fulgham: A Tale of a Petty Jerk

"I was the mission director in Afghanistan. And this person didn't want me to go out there. He came to my swearing-in ceremony and did the worst job of explaining why I needed to go to Afghanistan. He read a note from the assistant administrator and then didn't endorse me. Everybody saw that.

"He came out after I'd been there three months to check in with the ambassador. The ambassador reported, 'He's doing a wonderful job.' I get an A on my annual report card, with a glowing review from the ambassador and one from the commanding general. Everybody reported I was doing a stellar job. When it comes time to get the bonuses for Afghanistan, I got a smaller bonus than my deputy. He tells the committee I was just a figurehead, that the deputy was the guy who was really running the mission. And the committee went along with it. Because he didn't appoint me to that job, he didn't think I deserved it. The AID administrator and the assistant administrator didn't know about it.

"Later, I was up for an award for the work that I did in Afghanistan. The State Department said, 'You should nominate Alonzo.' So he had my desk officer write my nomination. And then he had someone who was in counsel with the president at the White House write his. I'm the one out there putting my life on the line every day for a year. And he got the award."

Alonzo Fulgham's experience illustrates the added difficulty you may have if people within the bureaucracy perceive that you jumped the line, attaining a position before your due. He had never been a deputy or a director when he was appointed USAID mission director to Afghanistan. But he had attended the War College, and he had participated in interagency meetings, gaining understandings and building relationships with agencies and people that were critical to success in Afghanistan. He was the right person for a very particular job at a particular time. People in bureaucracies don't always see that. They expect everyone to play by the same rules (well, except when it comes to race and gender).

■ *We've all worked for really tough people. And as long as they treat everybody the same way, then it's not discrimination. For example, early on in my career in AID, I served in Honduras. There was a senior guy in the mission who treated everybody badly. Everybody got treated with the same lash all the time. He would embarrass you if your work wasn't up to his standards. So there are people like that. And it's hard to discern when it's racism versus this person has a bad personality or a total lack of human interaction skills.*

▶ You can never stop dreaming of wanting a better world that is without injustices or without strife. It is what so many advocates throughout history fought and died for. But you also have to be grounded in reality and understand the world that we live in. So, let's look at how you can respond constructively when you are challenged by racism, sexism, jerks, and bullies.

Putting It into Context

Putting challenges and affronts into context is important. When deciding if and how you want to fight, you need to understand the prospects of success, the risks involved, and the importance of the issue and the fight in the grand scheme of things. We have already seen examples of how sometimes such challenges, while devastating in the moment, can lead to better opportunities to grow and thrive, as for Sanola A. Daley (Box 5.2), or may lead to greater opportunities you could never have imagined, as with Aaron's service as USAID mission director in a Nelson Mandela–led South Africa. Sanola and Aaron determined that either the fight was not winnable or victory would come at too great a cost. When that happens, it's no reflection on you. You can live to fight another day. As one of General Barrye Price's mentors put it, "When you fall on your sword, even if you win, you still lose a lot of blood."

Some of our giants had ample experience encountering racists, and that helped them to navigate these questions. Katherine Lee grew up in Alabama and feels it taught her what she needed to know: "Do I accept this? Do I reason and say no? Or do I walk away from the situation? Just get out of the situation? Those were skills I brought having grown up in Alabama." Ambassador James Joseph drew from similar experiences growing up in the South.

Make no mistake, this does not mean you shouldn't fight. As Ambassador Ruth A. Davis put it, "Had I chosen not to fight, I would not have been able to do my job. I would have been stifled." But, she adds, "I think every battle is not worth fighting for. You can't have a battle a day. You have to pick them, and you have to focus on how you want to go about fighting these battles. You certainly want to make sure that you do no damage to yourself and that you succeed at what you're trying to do." Lauri Fitz-Pegado agreed: "You cannot fight battles every day. It will kill you." Later in her career, other priorities took precedence. "I was not the firebrand that I had been most of my life. It was self-preservation. I was divorced. I had a child that I was raising as a single mother. And I needed the job. So I picked my battles carefully."

Alonzo Fulgham shared another experience that illustrates the calculus of costs and benefits in choosing when to fight. His troubles, once again, stemmed from leapfrogging to a position at a higher level than others perceived was his due. The question he was asked in Box 6.2 is one to remember.

Putting a challenge in its context requires understanding how the system works. If you have that understanding, you may be able to avoid some challenges. Context also determines if a fight is even possible. Ambassador Gina Abercrombie-Winstanley learned the cost of not knowing the system and provides a great example of resilience (see Box 6.3).

Putting things into a larger context is essential to managing these inevitable challenges. ■ *I think about Frederick Douglass in the 1850s and 1860s. He escaped from slavery, educated himself, and got support from the American Friends Society, the abolitionist movement. He became a spokesperson against slavery and for his people, ambassador to Haiti, confidant to Presidents Abraham Lincoln and Ulysses S. Grant, and so forth. He spoke out against what happened during Reconstruction. It's an unbelievable story. And so, when you think about what he went through during that time, the things that we face today are pretty minor in my view. Hard, but not the same. It's inspirational to think that a Black man in the 1860s was able to do what he did against all odds.*

Box 6.2   Alonzo Fulgham:
How Badly Do You Want to Be Right?

"I was the regional office director for Georgia and Azerbaijan, responsible for the market reform program. I had six PhDs working for me in privatization, energy, market reform, stock market, etc. This one guy didn't do the things he was supposed to do. And every time I told him to do something, he looked at me like, 'Hey, Sonny, I have a PhD. You don't tell me what to do.' And, by the way, his wife was the mission director's secretary. This guy was saying things to the mission director like 'I don't think he's got the right pedigree. He doesn't know this.' Meanwhile, all of my outside constituents love me. The government loves me. The European Union loves me. I'm in all the key working groups and they love me.

"This guy blew up something. Everybody knew he had screwed up. When word got out that I was about to fire him, the mission director wrote a note telling me why I couldn't fire him, that part of the problem was me, not the guy. So I was fit to be tied. I knew I was right. He copied Washington on that letter. So now it's a political problem. He's basically put it on the agenda that there's about to be a blowup. And he's wondering how I'm going to handle it. Am I going to bring race into this? Is this going to be a fight?

"I started writing my rebuttal. If smoke could come off the keyboard, it was coming off those keys. Colleagues in Washington were saying, 'We saw the letter. We all know it's horrible. We all know him. He's a horrible manager. We feel bad for you.' One colleague said, 'Alonzo, I know you wrote a response. I know it's going to be thoughtful. But how bad do you want to be right?' What they were saying to me in code was 'You're going to write a response that's going to make him look really bad. But the people who put him out there are behind him, and now you created a problem for them.' He said, 'Just think about it for a couple of days. Please don't send it.'

"I sat and I thought about it. And I knew there were bigger fish that I wanted to fry. Even the ambassador knew he was a knucklehead. Sometimes you're dead right, but fighting could create such a firestorm. And that's the thing you learn as you go along. The fact that everybody else was apologizing to me and told me this guy was a fool—am I going to waste my ammo on this guy when they already know he's a failure? Don't do it. Keep your powder dry. Sometimes people are giving you signals. They're not going to tell you not to do something. They're trying to help you create a process in your own brain of how to manage people. I went on. And he had to sit in that room for three weeks and witness the good-bye parties and nice things people said about me. That's justice. Ten years ago, I was going through stuff and discarding files. I read the letter again. I thought, 'God, I'm glad I didn't send that.'"

**Box 6.3   Gina Abercrombie-Winstanley:
              Learning to Be Resilient**

"I was tapped to be US ambassador to Oman in 2004. I spent the morning at White House presidential appointments, where Dina Powell was saying, 'Congratulations, we're going to be announcing your name in the next couple of days. Your family must be so proud. What do you hope to accomplish?' And then I went to the assistant secretary in the afternoon, who said, 'We're pulling your name.' It was the same day. I reached out to the ambassador for help, and he told me, 'No. No.' It was after the [al Qa'ida] attack on the US consulate in Jeddah, where I was serving as consul general. I was told I couldn't speak to the press about the attack. I kept saying I'm not allowed to speak. Ted Koppel's very last *Nightline* was on me. And it was so humiliating. On television, they said, 'She declined to speak.' The assistant secretary told me the institution is more important than the individual, and I was going to take the hit for that. So they withdrew my name from the White House after I'd gone through all the vetting.

"Largely, I hold myself responsible. You better know the system. You've got to understand the invisible furniture that is in your organization. It was my fault that I got dinged by the ARB [Accountability Review Board—convened when there is an injury or loss of life attributable to security issues], because people tried to warn me, and I didn't believe them. The OBO [Bureau of Overseas Building Operations] knew that we had a vulnerable gate. We had reported it, and they told us we were getting a new one in two years. I didn't control the timing for a new gate. I was so certain of my position and my rightness and that I'd done everything possible to keep people safe. I helped my people through a terrorist attack. I had to go out and console families. Why would I get in trouble? Well, if I had known the system better, when they told me the timing of the gate, I would have put my concerns in black and white: 'I am telling you this gate is dangerous.' I didn't protect myself. I stumbled on the invisible furniture. I had been warned by people. I just didn't believe it because I didn't know the system. I thought that because the assistant secretary had put me forward and I was going through vetting, nothing could change that.

"The principal deputy assistant secretary in the Office of the Director General, Ruth Whiteside, found me a place to go when no one else would hire me. She saved my career. Because not only did people not help me, I was shunned. She told me to go over to FSI [Foreign Service Institute] and run the training for diplomats going to the Middle East. Professionally, I always did my best, and I did improve the training. But I have since apologized to my colleagues, because, certainly at the beginning, I wasn't a good colleague. I was resentful because I should have been an

continues

Box 6.3   Continued

---

ambassador, not filling a mid-level position at FSI. It was a GS-14 job
to do that. And I was a senior Foreign Service officer. I was supposed to
be an ambassador. I was in a tiny little office, in one of many. I was
extremely bitter and betrayed and angry. And it took someone who asked
me what happened. I told him the story. I was expecting love and comfort and 'You poor thing.' And all he said was 'Boy, you sure are bitter.'
And that's what flipped it for me. That's when I knew that nobody wants
to work with bitter, and my pity party needed to end immediately. And
that's what it took."

Ambassador Abercrombie-Winstanley was later recognized with
Department of State Meritorious and Superior Honor Awards, including
"for acts of courage during an attack on the US Consulate General, Jeddah, Saudi Arabia on December 6, 2004, by al-Qa'ida terrorists." She
was named ambassador to Malta in 2012.

Accept and Move On or Around

Many of these experiences demonstrate the need to sometimes choose
not to openly fight, to accept things as they are, and to move on or
around the affront. In Chapter 3, we heard from Ambassador Rea
Brazeal: "Early in my working life, I decided I would never know why
I got support or didn't get support. . . . I would never know whether it
was because I was Black, because I was a woman, because I was young,
because I was tall, because I was fat. And that way lay madness." She
shared great examples of how she worked around these issues wherever
she could and even used them to her advantage (see also Box 8.10). For
example, when she arrived in Japan, she didn't like the commercial
counselor, who she felt was a male chauvinist. "He had control over who
got a newspaper subscription. I wanted a newspaper. And he said,
'You'll get exactly what your predecessor got.' Since I had no predecessor, I knew I'd get nothing. Other women officers wound up in shouting
matches with this guy, but I went back to my office, and I sat and
thought about it. I solved it by always getting to the embassy before he
did, and I took his newspaper." Dr. Helene Gayle plowed through these
experiences: "I was just determined to do what I wanted to do." Her
stubbornness didn't allow any of these experiences to get in the way.

All of our giants went on and continued to excel to become the
giants they are today. In many cases, not fighting actually led to better

outcomes (as for Sanola A. Daley and Aaron Williams). But we don't always know in advance if that will be the case. ■ *You don't know that. And it's hell you're going through at the time. You're angry, but you've got to keep your head on your shoulders. You can't let your anger and emotions get the better of you. You've really got to play a cooler hand. And you have to let the people who are your friends and supporters give you the support you need.*

When I lost the position leading the Inter-America Foundation (see Chapter 5), I went home that night and wanted to throw bricks through the wall. And I decided I was just going to have to swallow this and walk away. But before I did that, I went back to the Republican staff on the Hill and told them if I was going to go away quietly, I wanted an ironclad agreement that whenever I went up for the next job, wherever it might be, I didn't want any interference. I would want them to endorse and support me. And that's what they did when I came up for mission director in South Africa.

So you were humiliated in a professional opportunity. It's not the worst thing that can happen to you. It's not like cancer. Okay? Sure, it's really tough. There is an element of "What did I do that led to this? You're not that important, so why would they do this to you? You must've done something else. There's got to be another story here." You may feel like damaged goods. Can you show your face on Capitol Hill anymore? A lot of stuff goes through your head at these times. So you have to be determined and walk through it. I already had a stellar career, and I had plenty of allies and supporters, so I had something to fall back on. I would be fine.

This is all the more reason why, especially with the more minor but cumulative affronts, you've got to keep a sense of humor. Maya Angelou said it best. As her mother had done with her, she told her son jokes and encouraged him to laugh—at life and at himself. She wrote, "The Black child must learn early to allow laughter to fill his mouth or the million small cruelties he encounters will congeal and clog his throat" (Angelou 1991, 150). Philip Gary has lived by that sense of humor. He advises, "The sense of humor has to be for you more than anybody else because it keeps you balanced. It keeps you from going off the deep end because you're so serious. I had a lot of contemporaries who were steeped the same way I was, but it became a burden. You had this talented tenth mantle that you had to carry. You have to lighten up about it and just say, 'Okay, this is who I am.'"

Vernon Jordan was a great role model for this. He grew up with the casual and ubiquitous N-label in segregated Atlanta. When the wealthy man he chauffeured for caught him in the library, the man proclaimed to his family, as if astonished, "Vernon can read!" Vernon Jordan used that phrase as the title of his autobiography. As Robin Givhan reflected at his passing, Vernon Jordan wrote, "'Each of us has to decide for our-selves how much nonsense we can take in life, and from whom we are willing to take it.' In other words, this small, old man didn't matter. He was not someone to slay. Instead of fanning his racism with outrage, Jordan doused it with pity" (Givhan 2021).

Ambassador Johnny Young provided an example that was so absurd he could only laugh. He was supporting a US government del-egation traveling to Kenya to participate in the first-ever Africa-hosted meeting of the International Monetary Fund and the World Bank. It was a large delegation comprised of important VIPs. On the drive from the airport, a congresswoman expressed her excitement at being in Africa for the first time. He recounted her saying, "'I'm so happy. I can't wait to get to the bush.' Then she turned to me, and she said, 'Are you from the bush?' I said, 'No, I'm not. I'm a Foreign Service officer. I'm from the United States, Philadelphia.' It was really quite funny" (Young 2013, 56).

■ *To have a sense of humor about yourself and the world you live in, you also have to be secure. Barack Obama is known to be a very serious person. He also has a pretty strong sense of humor. And he is very secure. He would have to be to have become our first Black president. I don't think many people reflect on that part of personality and how it interacts with their professional development and career. A sense of humor also allows you to draw people in who might have significant cultural and professional differences with you.*

We all know, you cannot control others' behavior; you can only control your own. Maya Angelou, again, shares important wisdom: "When you don't like a thing, change it. If you can't change it, change the way you think about it" (Angelou 1994, 87).

Just Do Your Job

Sometimes doing your job must take precedence over that drive to fight. Whether it's the politics and policy you don't like or racist and sexist responses that provoke you, you need to be crystal clear about your com-mitments and responsibility. As we have already learned, Ambassador Ed Perkins took very seriously his oath of office to serve the United States and uphold the Constitution. So do all of our Foreign Service giants. With or without a professional oath, we hope you will keep center of mind your commitments and responsibilities to a particular mission and values, which often means serving interests beyond your own—values and principles, as well as organizations and institutions.

When You Question Politics

Ambassador Johnnie Carson has experienced many policy disagreements. As an expert on Africa with on-the-ground contacts and experience and superb analytic and political skills, he often has strong convictions about which policies are most appropriate. He has also been tasked with representing and enacting policies he didn't believe were the best course of action. He explains one has an obligation to follow the law, the Constitution, and the directives of one's superiors. He describes a menu of optional responses: "If a person feels that they are being asked to do something that violates a very personal moral principle, then they have the option of resigning, of asking to be transferred to another office or division, or of taking a leave of absence to do something different. When an action is illegal, against the law, or a violation of the Constitution, a person has an obligation to go up the chain of command and say, 'This is not in accordance with the law.'"

These issues were top of mind at the time we held our focus group discussions. The young people we spoke with were deeply concerned about serving in a presidential administration that was contrary to their values and policy aspirations. There is no one right answer to these moral dilemmas. Ambassador Linda Thomas-Greenfield offered the following perspective for younger people already serving or about to begin their service. "Hang in there. This shall pass. They're going to have to rebuild this thing. They need people who are inside and in the pipeline to help rebuild." Some of our giants did choose this time to either retire or resign. So, we asked, why would they advise younger people to continue working for the federal government? Ambassador Linda Thomas-Greenfield responds in Box 6.4.

■ *In fact, strategic resignation is an important aspect of your public service. When you are more senior, you have a rare chance that most young people coming in never have, to really make a difference and take a stand on the future of public service.*

Chris Richardson was appalled by the Donald Trump administration's Muslim travel ban. He responded with enthusiasm to a movement within the State Department to issue a dissent cable. After helping with the writing, he emailed his colleagues, urging them to sign it, but was disappointed with the response. "People were telling me, 'These things happen. Maybe Trump will moderate.' Some officers were hostile to even speaking out, saying the president has a right to make these kinds of decisions. That's true. But I always said that we have an obligation to speak up against things that we think might be wrong. For me, morally,

---

**Box 6.4   Linda Thomas-Greenfield:
Only Leave in Protest When It Matters**

"You're too young in your career for it to matter. You need to stay in, because if you quit right now, nobody cares. Nobody will care that you didn't come into the Foreign Service. People cared that I left the Foreign Service. I had established a name for myself. I could make a splash. The *New York Times* would come and interview me to find out why I left the Foreign Service. It is only at senior levels where these policies and resignations will matter.

"I came in during the Reagan administration. One thing Reagan did that I was personally offended by was he met with Sam Doe, who overthrew the government of Liberia. He killed nineteen of the most prominent international statesmen in the world, and our president met with him. I was a junior officer in Jamaica then, and I thought, 'I can't work for this guy!' Somebody said to me, 'Linda, nobody will care that you can't work for this guy. If the assistant secretary quits, everybody will care. Do your job and stay in so that when we need you to make a difference, you're there.' It was the best advice I could have gotten, because I eventually reached a point where I could make a difference."

---

it was a litmus test. Then, after the president made his comment about African countries, that was my final straw. I felt I needed to go do something else."[1]

When Race Becomes a Factor

Chris Richardson's decision to leave the State Department is not the end of his story. He wrote an opinion piece in the *New York Times* titled, "The State Department Was Designed to Keep African-Americans Out," which was widely read and cited. He has continued to write about and to organize panels and discussions on this topic, advocating for a more representative and just State Department. He has worked hard to move beyond mere resignation as protest and to exercise his ability to speak more freely from the outside. In Box 6.5, he identifies four systemic issues one has to deal with when it comes to race in the State Department.

If these daily affronts are not enough, sometimes racism is right up in your face. And sometimes actors in any one of these four categories Chris Richardson identifies may try to use race to intentionally knock

Box 6.5   Chris Richardson: The Four Systemic Race Challenges You May Face

"First, you have to navigate the fact that your white colleagues may be looking at you with a generational understanding of what the role of a Black person is in their lives and how you are challenging a lot of those notions just by your very presence. A lot of white people are not going to want you to tell them why they're wrong or to give them orders. If I, as a Black man, or God forbid, if a Black woman sits there and tells a white man, 'You're wrong,' that white man isn't paying attention to why they're wrong. They're paying attention to all the ways you've disrespected and crossed some subconscious boundary. Second, you have to deal with the local staff at the embassy who might be shocked that there's a Black guy who's in charge of them.

"Third, in dealing with American citizens, there's a sense that those people look at you and think, 'Are you the help?' I had a lot of people who said, 'I want to talk to a real American,' the implication being that I am not a real American. Fourth, even in a Black country like Nigeria, local citizens would say, 'We want to talk to a real American,' because the face of a white person is considered the face of authority. Yes, you need to do your job and be good at it. But while you're dealing with your job, you're also dealing with all these micro and macro issues just because of the color of your skin."

you off balance. And then what do you do? How do you still make sure you do your job? Ambassador Harry K. Thomas Jr. shares his wisdom and experience in Box 6.6.

Stop and Think

Chris Richardson's and Ambassador Harry K. Thomas Jr.'s experiences are good examples of making intentional decisions. No matter how egregious the affront—and one would be hard-pressed to identify something worse than what Ambassador Thomas experienced—it's important to stop and think before you react. There are three elements of that thinking we want to highlight: focus on purpose, protect yourself and your sanity, and recognize when reacting serves others' purpose and not your own. Navigating the issues and options is much easier when you can identify others to help you consider these elements and then support your choices.

**Box 6.6   Harry K. Thomas Jr.:
The Worst Insult in Zimbabwe**

"In November 2015, while I was waiting to get confirmed as ambassador to Zimbabwe, one of the desk officers brought me the front page of the Zimbabwe newspaper. The headline was 'Who Is This N-word Anyway?' That was the first of many times I was called the N-word. I had to be cool. You can't lose your temper. Every time that happened, Linda Thomas-Greenfield, who was the assistant secretary, would call in the Zimbabwe ambassador and dress him down, and he would apologize. They called me Uncle Tom. They called a Black woman, who was our political affairs officer, Aunt Jemimah. You never like it, but you get used to it. Whenever you spoke out on human rights, within two days you were going to be called something on the front page of the paper. Zimbabweans are brilliant people. They know right from wrong. They knew what they were doing. In terms of being a person of color, that was the worst thing that ever happened to me. And it happened repeatedly . . . in an African country.

"I did not let it influence my effectiveness. I knew I couldn't react. I didn't say anything to the Zimbabweans until a new government came in and we had a slightly different relationship. If you're leading a very diverse mission, no matter how painful it is, if you are a person of color or a woman or gay, my advice would be to complain to your spouse or your partner, your parents, your family, but do not show that to your mission under any circumstances. Otherwise, you lose your effectiveness. As a leader I had to be concerned for my staff.

"We were there for [Robert] Mugabe's fall. The Russian embassy was across the street from our embassy. And when the people marched down the street—the first multiracial, multigenerational march they ever had in the history of Zimbabwe—when they marched past our embassy, they were chanting, 'USA, USA.' They weren't chanting 'Putin.' And we were in tears. It told us that they were subjugated, not stupid. When the US sticks to our values, which are human rights and diversity and good governance, even if we think it's not working, if it doesn't change these thugs who are running these governments, the people understand. And they appreciate it. It gives them some hope."[2]

Focus on Purpose

You've got to know your intent. Do you want to gain something in particular? Do you want to create better understanding and build relationships? Or do you want to just express your outrage? Dr. Helene Gayle prioritizes relationships and understandings, because "if it's about getting it off your chest, it's because you want to feel better. But you won't really feel better if the person didn't hear you because you said it in a way that was alienating versus in a way that built understanding. I'm more interested in somebody actually hearing why what they did was inappropriate or demeaning or hurtful. If I feel like it's either not the right moment, the right person, or I'm not in the right frame of mind to be able to say it in a way that will be heard, I just don't do it." Valerie Dickson-Horton has a similar attitude. She shared, "A lot of people like going out to pound on the table. My advice is to listen attentively, take good notes so you don't forget, and always try to be politely honest with everybody. You don't have to demean someone to throw the truth out there. There's a way to deliver it." Ambassador Gina Abercrombie-Winstanley agrees: "You've got to be prepared to make your case and make your case without bitterness, without irritation. I have always been an impatient, get-out-of-my-way kind of person. And my mother always said, 'Honey not vinegar, not vinegar. Got to catch those flies, come on now.'"

Ambassador Johnnie Carson warns that if you are going to fight, it should be for an important purpose. "I've seen people fight in the wrong places: fight over an office space or where they sit. Maybe the boss said something to them that they find troubling. Do you fight there? Or do you fight on policy issues, with the notion that 'This is not the way I would do it'? I've got to make sure I can get to a position and a place where I can have some control, so that the kinds of things I think are important with respect to personnel, management, and policy issues are the rules of the day and not another person's." Ambassador Reuben Brigety advises, "You can't die on every hill, but there are some hills that are worth dying on. And understanding which is which is a matter of studying history, your personal judgment, and listening to your own internal sense." He adds, "You also have to be really, really good at what you do." ■ *If you're not professionally successful, you're not going to be able to win the big fights.*

And once you are in those influential positions, Dr. Jacob Gayle cautions, you need to be mindful of what you are fighting for—revolution or evolution—and how you can be most effective. He shared, "It's an honor and a privilege and a responsibility to be at the so-called table. So when we do have the opportunity to have a voice in leadership discussions, we have a responsibility for how we diplomatically use it. It's not always about saying the first thing that comes off of our head, or revolution versus evolution at all times. Sometimes it is being part of that larger understanding of how bureaucracy works, how protocol works, and then being able to work within that system. It's sometimes less glitzy and newsworthy, but if your goal is to really create sustainable change, sometimes it's a little quieter than it is necessarily loud, boisterous, and demonstrative." In the early HIV/AIDS epidemic, Dr. Jacob Gayle learned there is a role for both revolutionaries and evolutionaries. "We had to sometimes work together. Each of us might sit on different sides of the table, but we had to remember that we were trying to benefit the very same communities." While working for the Centers for Disease Control and Prevention, he would slip into Act UP meetings. They had a common goal and would keep each other informed.

Dr. Gayle's experience is a good reminder that change is a multifaceted process. It is not a Lone Ranger sport. You will not be the only one fighting the larger battles.

Let It Go and Stay Sane

Does it matter if it's racism or sexism? That was Ambassador Rea Brazeal's question. She didn't want to get embroiled in that debate; she just wanted to move toward her goals. When asked about how race impacted his career trajectory, Ambassador Harry K. Thomas Jr. warned, "When you go looking for something, a lot of times you find it." It's possible there are other factors at play. In reflecting on the international development field, C. D. Glin thought, "It's a big city with a small industry. Did race play a role in some rejections? Maybe. I sometimes thought, 'We're all going to apply. Somebody is not going to get the job.' So, do I want to home in on being Black? Or do I want to move on and keep trying? I didn't want to get stuck in that place of 'woe is me' because I just didn't see it benefiting me in the long run." Ambassador Gina Abercrombie-Winstanley reported her biggest challenge was others' low expectations of her (see Box 6.7).

Ambassador Ed Perkins knew he would face a lot of obstacles in his career because of who he was. He recounted, "I decided that I would never, ever look for excuses. I would always look for a path to overcoming. And the paths are not always clear. I also knew the person who was most important in solving this problem was myself." Beyond this eagle-eyed focus that drives out the painful noise of discrimination, we would do well to cultivate an attitude of simply not caring about these affronts. General Barrye Price advocates a stubborn don't-care attitude, even as he recognizes, "You will be judged by people who don't know you, never got to know you, may not want to know you. And these judgments are based in many ways on ignorance, on what they saw on the news or the last experience with so and so, or how I grew up or where I grew up. . . . And it's all foolishness. So we've got to say, 'If

**Box 6.7   Gina Abercrombie-Winstanley:
              Staying Sane and Focused on Purpose**

"I made a decision not to let others' low expectations of me get me down. Because it is corrosive. It's a drip of acid that you have to deal with. Even sitting at the head of the table as a United States ambassador, I had European American men challenging me as an African American woman. And I'm the ambassador! And I knew that these conversations, these questions, these challenges would never happen if I were a European American male. I had to hold onto my sense of humor, and my patience as well, because I was responsible for everybody's development.

"You don't want people to feel resentful and say, 'Oh, she's an angry Black woman' or 'There's something wrong with her'—all the things that get said behind people's backs. You need to educate them on why that was not the right move to make, not the right question to ask. Why it was inappropriate. And 'Let me help you do better next time,' in the most positive way. The honey rather than the vinegar."

you get to know me, you probably would like me. But if you don't, I don't care.' I'm okay with that."

Recognize When Fighting Back Serves Someone Else's Purpose

Your calculus in knowing when to fight has to include your greater purpose and intention, protecting yourself, psychologically and otherwise, and also understanding that your fight can be exactly what others want from you. You may be intentionally baited, or you may just conveniently fall prey to others' agendas. Imagine if Alonzo Fulgham had sent that letter (Box 6.2). Luckily, he learned that the only ones who would gain from his protest would be his accuser and the underperforming contractor. A simple disagreement, a competitive spirit, or, worse, insecurity or feeling threatened can lead a colleague to use race and gender to goad you into acting out in ways that may only hurt you. They have those extra tools in their arsenal. You do not.

General and Secretary Colin Powell learned these lessons when he was based in the South, living in a segregated society and commanding an integrated unit. It was his first experience with this type of racism. He writes, "I had to find a way to cope psychologically. I began by identifying my priorities. I wanted, above all, to succeed at my Army career. I did not intend to give way to self-destructive rage, no matter how provoked. . . . Nothing that happened off-post, none of the indignities, none of the injustices, was going to inhibit my performance. . . . I occasionally felt hurt; I felt anger; but most of all I felt challenged. I'll show you!" (Powell 1995, 43).

When Ambassador Rea Brazeal arrived in Kenya as the new ambassador, her politically appointed predecessor refused to meet with her. She described him as a racist, and, not surprisingly, the Kenyan government seemed happy to see him gone. But he did not leave without first trying to make her work more difficult. "He told people, 'A Black woman ambassador to Kenya? Kenya doesn't matter anymore.' Given human nature, there were enough white Americans in Nairobi, who were happy to tell me what he said. I said, 'Oh, thank you so much for telling me.' Of course, they told me because they wanted to be a friend of the position." Ambassador Brazeal played nice, building relationships and goodwill "to the point that as I was leaving, they said, 'You know, you're not bad.'" Ambassador Brazeal's behavior is a great example of turning lemons into lemonade. She did not condone racist remarks, but neither did she rise to the indignities. She killed them with kindness, leveraging relationships for other battles that were more focused on the job and her purpose as an ambassador.

Look for Support

A theme throughout this book and throughout the giants' experience is seeking support and being supported by others. When it comes to determining when to fight, knowing who will support you is key. The support you have may still not be enough to win your fight. Recall that Ambassador Johnnie Carson was unable to secure a visa to South Africa despite the strong support from the deputy chief of mission in Lagos, Nigeria, where he was then stationed. On the other hand, when he served in Portugal, the ambassador there promoted Johnnie Carson twice, even though the deputy chief of mission was unsupportive. Alonzo Fulgham benefited from the wise counsel of friends and colleagues in Washington and decided being right would come at too great a cost. He held on to his rebuttal letter (Box 6.2). When she faced a battle she couldn't win, Ambassador Gina Abercrombie-Winstanley received support from others who provided a place to land at the Foreign Service Institute (Box 6.3).

Chris Richardson tried to work through formal dissent channels before ultimately deciding to resign from the State Department. While his complaints were about policy, history has shown that formal systems for redress don't work well for underrepresented populations. Even more broadly, whistle-blower protections are notoriously unreliable. That doesn't mean you can't find support through less formal channels, and formal channels can work, especially when you have this additional support.

▶ Influencing change looks different for everyone. So far, I haven't had a problem with advocating for myself or the greater good, but I have come to learn that what comes easy to me does not for others. Finding the right ally/sponsor takes time. You can find them through existing support channels (friends, employee resource groups, mentors). Many of the tactics that the giants speak about on the topic of picking your battles are extremely effective when coupled with the right sponsorship. Personally, I look for allies who have an established reputation within an organization and a voice that is valued across a spectrum of opinions. This person can provide you with the necessary protections in difficult situations. Along with the cover provided by your sponsor, having a detailed record of any written correspondence related to the situation is critical. It's hard to argue what is in black and white.

Fighting the Good Fight

We've reviewed examples of not fighting. Our giants have advised you on the calculus of deciding when to fight. But what happens when you do choose to fight? What does the good fight look like? We want to support you in being as strategic as you can be so that once you choose the most important battles, you are most likely to succeed in your purpose. Fighting the good fight requires being brave enough to do the right thing, holding your ground and attaining your goal despite racism, having confidence to exercise your technical expertise, understanding human behavior, and applying all of these not just for your personal gain but for important, moral policy objectives.

Be Brave

It's hard to speak up when things aren't right. General Barrye Price describes this: "I think people put self-imposed caps on themselves—a threshold of pain that they won't push through or push beyond. Oftentimes it's driven by ambition or fear: fear that they may not be able to achieve all that they aspire to; fear that they might be persecuted or ostracized." But, he adds, "my experience has been leaders really do want truth. They really do want insights. They don't mind disruption, just in the right way." ▶ Think about the impact of the statement and who it is intended for. Once you have been identified as someone who is comfortable speaking about uncomfortable situations, your words will hold a lot more weight, for better or for worse.

Ambassador James Joseph understands that to be a critic is to be someone who cares, someone who is actually a friend to that organization. He writes, "I discovered . . . that the most effective critic is likely to be the one who is willing to be a servant and the most effective servant is likely to be the one who is willing to be a critic. I continue to be both" (Joseph 2015, 284). Verone Bernard brings this attitude to her work every day (see Box 6.8).

Box 6.8   Verone Bernard: Motivations and Strategy to Get the Job Done

"Being right and wrong in this line of work is never about me. I've been taught there can be no ego in service. And I recognize my decisions can directly or indirectly impact the lives of others who are hundreds of miles away. When confronted with choosing whether to speak up or stay silent, I have to ask myself, 'Am I saying this to stroke my own ego? Am I saying this because it needs to be heard? Am I the most effective mouthpiece for this message?' Being grounded and motivated by a greater mission helps me navigate these questions.

"I was leading a strategy session with a diverse group of stakeholders and partners for a proposal in Zambia. Among us were technical experts, who also brought invaluable lived experience. There was a difference of opinion on the design of our technical approach. A white colleague became irate and started spewing very problematic things, including reminding the room of his degrees and extensive research. 'I've lived in the jungle with the Pygmies, and I've eaten raw meat.' The room was completely awry. I suggested we break for coffee to ease the tension in the space. When we reconvened, I couldn't get us back on track. The damage was irreversible. When I tried to survey the room for the next topic to tackle, one of the participants responded, 'Ask the Pygmy.' I thanked everyone for their time and said we would try again tomorrow. They were greatly offended, as they should have been. He was beyond disrespectful, totally out of line.

"That evening, my phone was bombarded with WhatsApp notifications and voice notes from the participants. The resounding message was 'If this is who you are, then we want nothing to do with this project. We are going to pull out.' I thought, 'Yeah, I want to pull out too.' So I asked

continues

Box 6.8   Continued

---

myself what would be meaningful? I tried to approach my colleague to debrief on the earlier events. Unsurprisingly, he had no interest in engaging in dialogue with me.

"For a moment, I thought about letting it go. I figured if it came to it, we could replace the partners. My greatest concern in that moment was elevating the issue and knowing I would have to continue to see this person in the hallways of my organization. I feared my own reputation being tarnished as a tattler and someone who couldn't be trusted. I was too junior in my career. I couldn't afford that. It would be easier if I let it go. As my mind kept pacing, I knew I had to do something.

"That evening, I drafted a memo outlining my recommendations for corrective action and a plan to repair the relationships that were harmed. I settled my nerves and phoned an executive in Washington, DC, to explain what happened and the reputational implication of my colleague's episode. The response to my concern was 'Tell me what to say, whom to call, and please get some rest.'

"It was a transformational experience for me because I witnessed a range of leadership styles in such a short time period. What I took away from this experience was that sound leadership is reflective. It listens. And it doesn't hesitate to do what is right."

■ *It's tough for a junior person to do that. You really need the higher-ups to come in and support you. And that's when you learn about the kind of organization and leaders you are working for.*

Sometimes you are one of the higher-ups, but you still operate in broader systems of authority. The importance and the potential consequences of speaking out are all that much greater. Philip Gary proudly spoke truth to power as he believed he should, even when it resulted in a premature ending to his post as USAID mission director in Nepal. He tells the story in Box 6.9.

This was not the only conflict Philip Gary experienced with the ambassador, and he served in this post for only one year.

What About Race?

The perennial question. The good fight stories we've shared so far are about speaking truth to power in a professional capacity. What if the challenge is much more personal? What if it is about race? You may be

---

Box 6.9   Philip Gary: Holding His Own Against an Ambassador in Nepal

---

"AID directors are asked by the World Bank to give their opinion on World Bank projects that they are planning on setting up in the country. The World Bank was thinking about building a dam in Nepal. The cost of the dam was equivalent to one year of GDP in Nepal. Also, the dam only made sense if you could sell the power that was going to be generated to India. India did not have a national power grid, so that was a no-go. So, I did the quick analysis and concluded it did not make any economic sense.

"I was ready to send the cable, and the ambassador stops the cable and tells me she doesn't agree with this, that she would support the government, and I should rethink this. I said, 'I really don't agree.' And she said, 'Well, this is what I think, and I want you to agree.' Finally, I said, 'Okay. Fine. We'll say what you want to say. We'll send it in, and you sign it.' That was not well received.

"The country was limping along. It was a matter of principle. I couldn't sign on to something I knew was going to fail in terms of economic return. It was just going to be another rip off for a very small group of elites in Nepal. I felt I needed to take a stand irrespective of the ambassador's political agenda or connection with the elite in the country. I felt that I was there to represent the poor people in Nepal. My job was to make those decisions and give that advice."

---

personally offended and even stymied in your objectives, and you may choose to fight. But you still shouldn't just start flipping tables.

■ *The more you advance to higher levels, the less you have to deal with issues like this. Of course, today there is more cover, just like in the #MeToo movement, for you to check people upfront. Nowadays, such racial discrimination would probably not get very far, because there would be too many eyes on it. Too many people would smell a rat. Today, if you have a gut feeling that racial discrimination is holding you back, you can go through the channels of your organization to make a complaint. There is still a risk, but not as much as there was twenty years ago. You still need to be careful. You don't want to be characterized a certain way. In our generation, we always had to deal with what I call the "chip-on-the-shoulder syndrome," an assumption that you're super sensitive and overreact because you think Black people are always being discriminated against. That conjecture is still with us.*

Be Strategic in Your Timing and Competence

Aaron's observation on this topic underscores the need for strategy: knowing the context, knowing the players, knowing the risks, and building on your strengths—including the strong network of relationships you have been cultivating over time. This requires intentional study and support. Ambassador Ed Perkins shared that he was fortunate to have a mentor early in his Foreign Service career who, in addition to coaching him on his career path, would help him when he thought he had to take on a fight. "He would characterize what the battle entailed and how to go about it." ▶ Knowing when and how to deliver criticism can make the difference between advancement and being sidelined. It's easy to immediately check people in their tracks, but without actionable feedback the criticism holds no meaning. This doesn't mean you should shy away from the difficult conversations—craft your message so it can be received in the best possible way. You have to know how to challenge people so they receive the message. General Barrye Price learned this lesson the hard way (see Box 6.10).

Box 6.10   Barrye Price: Be Tactful, Avoid Embarrassment

"When you embarrass somebody, it becomes personal. All they can see is red, and the whole focus is to destroy you. When you take it offline, you give an opportunity for cooler heads to prevail. That's when you find the opportunity for reconciliation, for healing, for understanding. I'm very candid, but I don't speak candidly in an auditorium.

"I was a lieutenant. I had finished my program. The major who was over all of us lieutenants had us in the Friday before Labor Day. We were changing leadership positions weekly, and he decided that for the convenience of the office staff, we weren't going to change leadership positions anymore. This is a Friday. Labor Day is Monday. We out-process on Tuesday, and I graduate Wednesday. Mine was the only hand that went up. There were five hundred lieutenants in the auditorium. He recognizes me. I stand up. I said, 'Sir, Second Lieutenant Barrye Price. You've said to me for nineteen weeks that it's more difficult to lead your peers than it is your subordinates. You are now saying that because of the inconvenience to the administrative staff, you're going to deny all of these lieutenants the opportunity to lead.' When someone calls you by your rank, it's like your mother saying your first name. You know you're

continues

Box 6.10   Continued

---

in trouble. He said, 'Lieutenant, you don't have to like it. You just have to love it.' Utter silence.

"I realized that I embarrassed him based on this rank differential. He was a major. I was three ranks below him as a second lieutenant. That whole weekend I was saying to myself, 'Man, I sure got under his skin.' I was disappointed that nobody else said anything. It didn't affect me. I was graduating in two days. But I was reflective enough to know that probably wasn't the way to handle that. And I heard my father's voice telling me, 'One who stands alone often times is.'

"Tuesday morning, the major wants to see me. He said, 'So, tell me about yourself.' I told him about myself. And he said, 'You were right. I should not have made that decision.' But he said, 'But.' And I apologized because I realized I had embarrassed him and that wasn't my intent. I said, 'I thought we were having a discussion, and obviously you were being directive. You weren't asking for opinions.' And he said, 'You're going to do well. Don't lose that ability to speak truth to power, but you've got to find the right place to do it.'"

■ *General Price was very fortunate to have had such a thoughtful leader, one who recognized his potential and the fact this was a learning moment for both of them.*

It's important to be timely in your feedback and challenge. But, as Sundaa Bridgett-Jones affirmed, "no one likes surprises." She has been fortunate to have opportunities to share her perspective directly with her supervisors privately. She elaborates, "It's important to take the time, whether in writing or in person, in a very cogent, coherent, and often passionate way, to offer the opposing side and show what the consequences and risks might be. It takes a lot of courage to do that, and one has to be prepared. My one-on-one conversations have been more successful than voicing that minority opinion among a number of people. There are occasions when we do need to use those broader public spaces, but more often than not, pulling people aside and being able to share our perspectives and point of view works well. At the same time, let's not be afraid to use the public space. It may give us the visibility we may need, particularly when we have our ducks in a row."

In some cases, the right time to raise issues may be much later, once you've developed enough of a rapport that the other person may be more willing to listen and understand. Sanola A. Daley shared, "I've had issues with a person or a situation that at the time I didn't feel like I could address well. And then I'll be on a trip with that person six months or a year later, and over dinner I'll say, 'By the way, this thing happened, and I wanted you to know I felt this way about it. I'm bringing it to you not so you feel bad, but so you know.' I've used this approach as a relationship-building opportunity. It really helps drive up the respect and improve that professional relationship for the long term."

Some fights may not require this level of engagement. Bob Burgess relied more on demonstrating his technical expertise to assert what was technically right and less on engaging with people and rules in the moment. He describes his approach in Box 6.11.

Box 6.11   Bob Burgess: Killing Them with Competence

GTE Sylvania provided lots of training on how to do cost accounting for a factory before they sent Bob Burgess to run operations in Trinidad and Tobago. "I had all of this in school, and I knew what they were talking about. But when I went to Trinidad and Tobago, we were only twenty some people to start out. I had to change that whole system. It was too unwieldy for such a small operation. So I literally took their system and threw it in the trash can. And I put my system in.

"Then I got a telegram saying that two guys from the accounting department in New York were going to come down and talk to me. They told me that I can't change systems like that, and I asked, 'Why?' They said, 'Well, because you're not qualified to do that. We've got these systems and blah, blah, blah.' I said, 'I'm going to explain my system, and you tell me what's wrong with it. Okay?' So I explained the system. It sent the reporting that they wanted from us. It gave them an update on our business and our progress and everything. . . . They looked at it and said, 'Wow! We have no comment. You can use the system. In fact, we're going to send you to Costa Rica to look at their system and see if you can implement your system there.'

"The biggest challenges I faced in my career were cleaning up somebody else's mess and putting my own systems and culture in. Once you do that, people don't look at you as a Black person. They look at you as a competent manager. And then if you've got people who don't want to go along with what you're espousing, you just simply move them out."

Break the Rules for the Right Reasons

Bob Burgess broke the rules in order to fulfill his professional responsibilities as he saw them—to do the best job he knew how to do. There may be other times you need to break the rules, or break with policy, because what you observe is not morally right. Make no mistake, when you do such things, you risk your career. Only you can decide when the ethical way is so important that you need to bring all that you and your position can muster to set things right. Ambassador Johnnie Carson did that in Kenya, as he describes in Box 6.12.

Box 6.12   Johnnie Carson: Fighting and Taking Risks to Change Bad Policy

"When I arrived as ambassador to Kenya, I was tasked with rebuilding embassy morale and rebuilding our relationship with the country after the 1998 embassy bombing. But HIV/AIDS was ravaging Kenya as well. I went and talked to people across the board, saying, 'Tell me what you're doing on HIV/AIDS. Do you have testing and counseling centers? Are individuals with HIV/AIDS excluded from employment opportunities? Are you testing people for HIV/AIDS in their preemployment physicals?' I heard a lot of stuttering. Eventually, I heard, 'Yes, we're testing people's blood to find out if they have HIV/AIDS and if they are otherwise employable for the job. And if they're qualified but have HIV/AIDS, we don't employ them.' So, I asked, 'Do you tell them what their status is?' And I got 'No, because we haven't told them we were testing them for HIV/AIDS.' 'So you're testing them, not giving them a job, not telling them their status, and not referring them to counselling?'

"I pulled everybody together and said, 'We live in a different world now. We tell everybody that we test for HIV/AIDS and refer them to counseling if they have the disease. If the person is otherwise qualified but does not have a full-blown case of AIDS, we hire them if they're the best person. And we tell people. We ask their permission to do this first.' To increase HIV/AIDS awareness and prevention among our staff, we invited all of our local employees to be tested at our expense, and also their wives, up to two. And we established a program to provide some drugs and early HIV/AIDS prophylaxis.

"This is the only time I'm aware of that I almost got recalled back to Washington. The director general and some senior management officials were furious about my new policies on HIV/AIDS. But once other ambassadors in the region knew about what I was doing, they followed suit. The Centers for Disease Control [CDC] thought it was really courageous and forward-looking. And CDC gave me their highest award for civil servants because I was prepared to push really hard. I'm actually quite proud of what we did. Those are the things I fight for."

■ *What Johnnie Carson did was absolutely the right thing to do. It was the only decent thing to do. And it changed policy and practice all across the African continent. It is the kind of thing that would be worth losing a position for.*

The Particular Challenge of the Media

We want to close with a few words and experiences related to the media. The media is sometimes referred to as our fourth branch of government, or the fourth estate, because of the essential role it plays in a democracy. It provides a pathway for advocacy, as we see with Chris Richardson's work. It can frame policy issues. And it can fulfill important watchdog functions on individuals and government agencies. It can also ruin careers. The media can cast a broad net for muckraking—searching out and publicizing scandalous information—that sometimes snares people who are just trying to do their job. We have seen all too well how the media can become a political tool to castigate those who represent policies or political parties that powerful forces don't agree with. When you are early in your career, you likely won't need to worry too much about the roles and risks of attention from the media. But as you ascend to mid-level, especially if you become a visible leader and representative of particular policies and administrations, you will need to be aware of and carefully manage the media, if possible.

Susan Rice learned these lessons the hard way. She reports how she agreed to represent the Barack Obama administration in media appearances in the aftermath of Benghazi, where US ambassador to Libya J. Christopher Stevens and US Foreign Service information management officer Sean Smith were killed in an Islamist attack on a diplomatic compound. She was accused of downplaying the possibility that it was a terrorist attack. In her autobiography, *Tough Love*, she describes how her brother chided her for not sufficiently developing and calling on a support network when the media accused her of misleading the public. (She had represented approved talking points.) He told her, "When people see that you are under fire, you need them to jump in fast and be willing to battle on your behalf." She faults herself for not asking for help sooner (Rice 2019, 336).

Actions you take in your career can later come back to bite you—especially if your new assignment requires congressional approval. Sometimes criticism of your earlier actions can provide cover for racism too. Lauri Fitz-Pegado experienced that when she was nominated to be assistant secretary of commerce and director general of the US and Foreign Commercial Service. Gaining Senate confirmation took a year, and it was contentious. The focus was on her previous work, but she concluded, "Race was clearly a factor." See her story in Box 6.13.

Box 6.13   Lauri Fitz-Pegado: Surviving Media Attacks

"I was accused of having been complicit in not disclosing the name of a witness at a hearing about abuses of the Iraqis against the Kuwaitis during the occupation. It was the daughter of the ambassador from Kuwait, which to me didn't make any difference because her story actually played out. But the press went after me like red meat. I was attacked in the print media and in a *60 Minutes* piece for which I stupidly agreed to represent my firm because I thought the truth would set you free.

"A good lesson in my life was that for African American people and people of color, the truth does not set you free. It haunted me for decades. My biggest career challenge was the damage to my reputation that I had to overcome constantly. No matter what position I was going into subsequently, it would come up. The fact people can google you is a curse. I've done all this stuff. I've been to the best schools. I've worked so hard. And all of this could be destroyed by unfair, vicious reporting and probably some that was racist. Would they have tried to destroy the reputation of a white male back then?"

■ *When you're going up for a confirmation hearing, there's no worse place to be when you're under attack because the whole world is focused on you. And it becomes a story above the fold, as they say. I've always admired people who are able to pick up the pieces after that kind of attack and move on.*

So how might you manage the media? First, as Susan Rice's example shows, you need to pay close attention when you speak to the media and carefully scrutinize your script and the context. That may not eliminate media attacks, but at least you improve your chances. Second, you can use back channels to influence reporters, which helps if you have friends in the media. This was Aaron's experience. He used his support network to help him to manage media attention he thought could hurt him.

■ *When I lost the fight to be director of the Inter-America Foundation (Chapter 5), I had friends in the media who wanted to help. They wanted to write about it, and I learned they wanted to interview me. At the time, Jesse Helms was also trying to eliminate the budget for USAID. I knew further provoking him would not be good. Also, I had an "informal" agreement with some members of his staff and associates that I would go away quietly, with the understanding that he would not oppose my selection for another major leadership position in the future. Even if I had not been party to this story, Helms would see this as a direct attack by me. So now what do I do? You can't ask a major newspaper not to write a story. I couldn't approach them either. I needed to have deniability. So I sent other people to see the interested media person. I told them, "I don't know how you can stop it, but please figure out a way. I can't be part of this." And they did. They said, "Please do not do this. This is going to really hurt Aaron if you do this." And they never wrote the story.*

In trying to mitigate negative reporting, perhaps most importantly, you need to take great care in what you say on and off the record. No matter how friendly you think a reporter is, you need to be crystal clear about what is off the record, and, better yet, don't say anything you don't want to see in print. Our final story, on this topic, comes from Ambassador Linda Thomas-Greenfield (see Box 6.14).

**Box 6.14   Linda Thomas-Greenfield:
Say "Off the Record"**

"I was in Rwanda on April 6, 1994. It was a harrowing experience. People encouraged me to tell the story. The public affairs officers in the Kenya embassy set up an interview with a *Washington Post* journalist. I met with him, and he wrote something for the *Washington Post Magazine*. And it wasn't bad. But after the interview, after he put his papers away and his notebook away and we're sitting drinking beer at the bar, he started talking. And I didn't say it was off the record. I learned so much from that. I thought, 'I'm just shooting the bull with a press guy, another African American going through the experience of being in Africa.'

"And he talks about all the negative experiences he had, that as African Americans you can experience some prejudices, and particularly with Kenyans, who are used to white tourists, who see you just as another Kenyan and treat you in a way that we African Americans know how to define. He had gone through that experience. And I had gone through the experience. And I said to him, 'Sometimes living in Kenya would give you the impression of what it must have been like living in South Africa under Apartheid.' And he quoted me in print saying, 'Living in Kenya was like living in South Africa under Apartheid.' For years, if you googled my name, that was the first thing that came up. I've done so much since, so lots of other stuff comes up now. But it was such a misquote.

"Some said my career was over. But I had a mentor who called me and said, 'The same thing happened to me. We're going to learn from this experience. In the future, you always say it's off the record, and you never trust a press person. They will respect you if you say off the record, but you must say it.' For about ten years, I never talked to the press, and I'd tell them why."

Some of the jerks and bullies you encounter may be from the media. Some of the media may be friends and important members of your support network. You need to become savvy about how to manage these relationships—to use the media for advocacy and policy framing when it can support your cause and to protect yourself in everything you say and make public.

■ *A final lesson here is you better be careful about what you say and put in social media. It's never going to go away.*

Work to Change the System

Racism and sexism are systemic in our institutions. As Ambassador Sylvia Stanfield put it, "The experiences in State are not going to be 100 percent rosy; neither is a career in any other field. The State Department is a slice of the United States and American life that you'll find in every sector." You feel it very personally when it happens to you, but it is not necessarily personal or unique to you. That's why many of the giants have also worked hard to change the underlying systems in the organizations where they work. When they attain leadership positions, they become advocates for diversity and related programming; they participate and advocate for diversity and for individuals representing diversity in performance-review and job-selection processes; and they mentor others, providing guidance on how to navigate these challenges and helping them to feel supported.

■ *You need to work hard and be a realist about what it takes to be successful in your career. But among those who are successful, all reasonable, thoughtful people will immediately seek ways to give back to their community—as Ron Brown always said, "to lower the ladder to let other people climb up."* Ambassador Susan Rice wrote about her parents and grandparents instilling in her that "with good fortune came responsibility. . . . [T]herefore, my duty was to serve others, in whatever way best suited my talents" (Rice 2019, 19). ■ *Supporting others is an important part of who you are as a moral, just leader.* And it means you will not have to face these struggles alone—the topic of Chapter 7.

Notes

1. In January 2018, then president Trump referred to Haiti and African nations as "*hole [expletive] countries."

2. For a broader description of Ambassador Thomas's experience in Zimbabwe, see Ty McCormick and Tendai Marima, "An Emissary to Tyranny," *Foreign Policy*, January 6, 2018, https://foreignpolicy.com/2018/01/16/an-emissary-to-tyranny-zimbabwe-african-americans.

7

You Are
Not Alone

We're here for a reason. I believe a bit of the reason is to throw little torches out to lead people through the dark.

—Whoopi Goldberg

I realized I would feel comfortable anywhere in the universe because I belonged to and was a part of it, as much as any star, planet, asteroid, comet, or nebula.

—Mae C. Jemison,
the first Black female astronaut

Navigating a career through the morass of systemic racism and sexism, compounded by the behavior of jerks and bullies—whether you fight or not—can be exhausting. The young people in our focus groups identified a range of topics they wanted to know more about. We addressed imposter syndrome in Chapter 3. Our discussion there included the pressure to be twice as good and the frustration of others questioning your worth and why you are there. Taylor and Verone Bernard also remind us that these careers entail ▶ working in a white world, where others don't understand the pressure that Black and Brown international affairs practitioners might be under because most of this work is so close and personal. We're touching and impacting people who look like us and share our ancestry. All of these issues led our focus group participants to put mental health on the agenda. How have the giants maintained their mental health while facing the many challenges and meeting the many demands of their careers?

A common theme throughout our conversations was community. None of the giants ever felt they were completely alone. And they proactively sought shared understanding and support from others. As we address the sometimes difficult topic of mental health, we want to make sure you, too, recognize that you are not alone. Hence the title of this chapter.

In this chapter we will revisit some of the sources of mental health challenges and review how our giants coped with them, including the things you can do for yourself and the importance of turning to others. We'll also address the importance of nurturing a life outside work, including family. First, we want to address the tired yet somewhat enduring stigma against talking about and recognizing mental health as a priority.

That Tired Old Stigma

■ *For my generation, talking about mental health challenges was a sign of weakness. You were just expected to tough it out and ride through it. The stigma is a particular challenge in minority communities. Black people and Latinos are not going to talk about mental illness or mental health issues or psychological trauma. There's a stigma attached to allowing yourself to be portrayed as somebody who cannot handle stress. And that's got to change.* ▶ Even today, mental health is just so taboo in the Black community. The idea of talking to a professional about your struggles and your anxieties is still something that we don't really discuss openly with our families. Maybe we still worry about what they will think, and it sometimes prevents us from getting the help that could change our lives.

In her book *The Unapologetic Guide to Black Mental Health*, Rheeda Walker describes this stigma: "Our community has a long history and a devoted relationship with stigma, denial, and shame when it comes to health and emotional health issues. Behind the proud belief that we are a strong people is a practiced habit of hiding our illnesses and struggles, explaining away the troubling behaviors of our loved ones, and suffering our secrets in silence. Stigma is this unbelievable force in our community that says you cannot get help" (Walker 2020, 211–212). Walker sees the power of stigma decreasing, but only "at a glacial pace."

Chris Richardson pointed out that in the Black community, going to a therapist is maybe seen as "a white person thing. . . . [F]or a Black person it's just unheard of." He wanted us to tell you that "if you need to see a therapist, go see a therapist. There's nothing wrong with that. It isn't a white person thing. It's a person thing." Ed Grier agreed, "We all experience it. We really do. And if people can speak out about those things, about how they overcome them, then it can help others." Chris Richardson adds, "Being Black, you always have to have this tough exterior. But being willing to cry, to let it out, and to talk to people and not bottle it in is just really important. I didn't learn that until much later in life. It's something that we, as 'older' Black people, have to be willing to tell our younger counterparts: a lot of the things that we did aren't necessarily the right things. A lot of us struggled with these things, and we didn't talk about them. But they are real. And we have to be willing to talk to people and do stuff about them." Let's say it again—this is another quotation to write down: "Seeing a therapist is not a white person thing. It's a person thing."

It's becoming easier to talk about these things. Michelle Obama famously shared that she suffered from low-grade depression.[1] Among our giants, Lauri Fitz-Pegado similarly shared, "I've had my moments of depression. I will say that. Because I think it's important, particularly for African Americans who have hidden from and been ashamed by psychological or mental health issues." She did not necessarily seek the support she needed at the moments she experienced these stresses. But, she warned, "stuff catches up with you."

■ *One of the big breakthroughs of younger generations is, overall, I find that you are prepared to deal with the need for therapy when you face a mental health challenge. When I was coming up in USAID, as a junior Foreign Service officer, we didn't think there was stress in our jobs. We just thought this is the work we have to do. And we've got bigger things to worry about, like getting on with our careers, our lives, our families. We didn't think that there was a special level of pressure that was being applied to us. People are now less willing to accept that this is just the way it is.*

It's Normal and Everybody Faces It

There are many elements of foreign policy careers that will be stressful—for everyone. Ambassador Rea Brazeal recognized that as a Foreign Service officer, "you go through the same cycle everyone else does when arriving at a place—you first have a lot of high energy and then you go in the slump and then come out the other side" (Brazeal 2007, 30). Some of these stresses relate simply to operating in a new culture or position. As Victoria Cooper put it, "The automatic decisions are not there anymore." You need to learn to navigate every decision in the context of this new environment and this new culture.

People also have different thresholds for stress, no matter their race. Some are willing to go to posts that will entail extended periods of stress or even trauma. Or perhaps you just find yourself in these assignments. Verone Bernard expressed great concern for the normalization of such trauma, as she observed it backstopping activities in Afghanistan. "I would get emails like, 'Oh, we were bombed last night.' I would freak out and no one else would react strongly. Like it was normal. We can't normalize this. We have to take the time to check in with ourselves and to check in with our people to make sure that folks are okay. And we might need a larger effort for those who are working in conflict zones, and backstopping conflict zones, to make sure that they're healing not just as individuals but collectively." In retrospect, Lauri Fitz-Pegado recognized that she probably suffered from posttraumatic stress after Secretary of Commerce Ron Brown's plane went down in Croatia with thirty-five people on board. She was tasked with meeting survivors and escorting the bodies home.

These stressors will impact any person. The severity of the consequences will depend on your personal threshold, the depth and duration of the stress, and whether and how you pursue coping and healing practices. These stressors can also be exacerbated and new stressors can arise because you are Black and a minority navigating these spaces.

Mental Health Consequences of Being Black

The cumulative effect of micro- and macroaggressions based on your identity can be severe. Paul Weisenfeld wrote that his brother describes these "accumulated indignities" as the "'private shames' that many people of color carry around." He adds, "A lot of our [w]hite colleagues would be stunned to learn of their number and would wonder how we keep it all in" (Weisenfeld 2020a). Such indignities emerge in daily interactions, not just in the workplace but also in our society. They are compounded by professional indignities and more egregious discrimination in the workplace that create systems of racism. The work of Ibram X. Kendi, author of *How to Be an Antiracist*, and Alicia Garza, cofounder of the Black Lives Matter movement and author of *The Purpose of Power*, reminds us that related struggles and the need for support do not reflect your personal failures but are actually the result of the current systems succeeding.

Sundaa Bridgett-Jones (like Rea Brazeal) falls back on the adage "Never let them see you cry." She described (like Sanola A. Daley in

Box 5.2) the toll on her self-esteem of being underestimated, invisible, and never credited for her own ideas. Catalyst (a nonprofit that works to accelerate and advance women into leadership) calls this emotional tax, defined as detrimental effects on health, well-being, and the ability to thrive at work due to being different from your peers because of your racial, sexual, or gender identity (Travis, Thorpe-Moscon, and McCluney 2016). You may feel on your guard all the time, waiting for a slight or a more egregious experience of racism. The psychological health and well-being impacts can be very serious.

■ *As I mentioned before, there is also a lot of stress that comes from being a first or, nowadays, one of just a few. You know already you may not be welcome. So you know you have to be perfect. It's like, one false move and all of the wolves come up. Everywhere in our society, as Black people have moved out of menial roles into positions of authority and notoriety, they are judged as ambassadors for the rest of all Black people in America. The higher up you go, the more that's the case.*

Jacob Gayle agreed: "If I fail, next comes, 'Well, we tried a Black guy before, and he didn't work out that well.' All the pressure is on us." Ed Grier recalled being told he was being watched all the time. An early mentor at Disney said, "They know who you are. They know what kind of car you drive. They know what time you get to work. Trust me, people will be watching." He knew he was performing for himself, his family, and for every Black person to come after him. Chris Richardson put it this way: "You're basically the face of every Black person that came before you and every Black person that comes after you. If there's a Black officer who's doing a bad job, you fear that they're going to judge you. Whereas we don't have that ability to say, 'Johnny is a bad white officer, therefore all the white officers are bad.'"

If that weren't enough, the stress is worse when you have other responsibilities outside work, a particular challenge for many women. Lauri Fitz-Pegado shared, "I didn't have the luxury of failing. And I knew I wasn't going to be judged like white people were judged. That creates a great deal of stress. And as a woman who's a mother, a wife, and also is in these unbelievable positions of responsibility—I don't think people realize how much stress that is." She adds, "There is a price for high achievement. There comes a point in time where your body gives out." She recalled repeatedly losing her voice, as she lost sleep traveling all over the world on ungodly schedules.

■ *You don't even realize how much of that stress you internalize. We internalize it because that's the way it is, and so we just have to walk right through it. But we should consider Jackie Robinson, the great baseball player who broke the color line in 1947. Many people believed that he died at such an early age because of the stress he was under—leading to heart problems. And he was only fifty-three. We need to do better at managing this stress.*

What You Can Do to Cope

As with most things, the first step to coping is checking in with yourself and your own attitude. For starters, how are you defining the problem? Rheeda Walker has terrific advice to offer: "Realize that you have been mistreated not because of who you are, but because of something that is wrong with racist people. This could give you some measure of relief, as well as some sense of what you are dealing with. Your constant self-questioning of your own perceptions can end. . . . Despite the persistence of the messages you receive that Black people are the problem, this messaging is fake news" (Walker 2020, 80–81). Yeah, write that one down too.

Ambassador Ruth A. Davis reflected on how much Black Americans have been through as a people. She reminds you to take strength from that experience, know you are resilient, and use that to inform your commitment to making positive change. "As a proud child of the South, I bear the scars of segregation and discrimination, but these scars ignited in me a passionate desire to make the world a better place. You know the legend of the phoenix—the bird that rose from its own ashes and was more beautiful and magnificent than ever. Well, I was born in Phoenix, Arizona, and raised in Atlanta, whose symbol is that bird. Consequently, I always believed that from ashes you could make beautiful things, from chaos you could make peace, and from despair you could bring happiness—but only with hard work, dedication and determination" (Davis 2016).

A healthy attitude also includes feeling more comfortable with imperfection and being willing to invest in self-help. ▶ This career is not a sprint. It is a marathon. If we don't protect our energy and our space, we will never get to where the giants got in this profession. Operating at 100 percent every hour of every day doesn't serve you or the organization you are working for. Choosing yourself and your needs can be frightening and empowering. The more we normalize wellness in the workplace and strive for balance in all areas of our lives, the better professionals we will become. Rheeda Walker quotes Audre Lorde on this point: "Caring for myself is not self-indulgence, it is self-preservation, and that is an act of political warfare" (Lorde 2017, quoted in Walker 2020, 136). So let's talk about how you can empower yourself to thrive despite these stresses and build your resilience.

In Chapter 3, the giants already shared how self-talk can help you to adjust your attitude in the face of imposter syndrome. Sanola A. Daley advised that you should have your script ready. Hers is "You've done this before. You've seen the results. You know what you're doing." Victoria Cooper similarly pulls back to revalidate herself: "I don't question my values and what I believe because someone else behaves in a certain way. I revalidate myself every time." Sometimes she's done that by immersing herself in her hometown and with family. Amanda Gorman draws from her ancestors for her mantra: "I am the daughter of Black writers. We are descended from freedom fighters who broke their chains and changed the world. They call me."[2] Rheeda Walker reports on research suggesting that "when you have a positive sense of who you are, the threats matter less. Self-affirming messages about your ability to withstand threats to who you are can be very effective" (Walker 2020, 83–84).

We want to also remind you of our discussion of humor from Chapter 6. Philip Gary advised that a sense of humor has to be for you as much as for anybody else. Maya Angelou taught that you need to learn to laugh at both yourself and at life. Having a sense of humor is a form of self-preservation.

You need to know yourself well enough to recognize your need for solitude. When do you just need to be alone in order to cope and recharge? Ambassador Rea Brazeal always tried to incorporate some fun into her work and lifestyle. There was no live television in Micronesia, where she served as ambassador. She would go to Guam and stay at the commanding general's guesthouse. "I'm sure he thought I was crazy, but I'd rent a car. I'd go to the grocery store, and buy things we couldn't get: tomatoes, lettuce, a bottle of wine. And I'd turn on CNN. I'd stay in this guest cottage for hours. He'd knock on the door and wonder if I were okay. I was just overdosing on fresh produce and real live news. To me, that was fun." Those temporary escapes are not always possible. Ambassador Ed Perkins advised that one "learn how to be alone, even in a sea of people. I learned to cultivate solitude in the midst of controversy or in a raging river of conflict in order to bring myself back to a sense of balance. That lesson served me well" (Perkins 2006, 167).

Like Ambassador Rea Brazeal, you need to commit to making room for fun. Ambassador Johnny Young found his first posting as a budget and finance officer in Madagascar "too confining. I wanted to be with the people more and I wanted more contact with the outside world." He taught English as a second language for starters. And then he drew on an old interest from his youth: "When I was active in the YMCA, I did international folk dancing, dances from Romania, Bulgaria, Israel, and Hungary and different places like that." He decided to teach classes on international folk dancing. It enabled him to develop friendships outside the embassy and to get to know the Malagasy (Young 2013, 40). Similarly, Lauri Fitz-Pegado had studied ballet as a child and taught dance during college. It taught her "the ability to cope with pain, physical pain." She kept it up early in her career and has returned to it in her post–foreign policy career. Early on while in the Dominican Republic, she even performed with the Dominican Ballet Company.

Exercise is so important to mental health as well as physical health. Chris Richardson reported riding a bike, getting out to walk, and just taking deep breaths. Ed Grier has found combining exercise with his family to be especially powerful. When he received an unanticipated promotion to run Disneyland Resort in California, it meant uprooting his whole family from Japan. His family was happy for him, but the move was really tough on his sons. It was their idea to "do other things to physically take care of ourselves." So, he reported, "we would get up at 4:45 every morning to go to the gym, all of us. And it was a bonding thing."

What is it you enjoy? Ambassador Sylvia Stanfield advises, "You need your own hobbies. What happens when you're assigned to a post and there's nobody else to talk with or the security doesn't allow you to go out and meet various people? You need something that helps you to relax. Do you listen to music? Do you exercise? Do you like to cook and invite people over?" She enjoys reading, for example. She admonishes, "You have to have your own personal resources and something that keeps you grounded."

And it is amazing how much a little fellowship can do to boost your morale and help you feel supported. Sanola A. Daley reported the immediate sensation of relief when she arrived at the International Finance Corporation for her first day of work, entered the elevator at 9:00 a.m., and simply saw others who looked like her. "I took a breath and a sigh of relief. Because it was the first place I had worked as an adult, where I was not the only Black person around. I remember thinking, finally, I didn't have to prove myself as much as I used to have to, because I wasn't the only one in the room anymore."

Victoria Cooper calls these affinity networks "comfort food" or "comfort space." You need to find those spaces where you don't have to constantly worry about being misunderstood. Through our professional selves, we may become bilingual in a way. Ambassador Ertharin Cousin noted this among young professionals in the corporate world, where you develop skills "to ensure that you have the ability to communicate with those who don't share your experiences." But then you need "that place, that group of friends with whom you socialize, share experiences, understanding, and acceptance, where you can unabashedly reveal your true self." It might mean a community of Americans in general, Black Americans specifically, or just other Black people (like for Sanola A. Daley), depending on your context and your needs. ■ *You absolutely need people external to where you work who allow you to remain authentic to who you are. That's really crucial, especially when you're dealing with this bipolar reality, where you're on the inside but you're also a person who comes from a totally different background.*

For most of us, like for Ambassador Sylvia Stanfield, it just starts with "a good network of friends that was also family." Sanola A. Daley reported having a series of different communities, including friends from high school and undergrad that she's kept up with on WhatsApp, even though she doesn't see them very often, and different sets of caring people she developed from her time working in Puerto Rico, Costa Rica, at the Inter-American Development Bank, and in graduate school. She has friends who she knows "are always there. And so when anything happens, they're the first people I will go back to, regardless of where I'm living. They are my rock. We don't always see each other, but we're always checking in with each other." It's important to know you have people you can call on at the drop of a hat, even if you haven't seen them lately.

▶ *Your peers are so important. You sometimes forget how much you need those moments of fellowship to just be 100 percent you. You need those brunches, drinks out, a book club, or whatever it is—you need those mental health opportunities for restoration.* And you have to be intentional about it. Dominique Harris has a group of friends from graduate school who get together every other Monday to catch up on life and work. It is a priority inked into her schedule. Like Sanola A. Daley, she also has friends she's kept up with from when she was very young. People like that become witnesses to your life and to who you are. Dominique shared, "They've seen me grow and evolve. They've seen some of my bad habits that I've kept. And they've seen some of the ways that I've become more patient with myself and other people."

▶ *All of our giants found community. Wherever they were in the world, they experienced that joy of letting their proverbial as well as their actual hair down and being themselves outside the white spaces they had to occupy. And you have to be intentional about that, especially when you are advised differently. For example, I had a college professor tell us, "Don't go and congregate with all the Black people in the room. Make sure you're working the room." Sometimes that's important, but sometimes I think, "I hear you, but I need this community right now."*

You also have to know your limits. All of these coping mechanisms are important, but they may not always be enough. You also have to know (1) when you need to walk away and (2) when you need the professional support of a therapist. As you know, Chris Richardson opted to leave the State Department (Chapter 6). Beyond his own experience, he emphasized, "If you get to a point where your family is being threatened, or your own personal mental health is being affected, you have to be willing to walk away. It's just a job. Nothing is worth sacrificing your mental health and physical safety over." It's also important to recognize that your friends, family, and mentors—as important as they may be to you and as much as they may care—are not mental health professionals. Sometimes you really do need to talk to a therapist. Doing that does not replace these support networks and other coping mechanisms or reflect failure on them. Therapy can also help you do the harder and deeper work you may need to do in order to become your best self.[3]

Turning to Others

Having that comfort circle is so important. And it's important to build some fun into your life. Those two things together can be magical. But sometimes you need to look to others for much more than just fun or even understanding. Sometimes you need others to help you to understand a situation, navigate a problem, and just know yourself better. Other people can hold a mirror to you and also help you to understand paths forward. We've already discussed mentoring at length in Chapter 4. Sometimes mentors can fulfill some of these functions. Looking beyond individuals, you also need your handcrafted communities—as described above. Let's call them your tribes. And you can look to more specific affinity groups. Sometimes family members are just what you need.

Tribes

Beyond social time, your tribe consists of the people you can just call up anytime and for almost any need, people who can help to build you up when you're down. They are the people you can check in with to ask, as Dominique Harris put it, "Am I crazy? Or are they crazy?" You tell them what's going on, and they may be able to help you figure things out. Or not. Sometimes all you need is someone to say, "Oh, yeah. That. I've been there." Just knowing you are not alone in your experience can bring comfort. And with your tribe, that support is often mutual, not one way.

Dr. Helene Gayle reported that in every context she's always had a group of Black professionals, whether formal or informal, where "we can talk about our experiences, like how some idiot said something stupid to you today, and ask each other how do you laugh that off and move forward?"

Ambassador Gina Abercrombie-Winstanley cautions about where *not* to look for such support: "People who work with you are not your friends. That's what my dad told me. They're your colleagues, and they may be friendly colleagues, but they are not your friends. Do not confide in them. Do not look to them for succor, for support, for whatever. That is what your family is for, and that is what your friends outside work are for. Because we're competing against each other at every level in every position, promotion, job. We are in constant competition. And that is what makes the culture so cutthroat."

Ambassador Ertharin Cousin agrees that you should cultivate your tribe outside your workplace. She recognizes the need for a place to be totally honest and free in your sharing. For her, that meant a cadre of friends outside her work, because "sharing honest dialogue inside the system is not necessarily going to lead to your success." She had a group of friends she could vent to who, she said, "could help me continue to maintain my own self and stay true to myself while also navigating what many would define as foreign territory. For us, it was all foreign because we were the first in many cases." Ambassador Cousin was quite fortunate to have in her circle the journalists Gwen Iffel and Michele Norris. And Ambassador Susan Rice occasionally joined them too. "You meet up for a bottle of wine and share the things that don't go outside the room. That's when you can cry, you can kick, and you can get advice on how to position your thoughts better, how to ensure that you are heard in the room when your voice doesn't seem to have resonance. For me, that was critical."

Ambassador Cousin also warned that you need this kind of outlet so that you don't let your frustrations out at the wrong time and with the wrong people: "You're like a duck on water. You seem to just work your way through it, and you have this professional persona. Your coworkers and bosses don't need to know that underneath the water you're flapping like hell, but somebody needs to know. You can't keep that inside. You need an outlet. Carrying work baggage home too often will create misplaced emotional challenges in your relationships with your spouse or your children. So you need a place and people for unpacking and letting go without repercussion or reprisal."

Ambassador Ed Perkins also relied on his tribe for problem-solving and generating ideas. He called them his private brain trust: "three

[B]lack men who are not only fine professionals but personal friends: John Gravely, Herbert Harrington, and Harold Sye." They were the ones who suggested he make entering Black neighborhoods part of his "change-agent strategy." He wrote, "I consulted them confidentially, and their advice was invaluable. Aside from [my wife] Lucy and my daughters, these were the only people I talked with outside of official interviews. My three colleagues and I had personally experienced segregation in this country, and we knew the difficulty in getting people to change" (Perkins 2006, 255).

It's important to recognize that you will need different types of support, and these will necessarily come from different sources. The women who wrote *For Colored Girls Who Have Considered Politics* advise that you should "watch who's in your squad." They propose a "core team" comprised of a cheerleader, who "will keep your spirits high and keep you encouraged when your self-doubt rears its ugly head"; a coach, who will push you and "help you map a plan and stick to it"; a compass, who will be "your truth teller" and help you "keep it real"; and a confidante, who will be "your keeper of secrets" and with whom "you can be bare and raw and entirely yourself . . . and unburden your fears, voice your dreams, and check your ego" (Brazile et al. 2018, 306–307).

Affinity Groups

For many, the first and most important affinity group or comfort space is the Black church or one's mosque. Ambassador James Joseph certainly promoted taking solace in one's faith community—not surprising, since he was a minister. He referred to Maya Angelou's endorsement of the church as a place to go for support: "If you are [B]lack and still the last hired, still the first fired, still the butt of even white liberal jokes, find yourself a [B]lack church . . . because when these things hit you—and be sure they will hit you—you need to be able to join with people who understand what is happening to you; people who can embrace you and say I feel your pain; people who will know how to pray for you; elders, deacons and ushers who will say, 'Oh no, we cannot have that happening to you honey'" (quoted in West 1997, 196; Joseph 2015, 26).

Of course, your family is also key to helping you to stay true to yourself and your community, as well as feel supported—even when they don't always understand what you may be experiencing professionally. Dominique Harris shared, "My family doesn't know what I do. What they care about is, 'Are you the person who we raised you to be?

Are you a good person? Are you doing your part to make this world a better place, and are you giving as much as you're receiving?'"

Dr. Jacob Gayle emphasized the particular need for a tribe or affinity group you can turn to as you move higher up in organizations. "It's a cutthroat, lonely environment at the top, whether you're talking government, multigovernment, private sector, or even philanthropy. You need to have people whom you can trust." He also recommended creating that network outside your own organization. He suggested you could start by looking to formal affinity organizations, like the Professional Organization of Black Foreign Diplomats, the Executive Leadership Council, or one of the Divine Nine. He stressed, "You've got to have some kind of peer support and trust. You need to know that somebody will know what you're talking about even before you actually speak a syllable." Affinity groups can prevent you from becoming lonely and also keep you accountable. Dr. Gayle continued, "If you think that you're doing it alone, or that you've succeeded alone, someday you may realize you really are alone. Proper mental health requires knowing where your North Star is and also always remembering who your community is that has sponsored you to be who you are and to whom you feel accountable."

Affinity groups inside your organization also have their place, whether formal or informal. When she returned to Washington from overseas, Ambassador Rea Brazeal looked to her Black peers inside the State Department to gauge the state of race relations in America: "If things were not going well, then people would make eye contact and essentially recognize each other, because you knew you were in the situation together. If things were going relatively well, there was a little less eye contact, a little less of the group recognition" (Brazeal 2007, 10). Of course, internal affinity groups are much more helpful when they are intentional.

When Verone Bernard started out, she was part of a cohort of Black colleagues. She described, "We were all hired around the same time. And we were trying to climb through the ranks together. We depended and leaned on each other for advice about promotions. We would share our deliverables with one another for peer reviews before we would send anything up to our supervisors. And we would meet for coffees and lunches, where we would sometimes ask, 'Who did it this week?'" They were a sounding board for one another. She continued, "Those were the places we could share, 'This happened. How would you have handled it?' Or 'Did I handle this right? Should I say something? Should I just let this go?'" It was an organic cohort that they organized for themselves. Verone benefited enormously from this peer mentoring but recognized that, ultimately, they also needed to have more senior mentors who could bring experience and advice they didn't have. She is grateful to now count Aaron as one of her mentors.

More formal affinity organizations can be important sources of support. Dr. Jacob Gayle already mentioned the importance of professional and other associations outside your organization, especially as you work your way higher up into leadership. Formal internal affinity groups like the Thursday Luncheon Group, targeted pipeline and mentorship programs, and, more broadly, employee resources groups are designed to support not only individuals but communities of employees (and potential employees). These are the vehicles that enable you to have power in numbers so that no one individual has to face structural challenges or repeated offenses alone.

Looking Out for Each Other

Your tribe and your affinity groups work best when the support is mutual, when you give as much as you receive. Looking out for each other is something all of us can do. When you are in a leadership position, it is an even greater responsibility. And sometimes people are looking out for you when you don't even know it. Katherine Lee shares an experience in Box 7.1.

Box 7.1   Katherine Lee:
Isn't It Good to Know You've Got a Friend?

Katherine Lee was fortunate. Someone was looking out for her. Before she went to a post, she was told not to take her own car and to use the car assigned to the office, which she was to drive home daily since there was no parking at the embassy. She did her due diligence and verified that she could use the car. Her Washington Office told her she needed to keep a log of when and why she used it. When she got to the post, her assigned assistant told her otherwise. "You don't have to do that. Mr. so and so never did." But, she told us, "he was white. So I insisted. I kept the log." Later on, a friend of hers in another agency alerted her that inspectors had written up a report claiming she was misusing the car. Luckily, with her documentation, she was able to prove the allegations false. Her friend's warning gave her more time to make her case.

■ *Such optics alone could kill a career. We really do need to watch out for each other. What seems an easily resolved issue for someone else could be a career ender for a Black person.*

Our giants have made looking out for each other and others a core component of their careers. It's no surprise that Aaron had such a strong network he could tap into when he thought of writing this book. Our giants were more than ready to support Aaron for this project and are very eager to support you. Sundaa Bridgett-Jones emphasized how much Aaron and his wife, Rosa, supported her and others in South Africa. South Africa was her second overseas assignment with USAID, and Aaron was then the mission director there. "Aaron and Rosa invited me over to their house for dinner, not once but several times. There were a number of African American Foreign Service officers at USAID then and there. And we sat around and we broke bread and talked. That whole connection with families and having that family unit there allowed me to just be that person I wanted to be and have the inspiration of the people in front of me. Paul Weisenfeld was there, for example. And so many of the people who are leading in this field."

Aaron and Ambassador Ertharin Cousin reminisced about serving together in the Barack Obama administration. Aaron noted ■ *the great mutual respect and pure joy that we saw and continue to enjoy among ourselves.* Ambassador Cousin confirmed, "The comradery across the community of African Americans who worked in foreign policy: me and Aaron, Linda Thomas-Greenfield, Johnnie Carson, and even Susan Rice. Just knowing that I could pick up a phone and call any of you for advice and you would answer." She added, "We owe that to each other. Young people should not be afraid to build relationships with people who look like them early in their careers, because those people will ultimately sit in rooms and can invite you into those rooms. You also share a set of experiences that are valuable to your own growth."

In Chapter 4 Ambassador Cousin recounted how she called Ambassador Linda Thomas-Greenfield when she found herself in a pinch. And she confirmed that your value-added increases enormously when you have the ability to call on such powerful networks when needed, whether for personal support, to advance a professional agenda, or to respond to a crisis. ■ *I remember when I was Peace Corps director and we needed to evacuate our volunteers from Mali, when al-Qa'ida in the Maghreb started moving south from Timbuktu down toward Bamako. Johnnie Carson was the assistant secretary of state for Africa then. I tracked him down on a Saturday morning and said, "I need to talk to you about the situation in Mali.*

Here's what I think we should do." He said, "You've got my 199 percent support. Do it. Anybody tells you anything different, let them know you talked to me. This is a go."

Dr. Helene Gayle reported that throughout her career, for both Blacks and women, she would always "reach out and make it clear to people that I see you, that I know you're there." For example, in her work on HIV/AIDS in Africa, she was always careful to bring people along. They are now global leaders in the field. She always wants others to know they have a place to go to. And, she recalled, it's the same thing that Aaron and John Hicks, then USAID's assistant administrator of Africa, did for her when she arrived at USAID. "I landed in this foreign planet where people were skeptical about me coming from CDC. People, including people on my team, were asking, 'Why did they have to bring an outsider?' I didn't initially get the warmest welcome, and you and John just being there and saying, 'Let's have lunch,' made a big difference. So, that's what I try to do for people in those environments, reach out to them, make them realize that I'm there for them, and make them feel maybe a little more comfortable than they might in an environment that sometimes seems alien or hostile."

When you are a leader, you have a particular responsibility to look out for others. ▶ I have an amazing boss. She is highly regarded at my company. I, of course, had to come in and establish a track record for myself. But now that I have built up my body of work, I now have the trust that comes with that. Having the trust of your supervisors is so important. That gives me some mental release, like I can ease up a little bit. I don't have to be "on" all the time. In its report on emotional tax, Catalyst found, "When you feel that organizational leaders and team members 'have your back,' you are more likely to feel safe taking interpersonal risks." They refer to the psychological safety this creates, which enables you "to speak up about difficult issues, feel confident mistakes won't be held against you, and trust that co-workers won't undermine your efforts" (Travis, Thorpe-Moscon, and McCluney 2016, 5).

Ed Grier recognizes that part of creating that psychological safety is making sure people understand that "we're all human. Let's stick together." As the dean of a business school now, he is creative and unusual in the way he models that life is more than just the job. "Anyone can see my calendar in the whole school. I want you to see that there are things that happen in my life that are important. We all have dentist appointments to go to. We all want to go see our son's or daughter's dance recital. And I think those things are important."

Nurturing Your Life Outside Work

Ed Grier reminds us that one of the most important components of main-taining your mental health and building resilience is protecting your per-sonal time from the encroachments of your professional life, including its stress. Your life can't just be the job. Ensuring that it isn't requires action. You need to intentionally carve out space that is just yours. Gen-eral and Secretary Colin Powell learned that from a mentor early in his career who told him, "Never become so consumed by your career . . . that nothing is left that belongs only to you and your family. . . . Don't allow your profession to become the whole of your existence" (Powell 1995, 158). Ambassador Rea Brazeal was passionate about participating in the civil rights movement. She arranged to have more assignments in Washington, DC, to do so. But she determined not to talk about her activism during her Foreign Service work.

Of course, when people consider what is called work-life balance or work-life integration, they most often think about how they will create, nurture, and sustain their family lives. Honoring this part of your per-sonal life can be a challenge in any profession. It may be particularly challenging given the structural change embedded in Foreign Service careers—not only changing jobs but also locations, often internation-ally. That puts a lot of stress on families, as every member has to make adjustments and sometimes uproot their lives.

Ambassador Rea Brazeal did not have children of her own. She cre-ated her family. "I had my mother with me in the Foreign Service for about fifteen years. She would travel around with me here and there. And I enjoyed that. She was usually the oldest person in the community. In Kenya, we had a young caregiver for my mother who came with us when we left Kenya. She is like my daughter, and her daughter is like my granddaughter. So in a sense, I created my family along the way."

No matter what your family looks like, it's important to hold sacred some time, attention, and energy for and with them. Leaders are far more understanding than they once were about making family time a priority, as Ed Grier's example demonstrates. Ambassador Rea Brazeal also expressed, "As a supervisor, I always appreciated officers who would have a clear delineation in their workday and leaving to be with their family. That's something that you can establish early on and stick to it—knowing, of course, that if there's an emergency you will be there. Supervisors have to understand that this is the way life should be." Maintaining family priorities is not easy. For Ambassador James Joseph, it required "a high degree of intentionality." He was traveling a lot when his son was only four. He wanted to be sure to attend his son's basketball games, "not because I wanted to come to cheer for his winning. I wanted to help him deal with what it means to be a good loser. So I intentionally made certain that I was present. And I had to work at that because it often meant juggling my schedule." Chris Richardson's experience can help to put these commitments in perspective (see Box 7.2).

■ *This is very true. It's hard to pursue that approach to life, but it's the essence of life. You have to be able to walk away when life and your career attack the 10 percent core of what you value and who you are.*

This doesn't mean you won't make adjustments for the job or that your family won't make adjustments for the job and for you. These careers are challenging, and they do entail a lot of moving around. Your home base becomes what you take with you and what you live every day. It is not a physical place. C. D. Glin said, "You've got to have the support at home." Many of our giants made big career sacrifices because of family concerns. Katherine Lee had been offered the opportunity to

---

Box 7.2   Chris Richardson: How Do You Live Your 10 Percent?

"When I was fifteen, I had bone and lung cancer. I nearly died. I went through chemo. I lost part of my right leg. I lost a part of my lung. The doctor basically sat there and told me I had a 5 percent chance of living one year. That was twenty-three years ago, and I'm still here. Cancer taught me that 90 percent of stuff in life is not important. Ninety percent of the stuff in life, you can let go, you can let slide. You don't have to fight and die on every single hill. But that other 10 percent matters. It matters to who you are. It matters to your core.

"If you get to a point in your life where that 10 percent is affected—whether it's your family, your loved ones, your views, your values, Black people in general—you should always have the mental ability to walk away or fight. I think 90 percent of stuff in life I don't let bother me, but when it came to the Muslim ban, the comment about the African countries, and stuff like that, no. That strikes at that 10 percent of what matters to me, as a person. As someone who survived cancer when I shouldn't have, I am not going to live my life not being true to that 10 percent.

"Every job tries to tell you that your job is your family. Your job is not your family. Your family is your family. The people you work with are your work colleagues. While what you're doing is great, if it affects your mental abilities, and if it really breaks you down as a person, walk away and go do something else. Life is too short to be a slave to something that isn't for you."

pursue an ambassadorship but declined. "It was during a time when my brother was dying of lung cancer. I knew he had only a few months to live. My mother was eighty-nine at the time. I had been abroad so long." Her family had visited her at her different posts. Now it was time for her to come home to the United States for a while.

Adjustments go both ways. Victoria Cooper described how her daughter's needs informed her career decision (see Box 7.3).

■ *Victoria Cooper left the confines of a great corporate situation, with all the trappings and salary compensation and support systems, to go out on her own. That's a big step. That takes a lot of courage. And the fact that her daughter's well-being was a primary motivator is truly commendable.*

The challenges of nurturing family while being a professional are particularly acute for women. Ambassador Linda Thomas-Greenfield shared, "When I got pregnant, they were treating me like I had committed a crime. I remember someone saying, 'Oh, we have lots of single parents in the Foreign Service. Why are you trying to get an assignment with your husband?'" Things have gotten so much better since the days when women Foreign Service officers couldn't be married and men were judged for promotion, in part, on the basis of how well their wives would perform in social roles (ended in 1972) or the days before the Allison Palmer class action suit (filed in 1989) about discrimination in the promotion of women at the State Department. But all women, regardless of profession, often struggle with balancing family and work responsibilities and career ambition. Ambassadors Linda Thomas-Greenfield and Gina Abercrombie-Winstanley are blessed to have understanding, supportive, and capable partners. As they describe in Box 7.4, together with their partners, they determined their priorities and lived them in partnership.

**Box 7.3   Victoria Cooper:
For the Love of My Daughter**

"When PricewaterhouseCoopers wanted me to move to South Africa or Abuja, my oldest daughter was already in college, and my youngest daughter was in the British system, going into sixth form. I thought, I can't pull my daughter up and take her to South Africa. This is not an experience I want for her. My daughter also told me that she was not going to go to boarding school. She was sixteen and decided that my career was not going to uproot her life. Her dad had gone to boarding school in England, and I had made the arrangements at a boarding school. But she was in serious protest. So I stayed in Ghana. And I built my own consulting firm there because that's where my clients were."

**Box 7.4   Linda Thomas-Greenfield and
Gina Abercrombie-Winstanley:
Living Your Priorities in Partnership**

Linda Thomas-Greenfield

"I was in French training for a post to Côte d'Ivoire. The post was cancelled, and we were all set to go to Nigeria. I got a two plus in French, and I needed a three to get off of language probation. I called my career development officer, gave him my score, and he wanted me to do four more weeks of French. I explained, 'I'm sorry. I have given up my babysitter. We've given up our house. I don't have any place to live. You're not giving me per diem. I think I'm going to go to post.' And he said, 'No, you're not. You've been asking for favors because you have a baby since you came into the Foreign Service.'

"I was ready to quit the Foreign Service. My husband said, 'I can go to Lagos. I can get a babysitter that will cost us a tenth of what we're going to pay here in the States. You can concentrate on your French for four weeks and not have to worry about coming home to take care of the baby.' And I said yes. My mother thought I was the most horrible person in the world that I would send my ten-month-old baby to Africa with his dad.

"Later, when I served as staff assistant to then director general Ed Perkins, the hours were so long, I thought, 'I've got two kids at home. I can't do this.' Fortunately, I have a wonderful husband. He had a job that was seven to three. He got home at three o'clock and took care of all of the children's needs.

"We never had a separate assignment because we set our priorities very, very early. Our first priority was our children. We were only going to go to posts that had schools for our children. We weren't going to put our kids in boarding school. Our second priority was each other, which meant that if I got a job, there had to be a job for him; and if he got a job, there had to be a job for me. And our third priority was the job. The job was never the top priority. So we ended up taking jobs that were not necessarily career enhancing.

"For example, I took a refugee coordinator job in Pakistan that I didn't really want. My husband got a really good job in Pakistan, so I took the job in Pakistan. Then I got assigned to Geneva in a dream job: the head of the refugee and migration affairs office. There was not a job there for my husband. At that point he was an 02. And the job that was there for him was an 03. They had had a hard time filling that job with good people. He took the 03 job, even though he was promoted to 01 before he arrived at post. He was in a two grade down stretch in the political section, but nobody realized it.

continues

Box 7.4   Continued

"So we made some career sacrifices to ensure that we were together and that our children didn't get separated. You have to know what your priorities are and what your goals are. I wasn't working to become an ambassador. I was working to be a successful Foreign Service officer and to be an 01, and I was working to be a successful mother."

Gina Abercrombie-Winstanley

"I had heard in A-100 about the divorce rate. They'd warned us it was two-thirds, which is higher than the national average, which is already too high. I had a really firm conversation with my husband to clarify how we were going to approach this career. He was excited about it. He's a pirate at heart. He likes to travel. And he's an engineer and was doing development when we met. We said, 'Okay, we are going to make the decisions together, and any place you don't want to go, we're not going.'

"So, we set this plan in motion from the beginning. When the bid list came out, I didn't look at it. I took it home, and I presented it to him. He did the first cut of places where he thought he might be able to find work or had another interest in going. And then I looked at it with his cut and made my bidding decisions based on that. We're coming up on forty years of marriage. It has worked very well. And that's how we did it.

"My advice is to choose your partner carefully. If you choose the wrong one, it's not going to work. And be as clear as possible. My friends who are now divorced, or separated, they weren't completely honest about their expectations. And it's important to revisit these. Because these things change over time. And communication is so incredibly important.

"There were times when my husband was doing 80 percent—100 percent sometimes—at home because of my career demands. Certainly, with the evacuations. He had three days to quit his job and pack up our two children and get out of the country in Jeddah. Three days. Our children were six and nine. He had to pull them out of school and set up a household elsewhere. That is an enormous challenge for anyone. But for the guy to have to do it, as opposed to the woman, who expects to do it? Yeah, I have to give all props.

"I told him, 'I love this job, this work. I love it. But it is a job. And you are my life. And the minute you say that you're done with this, we are done with this.' And he knew I meant it. And I did. And that was that."

Ambassadors Thomas-Greenfield and Abercrombie-Winstanley had their guiding principles for their careers, their marriages, and their children. It takes a lot of skill to manage these priorities and your career. It's important to decide with your partner what your priorities are early on.

■ *Our family underwent some degree of stress in balancing our careers and educational opportunities for our sons in the Foreign Service, as we spent half of my career at overseas posts. I was extremely fortunate that my wife sacrificed her career in the United States and was my dedicated partner in managing our Foreign Service assignments. She expertly juggled the demands of the myriad of representational duties that are required of all senior embassy officials and the education of our sons as we moved from country to country. My wife and children met and overcame the challenges of living and going to school in different societies and cultures, despite the disruption that is common on overseas tours. Our goal was to assure that our sons would spend a significant period of time in the United States, see Reston, Virginia, as our hometown, and thus have an authentic American childhood, while living the life of global citizens. As we now look back at our collective past, the four of us believe that these experiences enriched us both as individuals and as a family. In this vein, I asked my sons last Thanksgiving how they felt about being dragged all over the world. They were unanimous that this was a great thing. It made them who they are: their view of the world, their ability to interact with people from all different cultures, speak foreign languages, and so forth. They were really happy about the experience.*

Luckily, family life overseas can be a very positive experience for everyone. Bob Burgess also reported that his kids thrived overseas, and the experience helped them to become the fine, accomplished people they are today. Dr. Jacob Gayle and his wife also managed a dual professional family. She is an accomplished gerontologist. They, too, took decisions together about which job locations would be suitable for both of them. Once he started traveling more with the Centers for Disease Control and Prevention, he reported, "I decided I needed to bring my wife and children along with me. We always envisaged that our children, too, would be global citizens and that through our opportunities we, as parents, would be able to expose our children to the world, to allow them to really live and grow and understand who they are in a global context." How to do that was not always clear. He shared, "I would always say our children needed to understand that they were global citizens. She would say, 'That's true, but they need to know what citizenship they bring to the global community.' So we had these debates back and forth. Are they American kids in the world, or are they global kids that have been born in America?"

All of our giants ensured they nurtured life beyond the job. As Ambassador Rea Brazeal said, "Because this is your life. I've met too many people who say, 'Well, when I retire, I'm going to have fun. I'm going to do this and that.' And then they don't do these things along the way." It's important to live your 10 percent as fully as you can every day. It's about being *all* of who you are, the subject of Chapter 8.

Notes

1. See "Protests and the Pandemic with Michele Norris," *The Michelle Obama Podcast*, August 2020.

2. Amanda Gorman, quoted in interview with Anderson Cooper, as reported in the *Los Angeles Times* (Saad 2021).

3. Rheeda Walker (2020) discusses the choice of having a Black or a non-Black therapist. If you prefer a Black therapist, she recommends the online resource Therapy for Black Girls (www.therapyforblackgirls.com), a directory of sorts where Black therapists provide contact information and a description of their expertise. While not comprehensive, it is a start, and more therapists are signing on by the day.

8

Being All You

However far a stream flows, it doesn't forget its origin.
                                                 —African proverb

You are a light. You are the light. Never let anyone—any person or any force—dampen, dim or diminish your light.
                                    —John Lewis, *Across That Bridge:*
                                Life Lessons and a Vision for Change, 2017

Being all that you are is a responsibility to yourself, to your family, and to the job. Recall from Chapter 1 that *your* participation, specifically, matters. It represents the fulfillment of the US Constitution and the promise of our nation for a better future for all. Your participation enhances the credibility of our foreign policy. When you bring all that you are, you can meaningfully deepen understandings across cultures and peoples in ways majority populations cannot. You support our nation and help to cultivate more informed US and global citizens by bringing those understandings home. And when you contribute your whole self— your professional skills as well as your unique talents—you enhance the effectiveness of our foreign policy and help to craft more creative and responsive policy solutions. Your participation matters for US foreign policy. And it matters most when you bring your whole self to it.

This is a tall order when our society, coworkers, and even foreign nationals sometimes question your right to be in these spaces. We have already reviewed how the consequences of these affronts can be damaging to your personal well-being. ▶ It really feels like, as Black people, we cannot bring all our authentic selves to work. Some of our white colleagues or non–people of color say, "No, I really want to know who you are," but they really don't. How do you bring your authentic self to the workplace? What is the fine line between code switching and being all you? And how do you do that in a fluid environment?

▶ A lot of things have changed, allowing us to lean into our identities, especially for the intersectionality of being a woman and being Black in this field, in ways that our giants weren't allowed to do. C. D. Glin, who has always embraced his African roots (see, e.g., Boxes 2.5 and 8.4), believes, "You are in an era where you can be more authentic and be who you are in ways that we never could have." At the same time, he recognizes, we have been experiencing political moments that have at once interrupted that progress and embraced it. The path is not always clear. The recent political divisiveness has led to a lot of mask wearing. ▶ We code-switch every day, and we have to continue to do that. It's almost like it's innate. We're taught that from birth. When are you wearing a mask, and when are you being authentic even as you switch codes for the context?

Standing tall and being all you is how you can personally thrive and be most impactful in your career. In this chapter we review how you can best do that, despite feeling like you may be operating in alien environments that do not recognize or value who you are. We start by sharing the wisdom of our giants on the importance of self-awareness and knowing who you are and where you come from. We include a discussion of the particular experience of women. We tackle the tension between your personal identity and the professional cultures you will need to operate in, responding to the tough questions we raised above. We conclude with examples of how to put your full identity to work for the best professional outcomes. We recognize that there are aspects of identity besides race and gender, as well as intersectional identities, that present additional challenges, implications, and strengths. We want to emphasize the importance of bringing the whole of your identity to your work, beyond those components we directly address below.

Knowing Your Roots

▶ My mother, who did not graduate from college, was going to make sure that I went to the best school. I was around people who were college educated. I was in activities that were going to broaden my horizons more than just 106th and

Emerald on the South Side of Chicago. But she never let me forget where I came from. It doesn't matter how many countries I go to, how many rooms of power I sit in, how many heads of state's hands I shake, I will always be the little girl from the South Side of Chicago.

In Chapter 4 we shared how Ambassador Ed Perkins sustained his relationships in Portland, Oregon, which kept him "grounded." He shared, "They have been my true north, the place I return for replenishment" (Perkins 2006, 71). And we noted that Ambassador Johnny Young held his swearing-in ceremony at his vocational technical high school in Philadelphia to provide "a symbol of what is possible for kids coming from that kind of school" (Young 2013, 221–222). Ambassador Susan Rice reports that her parents and grandparents "raised me to remember where we came from. To honor the richness of my inheritance, value myself, do my best, and never let others convince me I can't." And "with good fortune came responsibility, they taught me; therefore, my duty was to serve others, in whatever way best suited my talents" (Rice 2019, 19).

Victoria Cooper was the only one of our giants who chose to make a home in Africa independent of a career in US foreign policy. She didn't go to Liberia to "run away from the American experience, to get away from what was happening in America." She moved there for love (Box 2.12). "I'm always one to say, 'To thine own self be true.' We have to know ourselves. I'm grateful that I am from a family that respects and grounds ourselves in our African American experience." When she was feeling particularly challenged, she revalidated herself by immersing herself in her hometown and with family (Chapter 7).

Beyond solace, support, and the responsibility to give back, grounding yourself in your roots can help foster the empathy that can make your career more impactful. As ambassador to Ethiopia, Rea Brazeal observed that some of the other donor countries had the attitude that "Ethiopians starve to death all the time." "I just couldn't accept that. No, no, no." As the children of immigrants, Verone Bernard and Sanola A. Daley use their identities to connect to the work. In Box 8.1, they share how they stay true to what development is supposed to be and how they stay motivated.

Life is also fluid. Our experiences change us. But they don't have to change our core. Paul Weisenfeld became aware that, after his law education and experiences abroad, "if I went back home and talked to friends I grew up with, my language changed. It doesn't change as much now, but it did when I was in my twenties." ■ *I would always go back to Chicago, after I got back from the Peace Corps and then during my professional career. When*

**Box 8.1   Verone Bernard and Sanola A. Daley:
Connecting to the Work**

Verone Bernard

"We often talk about making sure that we're centering our work around the most vulnerable and the folks who need it the most. My mom, a Haitian immigrant, is the strongest person I know. She lives with a mental illness and continues to navigate in a world that doesn't care about poor, uneducated people. Her story reminds me that those can't be just talking points. The way that we decide to see people and care about people, the way that we allow our words to transform into action, really matters. Being so close to someone who needs so much is a constant humbling reminder for me to always stay true to this work. I joke about, 'Yeah, the beneficiaries of our programs are probably my cousins,' but it is true. I'm zero degrees of separation away from the amazing work that's being delivered. My mom and our situation are my constant motivating driver to always make sure that I'm staying true to my values and centering the experiences of the people whose voices are often neglected."

Sanola A. Daley

"My remedy, pre-Covid, was to go to the field and spend as much time close to the real people, with the real situations, as I could. It's really easy when you're in DC, buried under paperwork, to forget why we're doing this. That's why the pandemic was hard. It was so hard to not be in the field, not be talking to the local men and women, not be looking at working conditions, not be hearing about the challenges. So as part of my own mental health, given the pandemic, I went home for a month. I went to Jamaica. I took a month off, and I was just at home in a developing country with all our development challenges: the urban planning, the recycling issues, the gender issues, the health care infrastructure, and the pandemic issues. And it reminded me why I was here and why I was doing this work.

"What I try to do and try to encourage is to just connect back with the real purpose of development work—the people, the situations—reconnect with the real thing and then let that guide you when you're not there so that you can still stay authentic to it. That's how I feel that I'm really working on something that's relevant and not far from where I came from."

I saw people in my neighborhood, I wouldn't say to them in the morning, "I've looked at the whole array of issues that I need to deal with today, and I think this is the most important." I would say, "Got a lot of stuff going on." I mean you would change, right? Because if you didn't, people would think you were trying to be special, different. That you thought you were better than they were.

The point is, we are constantly adapting to different environments. But when we make adjustments in how we *present* our core selves, how we speak and maybe how we dress, even with our family, we are not changing our *core* itself. We carry our true selves in different packaging for different occasions. More on that below. First, let's explore more of what that core is.

Knowing Yourself

You are complex. You are unique. We can talk about particular identity categories that may resonate for you, but ultimately only you decide who you are and what matters. What's important is that you decide—not others—and that you make that identity front and center in your psyche so you can value, protect, and nurture it. We'll explore Black identity, class, values, personality, and gender here. Of course, your identity is also informed by your experience, your faith, and the many roles you play in your life—sibling, parent, community member, and so forth.

Black Identity

Ambassador Rea Brazeal reminds us of how perceptions of Black identity change over time. In her oral history, she interspersed the various labels that come with that identity. As she put it, "I was born a Negro and I grew up being Black and I am now an African American, but I've always been a woman." At any one time, there has never been consensus about Black identity and those labels. Nemata Blyden reviews this complicated history, as well as the complex relationship between Black Americans and the African continent and peoples, in *African Americans and Africa: A New History.*

Dr. Helene Gayle describes her journey in Box 8.2.

This pan-African perspective and focus on a shared Black experience is core to many of our giants, even if the specific experience varies from place to place. Ambassador Harry K. Thomas Jr. reported Nigeria was his favorite country to serve in. "I will always love Nigeria because it was the only place, and I repeat that, the only place, including Zimbabwe, where I've lived where it was an advantage to be dark-skinned."

In her insightful piece titled "We Need to Talk About the Pressure of Black Excellence," Elisabeth Fapuro warns against the homogenization or unity of a Black identity, countering those who would become

Box 8.2   Helene Gayle: An Evolving Black Identity

Dr. Helene Gayle was an early activist, focusing on Black power. "We were the post–civil rights children in a way. We were much more into being militantly Black, which to me also then started extending into Pan-Africanism. So I got very interested in the African diaspora more broadly. And that went from the childhood experience, to this political conceptual notion of how important Africa was to us as Black people and redefining who we were as inferior beings without a history, to really understanding that we had this incredible historical past. When I was in college, there were both the Black Student Union and African diaspora organizations. So I got very involved with the Caribbean students and the African students, and that was also very important to me in terms of starting to have an experience with African peoples from all parts of the world."

"authorities of [B]lackness." She wants to make sure that individuality does not become yet another exclusively white privilege. Unfortunately, white people most often assume there is only a singular Black identity. ▶ We're forced to just be in this one box, like the Black experience is a monolith. I see the world and view race very differently from someone who grew up in white, suburban America, where she was the only Black girl and may have never really thought about her identity as a Black woman until she left that space. It's hard to counter that singular narrative when people in the workplace have such limited experience with Black people. There are often still so few in a particular place.

Let's face it. These differences have implications for how challenging you may find it to adapt to the State Department culture or US foreign policy professions more broadly. Philip Gary explains in Box 8.3.

▶ My experience crosses over between those two buckets. I grew up in an inner city, but my family is middle-class. I didn't go to an Ivy League institution, but I went to one of the best Black universities in the country. And I had international experiences much earlier than the average Black female in this country. I think, today, whether you are low income, middle-class, high income, no matter what school you went to, the topic of being authentic is something that we share across those lines.

Whatever your Black identity means to you is what matters most. The main point is that you are proud of your Blackness and consider it a source of your strength. Dr. Rheeda Walker, in *The Unapologetic Guide to Black Mental Health*, argues that having a positive sense of

---

Box 8.3   Philip Gary: How Different Experiences Influence the Need to Adapt

---

"It depends on what Black community you come out of. I grew up in the inner city of DC. If you come out of an inner-city experience, and you go to a small public university or a normal public university or an HBCU, you've had a set of experiences that have shaped you, most often in ways that don't lead you to the Foreign Service. That's one type of person of color. Many other Black people in the Foreign Service came from upper-middle-class families, went to Ivy League or very good public universities, and were socialized into the Black experience. That's also a Black experience.

"Those are two very different groups of people. And I think it's absolutely critical to know not only which one of those groups you come from but which does your being represent? If you come out of the upper middle class and have gone to Ivy League–type schools, you're much more comfortable with how the Foreign Service works, because it's much more consistent with what you've come up through. Now, there are still times when you can run into 'how can I be my authentic self?' But it's very different for somebody who's not been exposed to that body of experiences. Their authenticity reflects where they have been, and little or nothing of where they have been prepares them to be in the context of the Foreign Service."

---

who you are as a Black person is the key to thriving in your quality of life and well-being. As part of the first Peace Corps volunteer group to serve in South Africa after Nelson Mandela came to power, C. D. Glin not only found himself embracing his Black identity but discovered a mission to encourage that in others too (see Box 8.4).

Values

Values and identity are impossible to disentangle. Our values are an essential component of how we express ourselves. Verone Bernard and Sanola A. Daley (Box 8.1) and C. D. Glin (Box 8.4) all expressed how their values—and identities—connect them to the work of US foreign policy. Through their values, they can embrace the work they are doing and why. Sometimes your values will cause you to question the work and reassess your fit. In Box 8.5, Lauri Fitz-Pegado shares her story about why she decided to leave the Foreign Service.

Box 8.4   C. D. Glin: Embracing Black and Inspiring Others to Do So Too

"I'm somebody who had embraced, loved, and was unapologetically Black. I like who I am. Most of the environments I'd walked into, I was welcomed. I was used to being seen as interesting and being accepted. Going to Peace Corps South Africa was really different. We landed in Cape Town and were greeted by Thabo Mbeki and Al Gore, then vice presidents of South Africa and the United States. I was in a *Washington Post* story: 'Howard grad blazes trail to South Africa.' It was the perfect storm of my life.

"And then we got to my village. The community had been expecting us. We would be working in schools. And as the Land Cruiser is going through the community, the kids are yelling and screaming, and they're happy. And then the car stops, and I hop out. I have little baby dreadlocks and a big smile, and I'm happy. 'All right. Hey, I'm here!' And it probably didn't literally happen like this, but it was like all the clapping stopped and everyone looked around. And they were like, 'Where is our American volunteer?' And so almost for the first time of my life, when I thought it was going to be the pinnacle of what I had studied, what I believe, everything, I was greeted with disappointment. They were like, 'We thought we were getting a real American.'

"That moment was a turning point in my life where I said, 'Okay, fight or flight, be bitter or get better.' I said to myself, 'I have a job here. And my job isn't what the Peace Corps has given me. My job here is to literally show a new face of America so that they never have this reaction again.' At that moment I had to decide whether I'm going to be pissed off because they don't like how I am, or how I look, or am I going to try to share who I am so that we can really move forward? South Africa in the 1990s was my first time being in Africa with Black people who weren't that positive or happy about being Black. I had been in environments where Black people loved themselves and loved other Black people. Here I found, 'We're Black, and we don't like it. You're just as Black as us. We thought we were getting someone unique, exotic, a Ken doll. You're not six feet. You're not blonde. You're not blue-eyed. You're barely five foot nine with dark skin and some dreadlocks. How are you here to make us feel better about ourselves?' I get to my community, and they literally said, 'We wish we could be white.' 'white is better.' And 'You want to be white too, don't you?'

I knew that healing had to happen. I gave testimonies and speeches, and I trained teachers. We were basically bringing the community and parents back into schools. Under apartheid, parents weren't allowed to be involved in their kids' education. Schools had been a political tool to undereducate. We were telling the community that they could be involved,

continues

Box 8.4 Continued

they should care about their kids' education, and education is a powerful force for them to grow. It wasn't like, 'Okay. There's no more apartheid, and now they're equal and their lives have changed.'

That resonated with me as an African American because you're not going to be able to change how you show up. My skin is my skin. What am I going to do with it now? So, it's what every young boy or girl here, in an African American community, knows: you're going to have to be better. That's just how it is. But if you are better, and if you work hard, if you show up in a certain way, it will be okay. Progress will be made. As I was sharing with South Africans about being Black in America, I was hearkening back to things my parents told me about showing up. Apartheid happened. It was horrific. And now you have this anticipation and apprehension of what life can be. But it's not going to be a light switch. It's not going to happen immediately. I shared, 'We're going to have to work hard. But if we work hard enough together, I can tell you that your future will be better, and your kid's future will be better.'"

Box 8.5 Lauri Fitz-Pegado: I Just Can't Do It Then and There

"I had been an activist for many years, starting in high school. I was in the African Liberation Day marches every year, antiapartheid protests, and battles at Vassar College for increased board and faculty members of color. So it was difficult for me to decide to join the Foreign Service, frankly. I had made that decision after lots of conversations with mentors, my family, etc. It was considered to be quite an honor, and how could I, with this opportunity, think that it was not appropriate or that it was contrary to my beliefs? 'Get over it,' was what I had to do. That was a really big decision for me back in 1978. I felt very uncomfortable about being the face of the United States government and 'telling America's story abroad.' That story was not one I was really comfortable with. And as an African American woman, to be the voice and the picture of that story, I felt was a bit much for me to swallow.

"I was assigned to Dar es Salaam, after assignments in the Dominican Republic and Mexico. I was to be one of two people at the embassy required to meet a Kiswahili language requirement, because I was going to be the information officer/press attaché. I would be the face of the

continues

Box 8.5   Continued

embassy in Dar and probably the only African American officer in Dar. This was the time of apartheid in South Africa. Tanzania was a frontline state. Through Africana courses at Vassar, I had become a real admirer of Julius Nyerere, the president of Tanzania. I really had a sense of conflict for being in a country where the president was someone I had admired so much. He was a real icon in Africa. And here I was going to this country to compromise my beliefs, to sell American policy that I didn't believe in. So that, along with my opportunity to go to graduate school, health issues in my family—all of that was the perfect storm for me to decide it was time to go."

The work of US foreign policy is inherently in the service of the United States. Though you may work for nongovernmental organizations—or even in the private sector—much, though not all, of the work may be funded by the US government to ultimately promote US interests in the world. This is something you need to consider not just once in your career. You will probably need to reflect on it at various points as your jobs and political contexts change. It's important to think about your specific role and whether or not it advances, or at least does not contradict, your values. Philip Gary reflected on this with respect to his work at USAID (see Box 8.6).

Philip Gary worked for change he believed in alongside serving US interests. Many of our giants recognize the importance and power of creating change from inside systems that need to change. Dr. Helene Gayle reported, "The reason I'm on the Coca-Cola board is because I believe companies have an ability to not only create economic value but also social value. I am often asked, How does a public health professional join the board of a 'soda company'? My belief is that you can often change things more from the inside, and if I can help this company think about their obligation to public health differently, I'll make at least as big a contribution to public health than anything I can do." Dominique Harris was initially wary of working in the private sector. She stays clear and committed to her values: "Before I started, I made a promise to myself. I said, 'If I feel like I am losing me, and I am losing my value and my ethos, I'll walk away from it all.' And to this day, if I feel like I am not fulfilled, or I am not meeting the expectations that I've set up for myself, I'll walk away."

**Box 8.6   Philip Gary:
The US Self-Interested Nature of the Work**

"The development paradigm is based on a belief that if you could improve the situation in developing countries, you would improve your own situations. Societies would develop to the point where they would be better trading partners and better alliance partners. It is overtly set up with the US self-interest being at the center of the proposition. If you go into a Foreign Service government agency, you're representing US interests. You have to know that walking in the front door. If you're uncomfortable with that, then you should never come through the door.

"Having said that, it seems to me that what Aaron, myself, and other people ask is 'What is it that this organization does that's worth us doing?' Take where I started, for instance, the Office of Housing and its Housing Investment Guarantee Program. The money for the housing programs is generated off the US private sector. US banks make money off of this program. But the program is to build housing for low-income people. You had to be below the fiftieth percentile in that country. So you build housing for people who otherwise would literally have no housing. You have to decide if you think that's a worthwhile proposition.

"The US government is not a benevolent organization. It is not doing things out of the pure goodness of its heart. It's an enlightened self-interest venture. What you're asking yourself is, inside that self-interest venture, are there things that it does, that you can do, that sufficiently improve the lives of your target audience that you're willing to do that? Part of this concerns your willingness to put up with people, including yourself, questioning you, challenging you, and even sometimes putting you down for being a part of this. You do this because you believe that, in the great scheme of things, it makes things better than if you weren't doing it. If you don't believe that, you ought not do it. If you believe that, then you put up with all the BS and all the slings and arrows that come with it. But you know that that's part of the territory."

Personality

Knowing yourself is also about understanding your unique personality. What drives you? What drains you? What informs your behavior? How do you prefer to interact with others? Philip Gary is a pillar of self-awareness. He speaks very candidly, in Box 8.7, about how understanding his personality has served him well.

■ *Philip represents the highest degree of integrity about who he is, what he represents, and how he views things. He has always been candid and direct. That takes a lot of courage, and it requires being so secure in who you are that nobody can assail your fortress, no matter what the issue, the country, or the challenge.*

Box 8.7   Philip Gary: Unabashedly Himself

"One of the things that helped me throughout the Foreign Service was a character of my personality, and that was always feeling like a little bit of an alien in the world I was in. That gave me a bit of a shell that let me work my way through without being as emotionally vulnerable, as some of my colleagues were. Being able to be within myself took me through that experience so it did not permeate my being in the way it did some people. I had a sense of self that helped me deal with a lot of the things that came at me professionally without allowing them to become overly personal.

"I'm middle-class. My parents both went to college, Howard. My grandfather went to college. And they were, quite frankly, DuBoisians. They clearly believed in the Talented Tenth concept. They believed that you should dress and look a certain way, which I did. I have a costume, a way I dressed throughout my time in AID, in the Foreign Service, and working in other contexts. That costume, that set of experiences, that set of DuBoisian principles, came with me. Authenticity, to me, was living inside that. And because I was introverted and encapsulated, in some ways, I think my embrace of the organization I was in was never so personally great that I had the opportunity to be inauthentic. All the things that I had been steeped into being, I was going to be that. That was going to be an anchor for me. It was as rigid to me as my skin color. And so, if I had to navigate some particularly difficult situation, I had a basis to do so. And I never thought about imposter syndrome or inauthenticity because it just didn't seem like an option. I never felt enough of an insider to the institution to feel that I was in a position to be an imposter or inauthentic.

"In terms of dress, I have a suit and tie on, and underneath it, I have on a T-shirt, and it bears a quote by Einstein: 'The difference between genius and stupidity is genius is limited.' I have a sense of humor about this sort of thing. I hope you folks do know that I am saying this with a good deal of humor."

Ain't I a Woman?

Women face particular challenges in any profession. We addressed some of those challenges in Chapter 7 as we discussed nurturing a life outside work. You may also face challenges specific to being an American woman, in the context of other cultures, and being a Black woman, in the context of women's organizations. Despite ongoing challenges of discrimination, sexism, and the continuing stream of #MeToos, American women, especially professional American women, have come to expect respect as professionals regardless of where they work. And they expect that respect will not be contingent on their marital status or whether they have children. Sexist encounters with less liberal cultures can be subtle or jarring. Victoria Cooper shares her experience in Box 8.8 and how she used her identity and sense of self to get through it.

Box 8.8 Victoria Cooper: Navigating Gender Norms in Ghana

"I was a partner at PriceWaterhouse, based in Ghana, when they merged with Coopers & Lybrand in 1998. I was an African American woman in a partnership with five Ghanaian men. Before, I could make my decisions with my team. Becoming a partner, I became, in their minds, somehow a threat and needed to conform to their social construct. By this time, I was divorced, and I had my daughters with me. As a partner, I had my consulting business, representing the company across the government. I was visible and out there. People saw me. And the partners started putting pressure on me to conform to the social constructs. They would say, 'Oh, but you're not married.'

"This became really difficult. I was beginning to get high blood pressure. I'm usually a very calm person. I've lived in someone else's culture all of my professional career. So what do I do in these situations? I reflect and decide how I'm going to revalidate myself. I have to be true to myself, as Vicki, where she comes from, what she believes, what my core values are. So I needed to go home for a minute. I needed to spend some time talking to my family about this, my sister, my mom, my sister-in-law. They know me. They know that I'm nonconfrontational, that I'm going to analyze the situation. When my sister-in-law said, 'Curse them out,' I said, 'I can't do that.' She said, 'Well, figure out how you can do it the way you do it.'

"I began to reflect on the interpersonal skills that I had, my persuasive skills, how I am usually adaptable. What are the things that I've done that have allowed me to be successful? How do I usually problem-solve? This was very intentional and deliberate. My responses were not going to be impulsive. I was not going to allow my emotions to take over. The Ghanaian partners pushed in every possible way, and I had to figure out what I had in my toolbox. Much of that toolbox came from who I am as an African American in my family structure, and how we problem-solve, and how we build relationships. And I know, for them, family is family, and the African relationship structure is so key and important. So I worked on those relationships, got to know them, got to know their wives, got to know their families better. So they didn't just see me in the office. They got to know who I was. And that allowed them to calm down. And it allowed me to go ahead and work the way I work. I was always the one who would push them, who would press them, who would let them know that I wouldn't compromise. I would hold the standard because this is what our business required."

Sanola A. Daley has long been an activist, promoting women in the profession, for example, through leadership positions at Ellevate. Given her identity as a Black woman, she is very strategic in how she invests her energy to support other women, as she describes in Box 8.9.

If you are a Black woman, you experience slight upon slight for that intersectionality. Our final story for this section concerns a different kind of "leaning in" to that identity. In Box 8.10, Ambassador Rea Brazeal shares how she used dismissive assumptions to her advantage.

■ *Ambassador Brazeal and her colleague had the audacity to trigger actions by their respective bosses, unbeknownst to them. That takes a lot of courage and savvy. Bravo.* ▶ And using others' weakness—prejudiced assumptions—to your advantage? For a young Black woman, this is the ultimate playbook. Ambassador

---

Box 8.9   Sanola A. Daley: Strategically Investing in Women's Organizations

"One of the things that I found a little bit distressing is that the gender space in DC in international affairs and just in general can be elitist and not look diverse. I have stayed away from certain conferences because I knew I did not look like people who tended to go to those conferences. There are organizations that I knew I would not get into because I did not look like, sound like, or have the profile of the average person who worked there. Especially when you look at the career-development side of gender and women being entrepreneurs and women progressing into leadership positions, there's an undertone assumption of who those women are, what those women look like. And so I try to show up in places where there is a space for diversity, for different women to show up and share their experiences, because they're not all rich white women who are like Sheryl Sandberg. *Lean In* drove me crazy, because there are so many assumptions about the typical gender gap issues. Those were privileged white women issues. It was important for me to be in spaces where I could say, 'Yes, this is an issue in this developing country in *x* region. This is not the issue that these women over here are having. Let's talk about this one too.'

"I think it's important for me to share this, because, in addition to being Black, that's one of the struggles that I've dealt with as a gender person. I don't fall into the typical gender person look or the typical gender person background. I really think that's a fight that still needs to happen: we are not all poor women who are, for example, working in coffee cultivation. But we're not all Sheryl Sandberg. And we need to figure out who the women in the middle are and deal with them too."

Box 8.10 Rea Brazeal: A Mere Woman? Making It Work for You

"I never felt that I didn't have the ability to make policy in my Foreign Service jobs, even as a junior officer. In one position I had in the Economic Bureau, for example, you meet people in the interagency. I met a Black woman at the Treasury Department. She and I are friends to this day, because, of course, the Treasury was, along with a few other agencies, the last plantation. So having a Black woman at Treasury in a position of doing international work was startling, important, and she was sharp as a tack. So we'd talk on the phone, and we'd agree that we needed to move a certain issue up and get a decision. Then she would run to her boss and say, 'The State Department is interested in this issue.' And I would run to my boss and say, 'Treasury's interested in this issue, and we've got to move it.' And, of course, we'd already written the memos. So we could produce the memos, give them to people, and move the issue up the line and get a decision.

"This was a job that did development finance and helped develop positions on how the United States would vote on different loans to developing countries. So USAID played a very important role. I had a friend at AID who would tell me when his boss was going to be meeting with foreign delegations from other donor countries. So I would pick up my little steno pad and pencil and take off to his office and walk in, sit down—in the back of course—and take notes. My boss was always startled that I knew what AID was thinking up. The AID people just assumed I was some young, female note taker of no importance working for AID, and so I would just go to these meetings.

"I was taking advantage of how I knew people thought of young women. Most cultures around the world are male dominated. So as a young officer, I could go to people in the host nation and say, 'Golly, gee, I don't really understand nuclear power. Could you explain it to me?' They would, because they expected young people to be that way, especially young women. So as you age, of course, you have to take on a different persona, as an older woman. But as a young woman? Exploit it. That's how I felt, especially with Americans."

Brazeal's story also illustrates the power of solidarity and what you can achieve when you develop shared perspectives and priorities, even across organizational boundaries.

One more point about Ambassador Brazeal's experiences: like Victoria Cooper, she had her fair share of challenges from the cultures she worked in. "In the local cultures women are way down on the totem pole." When she left the Federated States of Micronesia, where she had served as the first US ambassador, the president threw a farewell party for her. She reported, "He said, 'Well, sorry you're leaving. I hope your replacement comes, and I hope she comes soon.' I felt that I had made some minor inroads on gender issues" (Brazeal 2007, 83).

What Is Inauthentic?

Now that you have some reinforcement of your unique identity and what these various components mean to you, it's time to tackle the vexing questions. What does it mean to be inauthentic in the workplace? Let's first consider the role you may play as a professional and the particular cultures you may work in.

No one has the luxury to be wholly themselves in the sense of making decisions and setting agendas independently of their organizational context and the professional oaths they take. In some respects, Philip Gary argues, "People being inauthentic has nothing to do with ethnicity. For white and other groups of color in an organization like the State Department, lack of authenticity is almost a generality. You're in an organization that has an ethos and a program. I would not be comfortable with the suggestion that that ethos and that program are drastically or naturally more alien to Black Americans than they would be to other Americans. In the Foreign Service, you take an oath; you work for the government; you follow the political leadership. You do not set the agenda; you don't make the policy per se. You follow it." For Philip Gary, being inauthentic, as he observed during his career, has to do with "people of color allowing themselves to be marginalized, in terms of their skills; being willing to take positions or jobs within the Foreign Service that did not highlight their skills. Where I found inauthenticity is when people were marginalized, knew that they were being marginalized, but weren't prepared to walk away."

Cultures differ from organization to organization, but most so-called professional organizations share some general characteristics. Depending on your own background, you may feel more—or less—need to adjust. ▶ I've met people who say, "I'm my authentic self every day. I bring who I am to my job without watering myself down for my colleagues." And, actually, it seems they may not need to be intentional about that because, from such an early age, they may have been moving through these spaces and don't really know anything else. This goes back to Philip Gary's earlier point about whether you grew up in a suburban middle class and/or attended predominately white schools. If so, these organizational cultures may not be as alien to you. You may feel more comfortable surrounded by those with the Ivy League credentials, for example.

Ambassador Ruth A. Davis, empowered by her family and her Spelman experience, was going to be herself no matter what: "A lot of my colleagues came from Ivy League schools, and I didn't. I was not as polished as some of them, but I decided early on that the Foreign Service had to take me or leave me, as I am. I think that that was probably the best decision that I ever made in my life, that I wanted to be myself and I wanted to project myself and not try to be an image of somebody else that I thought would be more appropriate." (At the same time, recall that Ambassador Davis was also the mentor who taught Ambassador Ertharin Cousin the dining etiquette she needed to succeed; see Box 4.2.)

Dr. Jacob Gayle shared a story from one of his mentors. Having repeatedly had that common experience of raising an idea, being ignored, and then having someone else raise the same idea and get praised, his mentor reached a certain point in his life when he realized, "You know what? The next thing I have to say is, 'Hey, wait a second. I just said that very same thing. Did any of you all hear what I said?'" He added, "Many of us don't get to that point, because we do feel like, 'Okay, nobody's listening to us. I'm going to give in. I'm going to succumb. I'm just going to sit silently at the table.'"

So should you dim your light or not? In *Covering: The Hidden Assault on Our Civil Rights*, Kenji Yoshino argues that everyone covers, or "tones down a disfavored identity to fit into the mainstream." Covering is another way of thinking about assimilation. General and Secretary Colin Powell believed in both knowing one's Black heritage and learning the foundations of our broader American culture, including white heritage: "My message to young African-Americans is to learn to live where you are and not where you might have been born three centuries ago. . . . Along with their [B]lack heritage they should know about the Greek origins of our democracy, the British origins of our judicial system, and the contributions to our national tapestry of Americans of all kinds and colors. . . . The corollary is equally true. Young whites will not be living in an all-white world. They must be taught to appreciate the struggle of minorities to achieve their birthright" (Powell 1995, 533–534). How far do you need to go to "fit in"? Or as Ambassador Reuben Brigety put it, "How do you navigate and develop the skills that will get you power, but also not lose who you are along the way?"

Yoshino outlines four types of covering: appearance, changing your physical presentation; affiliation, downplaying your cultural or personal connections (e.g., heritage, parenting); advocacy, not advocating on behalf of others like you; and association, avoiding relationships with others like you. These forms of covering concern how you behave. They can be subtle. They may be things you do automatically as a reflex, because of your experience and socialization, or more consciously, because you know it will be safer for you and others. For example, Dr. Jacob Gayle shared, "Anybody like me, who's a six-foot-four Black male and who stands behind somebody at an ATM, has tried to make sure the people know, 'I know I'm right behind you, and I may scare the heck out of you, but don't worry. I'm a nice Black guy. I'm not going to do anything.' I joke about that, and whenever I've said that to an audience, you'd be amazed at how many people, both male and female, that resonates with."

Claude Steele calls this "whistling Vivaldi." He takes the term from journalist Brent Staples. When Brent Staples was a graduate student, just his walking through Chicago's Hyde Park neighborhood would make white people uncomfortable, so he learned to whistle Vivaldi to put them at ease. Claude Steele writes about these responses to "stereotype threat" in *Whistling Vivaldi: How Stereotypes Affect Us and What We Can Do.* When you are in a situation that raises negative stereotypes about a group you belong to, you may try to distance yourself from that group. At an extreme, that could mean covering in ways that deny your core identity.

An organizational culture may expect certain elements of covering of everyone—for example, dressing a certain way. But when it comes to affiliation, advocacy, and association, there is no reason you should necessarily cover. There may be times you choose to do so to protect yourself from prejudice and discrimination. Ambassador Rea Brazeal chose to downplay her civil rights work with her colleagues in the Foreign Service. She had learned early on that not all colleagues were supporters of the civil rights movement. And this is the challenge. Oftentimes people cover to avoid prejudice and discrimination, a form of whistling Vivaldi. If you think about it, code switching is sometimes covering, because those who are already a part of mainstream culture have less need to hide a disfavored identity. The longer people cover to protect themselves from prejudice and discrimination, the longer mainstream culture's definitions remain limiting and discriminatory.

Yoshino's four categories can help you to reflect on your priorities and personal value limits in terms of acceptable forms of covering for you. For example, where do you draw the line in terms of what you wear and how you style your hair? How far will you go to hide your experience as a Black person or someone who grew up in an inner city or went to an HBCU—especially when your unique experiences can contribute to different ways of seeing things and to creative solutions? Will you avoid advocating on behalf of other Black people in your organization when they have experienced discrimination or subtler forms of disrespect? When you are at that networking event, will you intentionally avoid congregating with the other Black people in the room?

You and . . .

Recent work on diversity and inclusion characterizes belonging metaphorically as "dancing like no one is watching." Very few, if any, of us realistically do that in the workplace. Chances are, you will be yourself *and* conform to an organizational culture or professional style.
■ *You want to be authentic and be true to who you are, but at the same time, you need to figure out, "What is the corporate culture that I'm entering into, so that I can manage and be successful in this corporate culture?" Everybody has to do that. Black people, especially, have to learn how to be bilingual and bicultural in American culture. And the more deprived your background has been, the more you have to learn how to play that game appropriately to be successful.*

Making Adjustments

When C. D. Glin became associate director with the Rockefeller Foundation, based in Nairobi, he spent three months in New York to learn the appropriate culture and behavior for the job. "They paid for me to be in an apartment in Midtown Manhattan to learn how to do my job in Nairobi. The preparation part of it was like, 'How do you drink champagne? Which flute do you use?' I'm joking, but it really was an indoctrination in the Rockefeller Foundation's organizational culture. You are a steward of that legacy." Paul Weisenfeld's approach is to consider "What are the essential tools you need to be successful? One of them is adapting to the prevailing culture." The need for adaptation may be less extreme than it once was, but that will likely depend on the particular organization and profession.

Not all organizations will train you explicitly in expected behavior. You need to be observant, sensitive, and strategic to adjust your behavior in order to best meet your professional aspirations as you retain and celebrate the core of who you are. Ambassador Ertharin Cousin put it this way: "You have to maintain an ability to communicate verbally and nonverbally with those who don't share your experiences. That's quite different from presenting your authentic self, which should always center the inner you. Your authentic self includes the morals, the standards, the intellect that together define you. I am not suggesting that in your professional communication you in any way compromise your authentic self. I am suggesting you may need to adjust your communication style or how you dress. Despite a desire for self-expression, effectively representing those you serve when meeting with a foreign leader may require a wardrobe change, if you've always dressed hip-hop. You shouldn't define your authenticity by superficial, outward, relatively easy-to-change elements that help you succeed and don't necessarily define your genuine inner self."

Ambassador Ruth A. Davis believes that one of the essential tools for being successful is sensitivity to how you are perceived. "I was always sensitive to people around me, and I certainly didn't try to impose myself upon people. And that sensitivity is one of the things that I've worried about in our coming generations. Not to change yourself, but it's very important to see how you're being perceived by your audience. Sometimes you have to adjust how you come on to situations." This sensitivity relates to an important advantage you may not even realize you have. Chris Richardson explains in Box 8.11.

**Box 8.11   Chris Richardson:
Know This Advantage of Being Black**

"My great-grandfather, a long time ago, told me that Black Americans understand white Americans better than white Americans understand white Americans. What he meant by that was that as Black people in America, you have an understanding of white people and the codes that they're giving you, and you're able to pick up on things. What is being a diplomat but doing that?

"Being Black in America is like being a diplomat in the rest of the world. You have to know, okay, this white person is sending me a code by what they're saying. If this white person is clutching their purse, or this white person is giving you a look, you have to understand, as a Black American, what that means. You navigate your life trying to think about, how am I going to do something in a way this white person doesn't call the police on me, or this white person doesn't see me as being aggressive? How do I soften myself for these white folks so that they don't hurt me in that way? That's something I think all of us, as Black people, struggle with, but I think that, unfortunately and fortunately, that made me a very good diplomat. That made me very good at navigating the system and knowing how to survive it."

■ *I think that's right. As a person of color in the Foreign Service, you come in with a set of diplomatic skills that you've learned just by growing up Black in America.*

It's important to recognize that your choices about how you present yourself may come with consequences. Ambassador Ruth A. Davis continued, "There's a certain decorum. Earlier in the movement for dreads, we had a young officer who came to me and said, 'Ambassador Davis, they told me that you'd tell me straight out. Do I need to cut these dreadlocks off?' And I said, 'No, not if you don't want to. You can keep them on, but you might pay a price, and you ought to be aware that you might pay a price. You may not get the assignment to go to the foreign ministry, or you may not get the assignment to represent your embassy because of the way that dreadlocks are perceived. So, you decide. You keep your dreadlocks, but you might have to pay a price.'" She allowed that dreadlocks may be more acceptable now, but whatever your hair choice, you should know what the potential consequences could be.

You've probably experienced that people treat you differently based on how you dress. Many Black men have that experience, for example, when wearing a suit. Paul Weisenfeld shared, "Walking around New York in the late 1980s, wearing a suit and tie, people would say, 'Yes, sir.' And if I was not wearing a suit, people treated me very differently. So I got used to dressing nicely. Even today, it's just become a part of who I am. And I know this is true for a lot of Black professionals in my age group." He added, "I had several incidents in the 1980s when I was traveling and I thought I was not being treated professionally in the airport or on a plane. I'm always going to wear a blazer when I travel. Now, with gray hair, it's different. People treat you more respectfully because you're older."

In *More Than Ready: Be Strong and Be You . . . and Other Lessons for Women of Color on the Rise*, Cecilia Muñoz advises you to be sharp, both outside and in. She describes the importance of dressing for the profession, not just your identity. ▶ At Howard, we're taught to be proud of ourselves and the differences that make us who we are. And they polish and train us to be well-spoken and well-dressed so that we can assimilate into the rest of the world. But we don't have to tone down our Blackness. We don't have to be anything else but ourselves.

There may be small things you do to fit into a culture, be perceived as a player, and convey that you are worthy of respect. These adjustments can facilitate your success. They also mean you are not dancing like no one is watching. People are watching. They expect you to conform to certain norms. Dominique Harris is very clear about her expectations for bringing her "whole self" to work (see Box 8.12).

Box 8.12   Dominique Harris: Adjusting to Corporate Culture

"I think as a Black professional, there is always this notion of Langston Hughes, 'We Wear the Mask,' that goes to the heart of the things required of you to fit into various cultures. My hair is natural right now, and sometimes I wear it out. But my first few years, I always had my hair straight. There is a norm that you assume exists to fit into certain spaces and places. But at my core, I feel like I am able to be me and be wholly me. If I were not able to do that, I would find a new job, because I wouldn't be happy.

"In corporate America, especially, there is an element of understanding power dynamics and structures and being intentional in how you engage. It's a conscious decision of 'Here's how I'm going to show up. Here's how I'm going to present myself.' There are ways that I show up in my personal life with people I've known all my life that differ from how I show up at work. The environment is different, the priorities are different, and expectations may be very different. I think it is a gift, particularly for Black people, that we understand how to remain authentically Black and also how to fit in spaces that were not made for Black people.

"When I moved to Wichita, Kansas, I had to have candid, real conversations with people. There seemed to be this interesting intersection of authenticity and career, which seems to be at odds in some people's minds. I don't think the two are mutually exclusive. I'm very rooted in culture and very rooted in family history. But I also know how to navigate in corporate America in order to pay it forward, to open doors for other people. Even with the opportunity and paying it forward, there is an element of how you show up. People are watching and will form opinions based on everything from your appearance to how you interact. For better or worse, unconscious bias is real, and if you don't show up for the role that you want, you may not be seen as talent to move up through the corporation."

So you're making adjustments, and at times you may feel uncomfortable. And yet bringing your whole self to the work is what will make it fulfilling and impactful. Ambassador Harry K. Thomas Jr. summarizes for us: "Yeah, there are a lot of things that are going to happen in life, and it's hard for everyone. You understand that you've chosen to be in a competitive environment, so you have to do everything in that competitive thing. And if you are not doing your best, you can only lie to yourself. You know you can't lie to yourself."

Expect to Feel Uncomfortable

Initially, these cultures may feel very alien to you. But over time, as you adjust, they may come to feel normal, where code switching is second nature, like putting on a rain shell when the weather changes—you are still the same person inside. Paul Weisenfeld described his experience. "When I started working for law firms, it was the first time I was in an office setting. There were mahogany tables and mahogany walls, and everybody was wearing gorgeous suits. And everyone was white except for, worldwide, six people. And I saw maybe one of them once every three weeks or so. I definitely did not feel like I could be my authentic self. I have a very clear memory of being uncomfortable. What do I say? How do I act? And do I have to act differently than I do as a normal person? And then at some point I was comfortable in professional settings, and I honestly cannot say when and why that happened. I know it wasn't in two or three years. It was longer than that."

Ambassador Ertharin Cousin was direct: "Get comfortable with being uncomfortable." She cautioned that the room may not adjust to you or necessarily embrace your Blackness. She added, "You need to accept and recognize that success will not necessarily provide you with the emotional support and comfort often provided by your early career experiences." She stressed that being true to your core will lead to a more fulfilling and successful career: "The ability to stay true to your own ethical compass will determine not just how high you go but who you are inside as you go there."

Part of being uncomfortable is facing discrimination and microaggressions. Yet as you navigate your career, become more confident in your skills and who you are, and attain positions of greater power and influence, you will have a stronger foundation to withstand these slights and also to confront them when you choose to. Ambassador Rea Brazeal shared this story from her time as ambassador to Micronesia. "I was standing in the lobby of the embassy, which looked like a chicken coop, with the local staff. And this white American man came in the door. He looks around at everybody, and he says out loud, 'Nobody here looks like an American.' And walks out. So their mouths dropped open, and they all looked at me. I said, 'Well, if he comes back, we'll have to help him if he needs help.' I said, 'But before you help him, ask for some identification. And if he asks you why, tell him, because he doesn't look like an American.'"

Being the Best of You

Valerie Dickson-Horton posed an essential question, which is where we started, and which you should think about even before you enter these new arenas: "How comfortable are you in your skin? How comfortable are you being you?" If you aren't comfortable with you first, you may waste too much time and energy worrying about what other people think of you. ▶ I think that's something that a lot of people don't talk about. Be comfortable in who you are, the uniqueness that you bring, the edge that you have. I know I still have to pay my dues. I still have a long way to go, but I'm going to do it me all the way, 100 percent. And if you don't like what I'm selling, then there are ten other people who will. ■ *I think that's the right attitude to have. The giants in this book have always been authentic and always knew who they were.*

Dr. Rheeda Walker knows well the value you bring. "The truth you need to discover for yourself is that Black people may do things differently, but this is a difference and not a deficiency. The characteristics that make us different are rooted in something deeply creative and unique, so we do not have to be limited by others' imagination" (Walker 2020, 93). Verone Bernard understands this value. She shared, "I love what I'm able to do every day. The best part, which is also the hardest part, is being able to bring my identity into the room that I'm bringing solutions to. It's great that I'm able to come in as a first-generation American and first-generation college graduate who has all of these layered identities, came from an underclass neighborhood, and probably shouldn't have been in most rooms that she was able to be in. And because of that, I know the way that I understand problems is different, and the way that I want to approach problems is different than others.'"

Bringing in the best of your identity requires you also nurture it. Again from Dr. Rheeda Walker: "If you do not nurture the real you, with all of your imperfections, past failures, and different texture of hair in the front and back, you will stifle your ability to be your best self. You will stifle your talents and gifts because your fortitude is spent on overmanaging your façade" (Walker 2020, 207–208). Ambassador Harriet Elam-Thomas unabashedly celebrates her Blackness . . . and her hair (see Box 8.13).

Even in the military, where you are expected to conform, General Barrye Price performed as General Barrye Price and no one else. When you go into the army, you're supposed to be this vision that they want you to be, but he was still always himself. He challenged the status quo. And for himself and those he mentored, he made sure that, yes, you are serving a cause, you are serving your country, but you still have to be

Box 8.13   Harriet Elam-Thomas: Hair and Heritage

Speaking at a Delta Sigma Theta session titled "I Am Not My Hair,"
Ambassador Elam-Thomas spoke of "my hair, my silver braids pulled
back in what my niece Patricia describes as resembling intricately woven
African baskets. . . . I talked about how often first impressions are made
by hairstyles. It does not matter what color you are; it is how your hair
is coiffed. It makes a statement. I was delighted to share some of the
background of this coiffure that goes back thousands of years." She tells
how she felt after completing eight hours of braiding for the first time in
1988. "I came out a new person. The braids had a subtle dignity about
them. All of a sudden, I felt comfortable in my own skin. I wasn't the
diplomat who is [B]lack trying to be white."

She reports that this experience, and the woman who inspired it, "was
central to my accepting who I was as a person of color in the diplomatic
service. I no longer had to toe the line of being unnoticeable. In many
ways, that was a powerful identity statement. Yes, I was aware that some
of the corporate and government leadership and some of my colleagues
frowned upon and even prohibited their staff from wearing braids, no
matter how neat they were. They viewed it as a political statement, a
challenge, and perhaps it was. Thankfully, that is no longer the case. At
the time, however, I was proud of my heritage, even if it meant I would
always have to prove I was equal to, if not better prepared than, my white
diplomatic colleagues" (Elam-Thomas 2017, 173–175).

you at the end of the day. As Ed Grier put it, "Be who you are. Because
the easiest person to be is yourself."

Sometimes you may be advised to change things that, for you, are
beyond the kind of adjustments discussed above. When we addressed
the importance of networking (Chapter 4), Sanola A. Daley said, "I stay
authentic, because I can't do fake." She was advised to change in ways
that, to her, felt fake. She didn't do it. She tells the story in Box 8.14.

Ambassador Linda Thomas-Greenfield was her friendly self. By
just being herself, she made friends everywhere she went. This meant
that she sometimes would know things others in the embassy would
not. Sometimes that was challenging. She shared, "I remember an
ambassador came into a meeting, and he said, 'Oh, we're going to get
a meeting with the president on this day.' And I said, 'No, sir. I heard
from his wife, who I play golf with, that they're going to London next
week.' And he said, 'If they were going to London, I would know it.'
You hear that they're going to London through diplomatic channels

Box 8.14   Sanola A. Daley: I Don't Do Fake

"In my first performance review in Costa Rica, my one negative feedback was that I needed to work on a poker face. That was what my American boss told me: 'You need to work on your poker face because in every meeting, in every situation, I can read what you're thinking.' I laughed at the time. And he and I still talk every once in a while. And it's become a running joke that I still don't have a poker face. I can be very diplomatic. I'm very tactful. And people at work will tell you that about me.

"Those are skills I learned. I taught middle school and high school in Puerto Rico for one year. And I learned with those kids to be firm and to be honest and not to be a pushover. I remember one of those kids coming and saying to me that I could be really strict, but with a smile. That's me. That's a skill I retained from that experience: I will be very firm, I'll be very honest, but I will not be fake. Because at the end of the day, I need to live with myself. And if I'm not comfortable with how we got here, it's going to bother me. It will prevent me from sleeping at night, and I do not mess with my sleep. So that is my mantra: I will be honest, I'll be firm, I will be polite, I will be tactful, but I'm going to be myself. And that's what I've always done."

from the permanent secretary. You don't hear it from the president's second wife, who you happen to be friends with. And so that for me was a huge challenge." While these friendships may have seemed threatening to others early in her career, they are the bedrock of what has made Ambassador Thomas-Greenfield so successful in all of her posts: she makes a point to know people and build relationships. Dominique Harris's strategy is also to be friendly: "People tell me, 'Dominique, you're just so friendly.' I say, 'I have to be.' Ultimately, I know I'm going to do or say something that may rub people the wrong way. I need people to know me well enough to know that that interaction is not me all the time. Having rapport and a relationship with them allows them to show me grace when these interactions take place because they know me as a person."

You need to make your adjustments purpose driven. C. D. Glin advises, "Eyes on the prize." He shared, "People are going to see what they see or think what they think. You need to know that and still ask, 'What's going to lead you to the mission that you're trying to achieve?', whether it's for you or for your organization. At the end of the day, people get over some of the physical characteristics, and then they're going to sit down and be able to talk with you. So are you bringing a sense of confidence that you need to have, but without being sort of arrogant? There's got to be a sense of purpose of what you're really trying to achieve." Cecilia Muñoz reminds us that, as people of color, "we know things that the rest of the room doesn't know. And to do the work well, those people need to recognize what we bring" (Muñoz 2020, 37). To get that recognition, you need to hang in there and bring your whole self—the parts that matter.

Ambassador Ruth A. Davis loves her Black identity. She also reported, "It is more important for me to be defined by my professional accomplishments and my service to humanity, especially to young Foreign and Civil Service personnel in or aspiring to be a part of the foreign affairs community" (Davis 2016). Happily, loving your Black identity and serving humanity can go hand and hand. In Box 8.15, Ambassadors James Joseph and Ed Perkins demonstrate how your unique identity and heritage can make your contributions impactful in ways that would not be possible for others.

**Box 8.15   James Joseph and Ed Perkins:
Bringing Your Whole Self to Understanding**

James Joseph

"When I was with Cummins Engine Company, I had a unit reporting to me that did analysis of business opportunities from the perspective of both our values and investment returns. And I would often travel around myself and do some of these analyses. One of these, in the early 1970s, had to do with whether or not we located our regional office in Iran. It was the time of the shah. I went to the State Department, and then I went and spent several weeks in Iran. The State Department folks said, 'Oh, no. There's no danger of a communist rebellion in Iran or anything of that nature.' And 'You're likely to have peace and tranquility if you were to locate there.' But because of my religious training, whenever I did this, I also met with religious leaders. And it was there that I sensed that there could be some kind of a rebellion. I explored that. I came back, and I recommended to Cummins that we not locate our plant there, that we go to Athens, Greece, instead. And that saved the company a lot of money.

continues

Box 8.15   Continued

"When I went into government at the Interior Department, I had responsibility and oversight for the sixteen American territories, which included, of course, Guam and Virgin Islands, Puerto Rico, etc. So I got involved with people who were different in culture but in many instances looked like me. My most important experience was just the idea of being able to work with those folks in the same way I had with Black folks."

Ed Perkins

In his first interview with the South African press as US ambassador to South Africa, Ambassador Perkins was asked, "Why are you at this protest?" He responded, "Do you remember Marin Luther King Jr.'s *Letter from a Birmingham Jail?*" He wrote, "I often couched our change-agent activities in references to King's classic work of protest literature, and I did so now. 'I am here to represent the United States because injustice is being done. Human rights are being violated. That is something we cannot countenance'" (Perkins 2006, 321).

When he was ambassador to the United Nations, he shared, "there was a group of African nations who wanted to make sure that they were not forgotten and that they could make their points. The first thing I did there was to have a big cocktail party in the middle of the day to invite all of the African nations to come by and have a cup of tea or a drink or whatever, and just talk. One of them said, 'You know, Mr. Ambassador, this is the first time anybody's ever done this kind of thing at the UN.' Then I thought of the Black heroes that we've had. So I suggested that we have an official party uptown in Harlem, and we invited as many of the members of the UN as possible. When they came up and walked around the African American Wax Museum and saw some of the things that Black Americans had done, they said, 'Nobody ever told us that this was here.'"

Being All You

General Barrye Price paraphrased an impactful quotation from Søren Kierkegaard: "The greatest despair is not living who you are." ▶ My attitude is, you're going to take me as I am or not, because I know that I'm respectful, I do my job well, and I'm not causing any harm. I never try to be the next anyone. I want to be Taylor Jack.

Our giants want this attitude and love of self for all of you. C. D. Glin wants you to know that "it is possible to be who you are and to achieve beyond your wildest dreams. Conformity isn't necessarily the way to win. The way to really advance is to bring your whole self to the table and allow people to experience that. At some point in time, people will not only believe in it, they will want it. They want a fresh perspective. Having a difference of opinion isn't a bad thing. It is a contribution to the space." Dr. Jacob Gayle heartily agrees: "You weren't created to be the unique you that you are, just to sit at the table. We need you to be all of who you are. We don't need to have everybody the same, just in Black, Brown, Red, Yellow, and white versions. Diversity is the beauty of our strength." With support from mentors and peers, he stressed, "You are going to feel more free to be able to say, 'This is who I am. I'm bringing the best of who I am to the table,' and know that that's going to be appreciated greatly."

You will find that as you advance to positions of increasing responsibility, if you are mindful, you will find ever more creative ways to bring your whole self to the work, as Ambassadors James Joseph and Ed Perkins and many of our giants did. Leadership requires such authenticity. We will explore that more in Chapter 9.

9

The Triumphs and Challenges of Leadership

Have a vision. Be demanding.

—Colin Powell

Change will not come if we wait for some other person or some other time. We are the ones we've been waiting for. We are the change that we seek.

—Barack Obama

Don't give up—our country needs you now more than ever. This is a pivotal moment in the history of our country: Our ideals are at stake, and we all have to fight for who we are.

—Kamala Harris

Many books have been written about leadership. What we present in this chapter may not be entirely new. Still, some lessons here may be particular to these leaders, who have been shaped by their Black identity and related experiences—both personal and professional. Often we can read a lesson over and over again, but it doesn't really stick until we hear the same wisdom from someone we know and trust. We hope that, by now, you feel that way about the giants who have already shared so much of themselves with you across the pages in this book. From their professional biographies (see "Notes on the Giants") and the stories they've already shared, you know our giants are highly accomplished leaders. Many of them are firsts in particular positions and fields. Some have been celebrated for these achievements; some have excelled beyond the limelight. ■ *As I shared earlier, typically when you're in a senior level of an organization in America and you meet someone who is a person of color, you can be pretty sure this person is an exceedingly good leader, a competent professional, and has achieved a lot because they've had this journey.*

In this chapter, we explore what being a leader means—the good, the bad, and the ugly. First and foremost, it's about taking responsibility. It's also about working with and supporting others, forging and pursuing new initiatives, developing and sustaining a followership, and, all the while, projecting both confidence and humility. The giants want you to understand that leadership is about doing the right thing, even when success is not possible. And you will inevitably confront some failures. Through those challenges, leaders develop resilience so they can continue to do the right thing, with others following their lead.

Taking Responsibility

■ *Leadership is complex, both in theory and practice. It's difficult to do well. People have a lot of stereotypes about what leaders do and how they do it. A lot of people come to me and say, "I want to be a leader." I always ask them, "What do you think a leader does? What do you think are the attributes of a leader? How do you think they spend their day? What exactly is it that you think they do that makes you so certain that you want to do it?" The first thing to understand is you have to be available 24/7 for others who share the work. That's especially true if you take a servant leader approach. That commitment is something that most people don't really take into consideration when they say they want to be a leader. It's not like reading a book. Until you're in the thick of it, you don't really appreciate that.* C. D. Glin shared a conversation with his daughter: "'Daddy, you're the boss.' I said, 'Please, if I was the boss, you wouldn't see me so tired.'"

Several of our giants talked about making tough decisions. General Barrye Price said, "When in charge, you have to be in charge. There are people who advise, but advisors provide recommendations. When you're in charge, you really are making the decision." General and Secretary Colin Powell emphasized that leaders' decisions can be both welcome and infuriating: "I learned that being in charge means making decisions, no matter how unpleasant. If it's broke, fix it. When you do, you win the gratitude of the people who have been suffering under the bad situation." He also kept a saying on his desk at the Pentagon that "made the point succinctly if inelegantly: 'Being responsible sometimes means pissing people off'" (Powell 1995, 35–36).

Ambassador Johnnie Carson stressed the need for the right attitude when making tough decisions: "It's about being serious, focused, and purposeful." He always tried "to learn as much as I can. To listen more than I talk. To be coldly analytical about how I look at things. And not to let my hopes and aspirations get in the way of my analysis and the facts."

Beyond decisionmaking broadly, being a leader means taking charge in the sense of asserting your authority, assuming responsibility when things go badly, and having the vision and confidence necessary to lead others through the storms. Three of our giants share examples from their experience. We start with Ambassador Rea Brazeal in Box 9.1.

Box 9.1   Rea Brazeal: Asserting Her Authority in Micronesia

"I was the first US ambassador to the Federated States of Micronesia. Before we had an embassy, since World War II, it had been a US territory. I identified forty-four different parts of the US government that operated there. Most of these were domestic agencies, and they tended to incorporate Micronesia into their process as if it were another state of the United States. They didn't really have a consciousness of foreign policy. So I was always teaching government 101 to our fellow government departments. We could deny them entry clearance to come to Micronesia, and they were useful.

"I would tell them that the first thing Micronesians needed to hear from them was the word *no*. They seemed to be able to fund any idea that people had. And I told the Micronesians that they really had the best deal in the world in terms of money coming to them through this compact, but they'd never get it again. The circumstances would be very different by the time Congress had to re-up the compact, which hadn't happened before, so they needed to use their money wisely and not fritter it away.

"We had everything from the US Weather Service, to the Post Office, to the Department of the Interior. The monies flowed through the Interior Department. And Interior had a white supremacist mindset, as I would describe it, similar to how they would run the Native American reservations. In my briefings before going over, I had Interior people tell me that these people—'these people'—can't develop, etc. So I had a lot of fun because I was trying to restructure our relationship both inside the US government, so the State Department foreign policy would dominate, and with the Micronesians themselves, who needed to assume more control over their development."

It takes tremendous skill to assert one's authority and maintain good relations across so many individuals and organizations. Taking responsibility includes enacting rules and asserting authority as well as assuming responsibility for these relationships.

When you are a leader, you necessarily rely on others. And when they make mistakes, you own them. You are ultimately responsible. Paul Weisenfeld learned this as USAID mission director in Zimbabwe (see Box 9.2).

■ *Any smart press officer will tell you, you want to be the one to lead with your bad news. You want to frame the bad news and take away from the other guy the chance to characterize your mistakes.* ▶ Leadership is a long game. Like Paul Weisenfeld, the giants leaned into the mistakes they made. That's hard, because when you are at the top of your game, you're so exposed from every angle. But those mistakes are going to happen. The question is, Will you respond like a leader and take responsibility?

Leaders lead people, not just organizations. When an organization is in crisis, all of its people look to the leader for the vision that will guide them through; the confidence they need to believe in that vision and in their ability to help to achieve it; and the knowledge, expertise, and resources—or access to these—that is needed to survive and thrive. C. D. Glin was not expecting that so much would be required of him right at the start of his leadership of the US African Development Foundation, but he provided all the above and more (see Box 9.3).

■ *C. D. was absolutely the right leader at the time. If instead he had been a retired general or ambassador, he might not have had the energy, the knowledge, or the innovativeness to solve a problem of this magnitude.*

Building Your Team

C. D. Glin demonstrated great leadership in saving the African Development Foundation from the brink. But he did not achieve this on his own. Building an effective team is a primary task of any leader—even, as C. D. Glin faced, when you are dealing with a team you have inherited. ▶ The giants are great leaders because they are brilliant. They have forethought, and they have vision. *And* they have a wonderful team around them. They know whom to tap into, whom to call, whom to seek counsel from. And that's how they've gotten to where they are in the first place. President Barack Obama is an example of that. Yes, he is the formidable Barack Obama, but his team made him part of who he is. ■ *Taylor is right. His senior team reflected the intellect, strength, values, and determination that epitomized his approach to leadership. The people whom he selected for his senior team (including several who went to*

Box 9.2 Paul Weisenfeld: Taking Responsibility in Zimbabwe

"I was young for a USAID mission director, and I hadn't been a deputy director. A lot of people who worked for me were older than I was. PEPFAR was announced, the President's Emergency Plan for AIDS Relief. We were all trying to understand what it was. There wasn't a huge amount of information from Washington. We were in a tense relationship with the Zimbabwe government. At the time, Zimbabwe had the highest prevalence of HIV in the world. And PEPFAR had what were called focus, or priority, countries. It was a limited set of countries that were going to get the bulk of the money. And Zimbabwe was not on that list.

"The minister of health called me, yelling, 'We're the country most affected. PEPFAR has announced its humanitarian effort. Clearly Zimbabwe is not included for political reasons. You don't care about the Zimbabwean people! You're going to let them die!' And I said, 'Look, this is a new initiative. I don't really know the details. Let me find out more and communicate back to you.' I promised to send him something in writing. I had my head of the health office work on a letter, and it got cleared through Washington, and he sent it to me, and it needed a lot of work. I rewrote the letter. And it said that PEPFAR had fifteen priority or focus countries. So one of my edits back to [the health office head] was 'List what the countries are.' So he sent the letter back; I proofread it quickly, signed it, and sent it off.

"He made a huge mistake, and I made a mistake. I didn't proofread carefully. His list of focus countries included Zimbabwe, which was not accurate. When I proofread it, I got to South Africa, and my eyes skipped over. I didn't read the full list. When I called him afterward, he said, 'Oh, well I asked my secretary to fill in the list. Then she got confused and put in the list of SADC [Southern Africa Development Community] countries. So it's her fault.' I was stunned that he didn't take responsibility and blamed it on his secretary. Everyone who clears a letter, including me, who signs it, is responsible for the content. That's the whole point of the clearance process. At every stage you're responsible.

"It blew up. The minister of health called me and said, 'I am so happy that Zimbabwe is now on the list of PEPFAR countries. I've called President Mugabe and told him.' I said, 'Look, I'm really sorry. This is a terrible mistake. I'm going to send you a revised letter.' We ended the conversation with him understanding it was wrong. He was reasonable, but he was going to have to go back to the State House and tell them. I told my secretary to get the ambassador on the phone. Several of my staff advised me not to tell the ambassador, believing the issue would stay under wraps, but I just knew that was the wrong approach. It was a great example of something Aaron and others had told me: 'Deliver bad news yourself.' The ambassador was okay with it. I had been there long enough to develop a relationship with him, so this wasn't his first impression of me."

Box 9.3   C. D. Glin: Leading Through Crisis at the African Development Foundation

"I was working with the Rockefeller Foundation in Kenya when, in 2016, I was recruited to become the president and CEO of the African Development Foundation, an independent US government agency funded by Congress. It was my first CEO job. This is really great. The board tells me, 'We're hiring you for generational change.' No one has ever sat in this seat and been in their forties. The job was traditionally held by retired senior government executives. The board also tells me, 'We're hiring you to be a change agent. There will be transition. You get to build your team. This is the opportunity: you're going to take $50 million and leverage it to make it $100 million.' It's a big change to come back to Washington, DC, but this is how I wanted my life to go in terms of impact.

"Eight weeks after I take the job, there is a presidential election. When the results came in, I knew, from this point on, things were going to be very different. I'm head of a government agency concerned with US foreign policy in Africa, and I wasn't sure what the new US president thought about either of those. Also, I run a really small agency that's a blip of a blip in the foreign policy landscape. Right after inauguration an executive order announces a hiring freeze. A lot of the current leadership staff were on the verge of retirement, so they were going to leave. I took a job where I was told, 'Grow, scale, build your team.' So your starting players are leaving, you can't hire new people, and you're in this turbulent political environment. Thankfully, retirement-ready staff who had been thinking, 'We're going to clear space so you can build your team,' looked at the situation and now said, 'You can't hire anybody? We're not going to leave.' Then in March, on the front page of the *Washington Post*, the new president's budget comes out. The list of agencies to be eliminated is in alphabetical order. The African Development Foundation is listed as number one on the chopping block.

"My family hadn't made the move yet. And I left the Rockefeller Foundation on very good terms. I could make a phone call and say, 'This isn't really working out. Can I come back?' And I could have been back. This is the most important leadership challenge of my life because I have to decide right now, is it worth fighting for? Am I built to fight this fight? Can I do it with the team that's already here? Because I can't bring in reinforcements.

"Everything I had done up to this point prepared me for this moment. I've worked in the foundation world. I know development and grant making. I've worked in government before and under great leaders. I knew I needed to go to Congress, because the only way the agency could survive is to hug the appropriators, and they need to hug us back. They

continues

Box 9.3   Continued

would be asking, 'Do we believe this guy is fighting for something we think is good? Do we like him, his background and experience?' To support my proposal to save the agency, they will have to buck the system to say that this agency and I, as its leader, are worth saving. At the same time, can I keep the team here focused on the mission? Because everyone is testing us. I need all these troops to say, 'We're efficient. We're effective. We have impact.' Everyone needs to be on message, and everyone needs to keep 'killing it' out there. And I needed other advocates. We had never needed other people to say that we were valuable. We didn't have a US constituency. Who loved us? The Africans that we were giving money to? For Congress, 'They don't count. They don't vote. And you're giving them our taxpayer dollars.' So who cares about us?

"I was tested on every front. Am I a leader? Can I have staff follow me when it's an uncertain future? Externally, I'm going to the Hill and White House meetings briefing any and everyone. Internally, I'm telling staff, 'Keep doing what you're doing. I'll tell our story. I've got this part.' OMB [Office of Management and Budget] was asking question after question. What's your answer? Why this? Why that? We had to create materials; we had to do all these things to show we were efficient and effective.

"The authenticity, belief in the mission, being able to bring people along, being able to talk to different people and bring together different skill sets—all led to not only me staying at the African Development Foundation, but we became fortified. Now I can tell you that we have more money than we ever had. We're bigger than we've ever been. We're more known than we ever were.

"I came to the job with a lot of great ideas. But had I come in during peacetime, easy street, with no elimination threat, would I have been as hungry? Or do those tests really push you to levels that you never would have gone to had you not been tested? I sometimes sit back and think I would never want to go through it again, but I know I'm a better leader for it. It changed my thoughts around what I really value and when something is worth fighting for. This is the best job I've ever had, and it's tested me in ways I wouldn't have imagined."

Harvard Law School with him) had this unassailable, ferocious loyalty to him. I know some of these leaders. They are on his team because of who he is.

The giants surrounded themselves with the best and the brightest. And they were clear about their own limitations—from self-awareness, not from what others expected of them (or didn't). They know that leadership is a team game. Even when you inherit a group of people, as a leader, you will still need to make them into a team. C. D. Glin did that by exerting confidence, taking decisive action, and building trust with the people around him. He expressed confidence in his staff's ability to "keep killing it." They were all in it together. When we asked Ambassador James Joseph what he thought his major accomplishment was as ambassador to South Africa, he said his answer might surprise us. He built a team mindset, even when the players were numerous, varied, and beyond his authority. He describes his experience in Box 9.4.

■ *Ambassador Joseph is being characteristically modest. I was USAID mission director to South Africa at the time. It was a joy and pleasure to work for him, and we did work as a team. We had great respect and admiration for him and his incredibly deep knowledge of South Africa and of humanity in general. Everyone had to agree and step up to the plate to keep up with him at the level that he sustained. It was a textbook case of how to build a team and how to work with a team, even with people whom you did not select.*

Often new leaders will have the opportunity to bring in or hire on members of their team from the start. General and Secretary Colin Powell developed "Powell's Rules for Picking People": "What I looked for was intelligence and judgment, and most critically, a capacity to antici-

---

Box 9.4   James Joseph: Building a Large, Multifaceted Team in South Africa

"One of my accomplishments was the management of extraordinary growth at the embassy. We grew from 180 Americans representing seven federal offices to a level of 292 Americans representing twenty-three agencies. At the same time, the FSNs [Foreign Service nationals], local employees, increased to a total of four hundred employees. We became the largest US mission in sub-Saharan Africa and one of the largest in the world. And our most important accomplishment may have been our ability to work as a team, despite that growth and that diversity of where people came from.

"I saw myself as CEO with everyone working for me, even though they reported back to someone in Washington. If I had come up through the State Department, I might have thought of myself as a State Department employee. As a political appointee, I thought of myself as the CEO of the organization appointed by the president. Consequently, I worked with everyone as if they worked fully for me. And, of course, the people I selected myself were some of the best people in the Foreign Service. I could give you a couple dozen accomplishments out of my South Africa experience, but it wasn't me. It was the team. And I was most fortunate in that regard."

pate, to see around corners. I also valued loyalty, integrity, a high energy level, a certain passion, a balanced ego, and the drive to get things done" (Powell 1995, 355). Paul Weisenfeld emphasized the importance of fit: "If you're in senior management, your job is to manage other people. You're not doing the detailed work. The key is getting the right people in the right job. There are so many people who are smart, but, for example, if I'm going to be a laboratory scientist, I'm going to fail, obviously. It's not just being smart. You've got to be in the right job."

Building a strong team requires making tough decisions. Every leader has probably had the experience at some point in her or his career of not making tough personnel decisions early enough. People are the source of great ideas and brilliant work. And they can be in positions that don't play to those strengths. And, whether due to a poor fit or because of personality or what have you, they can be the source of trouble. Paul Weisenfeld talked about a "fixer" in his organization. She goes out to the field whenever there is a problem. She says, "What we really sell is personnel services. So if something is not working, that means there's a person that's not working." Paul Weisenfeld added, "In my experience, it comes down to the wrong person in the wrong job at some level. You have to give them a fair chance, but you also need to make decisions quickly."

Aaron shares his own wisdom about keeping and supporting great people on your team in Box 9.5.

■ *I learned a lot of this by observing others, including some of the giants in this book.* In our conversation with Bob Burgess, Aaron reflected on their time working together in Haiti and Costa Rica. He told Bob Burgess, "I saw how hard you worked. And, also, how much you enjoyed it. The people who worked for you loved working for you. Not just because you were the boss, but because you gave them space to engage as professionals and grow on their own." Bob Burgess responded, "Some of them are successful businessmen. They started their own companies. Others are general managers. They still tell me things like, 'When I get into a tough situation, I always ask myself, what would Bob have done?' And I thought that that was so beautiful. That was just terrific." Ambassador Rea Brazeal reflected on her experience working with a variety of ambassadors, both political and career Foreign Service. She said, "Those who are successful have some traits that I would like to encourage. For example, they use their professional staff; they don't make them into the 'other' or the enemy or push them away. They take into account the advice they get from the staff so that you feel that you're a part of a team. That doesn't mean they have to take everybody's advice, but they at least seek it" (Brazeal 2007, 63). Supporting others begins with respecting their talent and experience.

**Box 9.5　Aaron Williams:
The People Side of Leadership**

"You need to be able to mentor people who are on your team, and you have to be able to identify the best possible people to be on your team. I have made it a practice to ask people to join me in different organizations when I've moved. I've tried to keep my core team intact. For example, Paul Weisenfeld and I have worked together in three different places; Bob Burgess and I have worked together in two different places. I've really tried to develop people I saw to be great leaders, by giving them a chance to do what they do best. I've been very fortunate they have chosen to work with me two or three times. That, to me, is the ultimate compliment. People can say, 'I enjoy working with you.' But when you ask them to join you somewhere else outside their comfort zone and they show up, now you know.

"Whenever you assume a leadership position, you're going to have challenges. You better have people by your side and behind you whom you can trust. Of course, you also run into people who sometimes criticize this as cronyism, that you've got your own little select group. But if you have people who are high caliber, talented, and demonstrate these same leadership traits to the rest of the staff, it makes a solid team. And it's not an exclusive club. At the same time, you need to recognize the existing talent within your organization and give people within the organization opportunities.

"I've always believed in something that not many people believe in. It's often surprised people who have worked with me. I am always willing to let one of my top people go if they get an extraordinary opportunity that is in their best interest. A lot of people don't want to do that. They will hold on to you if you're good, no matter what, because that's in their best interest. But I've always felt differently. For example, when I was director of the Peace Corps, C. D. Glin was a member of my senior staff. When he told me that he wanted to go work at Rockefeller, I said, 'Pack your bags. You have to take this position.' How could you turn that down? He probably would have taken it whether I told him to or not, but I told him, 'This is the right thing to do.' And that has only strengthened our relationship long range. We've collaborated on a bunch of things since then. I was happy to see him move into a position of responsibility that no Black person ever had before at Rockefeller."

▶ Every giant in this book was poured into, and they poured into other people. And that's how you create a leader. Giving people opportunities and helping them grow is a commitment. It takes additional time and energy. It is also part of the job of being a leader. Ambassador Rea Brazeal recognized this, as she describes in Box 9.6.

**Box 9.6   Rea Brazeal:
                Committing to Building New Leaders**

"In the Foreign Service there is a hierarchy. At the same time, younger officers really want a flatter kind of organization, where their voice is heard. You simply have to balance. . . . I would take junior officers to be note-takers in my meetings. What this meant was I always had to take notes at my own meetings, because I needed to compare their write-up with what I believed was said in the meeting. I was willing to do it, it took more time, but that's how people learn. . . .

"I divide officers who work for me into two types of people. . . . There are officers who I call 'custodians': these are officers who when they take a job, they have to know the parameters, the job description, before they take it. They want to preserve the job as it is described, without having anything disrupted, and then leave it just as they found it. There are officers who I call 'activists': these are officers who impact their job, who come up with ideas, who make changes and, of course, these are the kind of officers I prefer to have work for me. But they're more challenging to lead, because they will ask questions and they will push the envelope. Thank goodness, because otherwise it is boring when everybody thinks the way you do. With custodians, it is very difficult to move forward on any policy issue because they just want to preserve what they find. . . .

"I think people should safeguard any tendencies they have to be activists and not have those skills damped down. I think this is important, because there can be supervisors, as I tell junior officers, who are not receptive to being questioned or not receptive to exposing them to wider experiences. The junior officer has to find supervisors who are willing to have them be activists and use that assignment to make themselves better" (Brazeal 2007, 101–103).

Sundaa Bridgett-Jones described the organizational culture at the Rockefeller Foundation, under President Raj Shah, as being one that supports activists. "Servant leaders welcome dissent. They see it as a point of strength. That's what they want from many of their colleagues." In thinking about when and how to dissent, as we noted in Chapter 6, she advises, there may be occasions to "pull people aside . . . but let's not be afraid to use the public space. It may give us the visibility that we may need, particularly when we have our ducks in a row. That's when we really need to have the courage to speak up and share our viewpoints. They might not have ever seen it that way." ■ *The most effective leaders are those who actually encourage dissent among their senior leadership and among the ranks. The worst thing is to be in a crisis and have only yes men. That said, you have to know what type of a leader you are working for so you can choose your strategy wisely.*

Supporting people, supporting your team, and getting the best they can offer requires taking an interest in them, and not just because of productivity. Ed Grier understands that well. He shared, "You have to build a foundation of trust early on. A small thing I've done to get to know my folks at work is just to know their spouse's name or their kid's name or what they're interested in. Whenever I come to a new position or area, I ask people, 'Do you mind sharing some basic thing about yourself?' And they say, 'What?' And I say, 'Just who you are and what you're like.' That's been very helpful for me."

And when you have a better understanding of people, you can also anticipate what they may need to further develop, to stay motivated, or simply to feel valued. Ambassador Rea Brazeal spoke about a Black woman who had served as the senior secretary on the Japan Desk for around twenty years. She knew the Japanese who came to Washington, but she had never been to Japan. "I couldn't believe this. So I arranged to use the mileage that we built up from flying back and forth so often to get a ticket for her. I arranged for her to be on a delegation. And when she got to Tokyo, she was feted by her Japanese contacts forever and a day. I mean, how could twenty some odd years go by and she could never have been in Japan?"

When Ambassador Sylvia Stanfield served in the Inspector General's Office, she learned, unfortunately, "We Americans should treat our local employees, the Foreign Service nationals, with greater respect. They have a lot to offer and to share with us. In all the posts I've served in, I found they had so much to contribute. They have the history. They generally are very proud to work for the US government. But sometimes we ignore them. We treat them poorly." And if you can't do that out of respect, Ambassador Stanfield warns, there are other reasons you want to pay attention to how local people are treated. "They can make your tour one of the most wonderful ones in the world and help you, or not. I've heard that one guy said, 'I always have bumpy roads, and I don't like this driver.' Jerky roads. Well, he thought he had a jerky driver. We act as though they don't understand English. They may not, but they do understand sufficient English to know what you may be saying in the backseat of that car. Your household effects may take longer to get to your next post." ■ *Respecting the local staff who work for American organizations is an important lesson that unfortunately some Americans must learn. In my experience, sometimes American officers treat our local employees as second-class citizens. And that is a great error. Ambassador Stanfield is right. They are very proud and will sacrifice themselves on behalf of the United States.*

It's one thing to convey a general attitude of disrespect. It's another thing to act on that attitude and treat people like they don't matter. Good leaders ensure all of their people are properly cared for and respected. Ambassador Rea Brazeal made this a priority for local staff (see Box 9.7).

■ *It's unfortunate that such things would happen in the world of diplomacy and that these practices might continue for years and years because nobody paid attention or cared. You need to be in a decisionmaking position to sometimes do the right thing and to change the way things are.*

Ambassador Brazeal's experiences are a reminder that leaders have a responsibility to question the status quo and to make changes as needed, both for the sake of the mission and because it's the right thing to do. In the context of supporting others, challenging the status

---

Box 9.7   Rea Brazeal: Taking Care of Local Staff in Kenya and Ethiopia

"In Kenya, in the 1990s, I don't know if I was the first ambassador to ever go down to the residence staff quarters, but I went down there. There was standing water. There were naked light bulbs hanging from the ceiling. There was an outhouse. So I came back up, and I said, 'Slavery ended a long time ago, and I'm not having this while I'm here.' So we arranged to rebuild the staff quarters. And I told them to put up a plaque with my name on it when it was finished, because I knew some white person would come along afterward and try to claim credit for it. My staff moved to the DCM residence and bused over every day while we rebuilt. I wasn't having that. Not on my watch.

"In Ethiopia, I was trying to get the Americans and Ethiopians to know each other a little better. The Ethiopians set up a sponsorship program where someone would volunteer to sponsor a new American officer or employee and show them around town—for example, show them where they could shop for certain things that they might be interested in. And it could be as long a relationship or as short a relationship as you wanted. That seemed to help a little bit. I tried to integrate the swimming pool. I wanted to allow Ethiopian employees to use the swimming pool, and Americans pushed back, I felt for racist reasons. That was going to be a harder nut to crack. And I ran out of time before I was able to push that through. But I did get Ethiopian employees invited to our Easter parties and other things at the embassy that they had not been included in before."

quo also means proactively supporting diversity. Ambassador Ruth A. Davis is very clear on this point: "It is incumbent on me as a leader to promote diversity. If I don't promote diversity, probably no one else around me will, and the status quo, which does not generally include a representative number of women and minorities, will remain acceptable" (Davis 2016). Especially as directors general, Ambassadors Ruth A. Davis and Ed Perkins took this responsibility very seriously. As we noted in Chapter 5, Ed Perkins wrote, "Women and minorities were not always given a good shot at assignments. . . . Sometimes I sat in on the meetings of the assignments panel, which surprised the panel members at first. I made it clear that they were there because as director general I had delegated that authority to them, and that I was reviewing that authority. I wanted to make sure that due process did indeed obtain" (Perkins 2006, 450–451).

■ *You have to be in the room to achieve diversity. If you're not in the room, the people in that room are going to go with the comfortable choice, unless they are compelled by law or the leader of the organization to direct them in a different way. It's not evil. It's not necessarily even racism. It's just the way human beings operate. The club remains the club.*

Ambassador Perkins worked decisively to support diversity on his team. He shared, "When I first became director general, my personal staff were all white. And I'm sure they were waiting to see what I was going to do. And I called everyone in and said, 'I do not intend to supervise a white-only staff here. So I'm going to bring in some other people, who represent the other kinds of people that we need to have on our staff.' I did that because I wanted to get the shock over with as soon as possible and not to do it in a gradual sort of way. Because people have to understand that life is not a bowl of cherries painted white. It's a bowl of cherries, some of which are black, some of which are half green, and so on."

These efforts are needed throughout the foreign policy arena, not just at the top of personnel administration. Every leader has an opportunity and a responsibility to support diversity on her team and in his organization or unit. Ambassadors Rea Brazeal and Johnnie Carson demonstrate in Box 9.8.

■ *These battles have to be continually fought. You have to keep pushing. First, you have to have the intake. Then you need to provide support and mentorship so that people have good career opportunities to grow and become successful. And then you've got to have people at the top who prioritize diversity and want to see people move forward. As leaders, today and tomorrow, this responsibility falls to us.*

Box 9.8   Rea Brazeal and Johnnie Carson:
Prioritizing Diversity

Rea Brazeal

"I often think I had the first all-woman embassy in Micronesia. I moved from one of the smallest embassies to one of the largest in Nairobi. I could see why a lot of white Americans got there and never wanted to leave because they had Black Africans working for them. They were in a position of being an expat and somewhat appreciated because they were American. I colorized the embassy intentionally. My political counselor was a Black woman. My economic counselor was a white woman. My consul general was a white woman. My refugee coordinator was a Black woman. My labor attaché was a Black man. It went on like that to the point that the Kenyans noticed and would thank me for changing it up a bit. I didn't realize until later that some of the American men would refer to the embassy as the hen house because there were so many women in positions of authority. But I could care less about that. I worked with other agencies to make sure they understood that I supported diversity.

"I found it relatively easy. Other American ambassadors would ask me how I did it. I said, 'It was fine. I put the word out, "I support diversity," and people apply. Isn't that amazing?' I said, 'The canard right now is that Black officers are mediocre. But I had a lot of mediocre white people work for me. So I don't find that a problem. People bloom at different times. So if you put the word out that you support diversity, people might apply. That works.'"

Johnnie Carson

"As soon as I came into AF [Africa Bureau] as assistant secretary, I populated as many places as I could. I feel pretty strongly about the level of minority, women, and Asian representation. I think we were probably the most diverse bureau there. People who did well, I pushed them forward for ambassadorial jobs. I also pushed the system on personnel issues as assistant secretary. I did it for a lot of reasons. We had capable people. And I wanted to short-cut others' efforts to muscle people into good African posts. We had forty-four missions and three or four consulates— a lot of places to fill. And all these people who were never going to get European assignments were being pushed to Africa. I also wanted to fill as many of the jobs as possible with people who had served in Africa, and done exemplary work there, and deserved to be promoted.

"If you wanted an ambassadorial job and wanted to be pushed forward to the D committee [which reviews candidates for senior positions],

continues

Box 9.8   Continued

I thought it was important that anyone the Africa Bureau put forward would have experience as a DCM or consul general or an office director, or some combination thereof, so you had proven experience. So I went to all of the D committee meetings when I was assistant secretary, because I felt obligated to step forward and say, 'These are my people. We've vetted them. They have great records. And they meet three criteria.' That's the pushback on the system. Anyone else should meet these criteria too. What I'm trying to do is open a door for good officers from the Africa Bureau. I feel very strongly about this. All of these people got ambassadorial jobs. I'm absolutely proud of that. They were all immensely qualified."

Creating the New

As this discussion so far confirms, leadership is about change: changing the status quo and setting new directions. Leadership is about creating new things to do and new ways of doing things. When she received the Distinguished Alumna Award from the University of Pittsburgh, Sundaa Bridgett-Jones spoke about transformational leaders, defining them as "people who deeply understand the world as it is, see the world as it could be, and work relentlessly to make it so." She quoted Maya Angelou: "Never, ever settle for normal. As Maya Angelou said, 'If you are always trying to be normal, you can never know how amazing you can be'" (Bridgett-Jones 2018). As General and Secretary Colin Powell put it, "Leadership is the art of accomplishing more than the science of management says is possible" (Powell 1995, 264). Leaders can do a lot of amazing things—working with others, of course.

If we think about Ambassador Brazeal's two types of officers on a continuum, custodians and activists, most leaders fall on the activist side. They question the status quo, propose new ideas and methods, and inspire others to help them make change happen. This is a tall order in bureaucracies that are more typically characterized as traditional and custodial. Every organization has its custodians, and they play an important role in ensuring continuity and stability and protecting values and traditions whose importance and worth others may not always understand at the outset. They can also make innovation more difficult.

Recall Bob Burgess's experience in his early years with GTE Sylvania (Box 6.11). He had to defy direct orders in order to put a more reasonable cost-accounting system in place given the context and size of his operation. He had complete confidence that he was right, based on his competence and experience, and he was able to easily demonstrate the effectiveness of his innovations. The headquarters staff were so impressed that they asked him to help put his system in place in other operations. ▶ This is what separates leaders from the pack. It's about being innovative and entrepreneurial. When you see a problem or an issue, identify it and make it better. And really push for your idea, even though you might get some pushback from the powers that be.

Sometimes you find you can't defy particular policies or traditions. But by finding common ground with others, you may be able to orchestrate a work-around. Ambassador Johnnie Carson did this for his HIV/AIDS prevention campaign in Kenya (see Box 9.9).

Box 9.9   Johnnie Carson: Finding a Work-Around to Do the Right Thing

"You would have been proud in Nairobi, if you came down Mombasa Road. Thanks to Coca-Cola and three CDC doctors I had previously worked with in Uganda, we had one of these giant AIDS awareness billboards. It was the largest HIV/AIDS poster in East Africa. And anyone driving down that road would say, 'In front of the United States embassy? A giant HIV/AIDS prevention poster?' I had that because I went to the Coca-Cola Company and asked them to put an HIV/AIDS prevention logo on the side of all of their trucks. The manager said, 'No. We can't do that. We have a strict policy about tacking on any social policy messages on our vehicles. If we put something like that on our vehicles, it would stigmatize more than it helps. But I see what you're getting at. AIDS is ravaging the community. Let's be helpful in other ways. Let's give you a billboard, and let us put this large poster on it, where you want it. It's all yours. We just can't put our name on it, but we'll pay for it and support it.' And that's what we did.

"People don't always reward that kind of stuff. And a lot of people don't engage in it. It's not just the politics. Any Foreign Service officer has to know as much about public health as they know about presidents, politics, and parliamentary procedures. They've got to know as much about climate change as they know about nuclear weapons. We live in a very dynamic time and place, and some have not been keeping up. Some have been missing the analytical changes and larger aspects of the world we live in. Diplomacy and leadership are about trying to advance a positive and effective agenda."

Sometimes that positive agenda is not technically in your scope of work. And yet, by virtue of your leadership position, you may have the ability to extend your authority and draw on your resources and expertise to meet a need consistent with the larger mission of an organization. As he shares in Box 9.10, Aaron had the opportunity to do that in support of one of the earliest Black pioneers and legends in US foreign policy, Ambassador Terence Todman.

**Box 9.10   Aaron Williams:
Stretching to Meet an Urgent Need**

"I had just been promoted to be the deputy assistant administrator for the Latin America Bureau and, of course, the first Black to ever hold that job. My first week on the job, there was an outbreak of bovine hemorrhagic fever in Argentina. Beef export is a significant portion of Argentina's economy. So I'm told, 'You have a call from Ambassador Todman in Buenos Aires.' I thought, 'That's strange. We don't have an AID program in Buenos Aires.' But I know who he is. In 1990, Ambassador Todman was the first Black American appointed as career ambassador, and was one of the State Department's most respected career diplomats. He had served as a US ambassador to six different countries in three regions of the world. So I said, 'It's an honor to speak to you, sir. I am a little puzzled as to what I can do to help you.' He said, 'We've got an outbreak of hemorrhagic animal fever here. I've called a lot of people in the State Department and the USDA. I can't get anybody to give me a straight answer. Can you help me?' He said, 'Even though I know you don't have a program here, you have access to resources in the American agricultural land-grant university system. See what you can do to find a team to come down here to help the Argentines deal with this right away, because this is a major issue for their industry.'

"I said, 'I don't know what AID can do in this space. I suspect not much, but I'm going to get you an answer. I'm going to find out exactly what needs to be done to help you work with the Argentinian government on this issue.' I said, 'I'm happy that I have a chance to work with you.' We identified experts at a major land-grant university and secured funding under an existing USAID program for this special assignment. We had to figure out how to get them there fast, so I thought, 'Let's request to use military aircraft out of Panama.' I thought, 'Ambassador Todman wants to get this thing done. This is important, and he's trying to take an unconventional approach to tap needed technical expertise.'

"And it worked. The team was there in forty-eight hours. I don't think it was the overall solution, but it contributed to solving their problem. That was one of my really proud moments in my career, first that I had a chance to connect with this amazing leader on a really important issue, and second that I was able to be responsive to him when other people let him down."

Both Ambassador Todman and Aaron understood that meeting the need and fulfilling the ultimate mission of helping Argentina's government should not be constrained by defined roles and responsibilities or organizational boundaries. And even as Aaron confronted custodians within the US military, he reached an activist leader who understood that too.

Ed Grier provides another example, in Box 9.11, of stepping beyond his formal duties to meet a greater need, this time to support Disney's partner in Japan.

Ed Grier's breakthrough came primarily because of his emphasis on relationships. His experience demonstrates that building relationships may take time, but that time is an investment that pays off over the long haul. Caring about others, responding to their needs, building trust—these are not often specified in job descriptions, but this is where the best leaders really excel.

Sometimes it is also necessary to take initiative in the absence of boundaries. Leaders do not wait to be told what is needed and what they should do about it. They listen, learn, and take action. That's what Ambassador Rea Brazeal did when she arrived at a post without any job description (see Box 9.12).

Box 9.11   Ed Grier: Innovating a Win-Win Solution

"I was warned before I left that there were some problems in our partnership in Japan. The Oriental Land Company owned and operated the parks and hotels using the Disney Brand. The Disney Company did not have an equity stake in Tokyo Disneyland. We took the royalties off the top, so the parks' profitability was not our primary concern. My primary responsibility, as the executive managing director of Walt Disney Attractions in Japan, was to the Disney brand. In fact, my predecessors felt their responsibilities ended there.

"We ended up having a breakthrough with them. My approach was, 'I'm here to help you to be more profitable.' And they were like, 'Why would you help us do that?' 'I'm your partner.' And so we ended up bringing a lot of Disney experts from around the globe to introduce Disney best practices to many facets of their organization. It became an amazing relationship. I built close working friendships with my Japanese counterparts. They would help me do things. And we would help them. Now it took some time to get there. They would invite you out to dinner, and that's when they would talk to you about real business. They would give you insights that you would never gain in the boardroom. And you couldn't say where you got those insights, but it came that way. This experience led me to my job in California as president, partly because I did so well there."

**Box 9.12   Rea Brazeal:
            Creating Her Own Job Description**

"My first assignment in Tokyo was to a new position in the economic section as a trade officer. Economic officers worked for both the commercial counselor and the economic counselor. I didn't have a job description. I asked my boss, and he wasn't very clear about what it could be. So I thought, 'Well, it wouldn't be very nice to go snatch some issue from the other officers that I would work with.' So I went around and talked to all of them and asked them, 'What issues did you think should be covered, but you never had time to do it?' In that way, I cobbled together issues that I thought could be in my portfolio that weren't covered and put together my own job description.

"I didn't believe that I should sit and do nothing. I didn't believe I should go and whine to my supervisors that they weren't telling me what to do. I figured I should find out how to be productive on my own. I enjoyed the challenge. Throughout my career, I have been asked to take several new positions and have enjoyed the creativity that comes from uncharted territory."

Followership

You may have the best ideas and the greatest technical expertise, but if no one follows you, these are not worth much. You are not a leader unless others follow you. And to be successful, you have to have followers in a variety of places: among your staff, your peers, and the leaders of your organization and also among external stakeholders, like funders, policymakers, and the leaders and people of the countries in which you serve. ■ *It's one thing to create a vision for your organization. It's another thing to make sure that you convince people and demonstrate that you are committed to that vision, and that is a day-to-day part of the job. That's not the exciting part, but that's what will allow you to execute a strategy that supports the vision.*

It should be clear by now that one of the first ingredients to inspire followers is to be authentic. That starts by sharing who you are as a person and inviting others to share with you. Earlier in this chapter, Ed Grier described this as part of his strategy to build a team. Ambassador Rea Brazeal put it this way: "You must have core beliefs and views that you share so that other members of your team feel compelled to follow you" (Brazeal 2007, 38). It also means being transparent about how and where you will lead. Ambassador Brazeal elaborated, "As an ambassador, you have to share your opinion on where you think the policy should go and what you think we should be doing. And you have to be able to explain it in a way to convince people to come on board, particularly your junior officers who have their own views of things and question a lot."

Dr. Helene Gayle shares her strategy for developing a followership in Box 9.13.

■ *People know when you are not really hearing them. They can tell when you're not respectful of what they think. But if you brought them into your counsel, you listened to them sincerely, and you valued their perspective, even if you make a decision that's contrary to what they would recommend, they will follow you.*

Paul Weisenfeld agrees. He puts it succinctly in Box 9.14.

■ *Beyond listening, Paul Weisenfeld reminds us that to be an effective leader, people have to know that you're a person of great integrity. For example, if you agree to do something, even when the higher-ups might override that and force you into a different position, they know it's not because you didn't follow through on your word based on what you laid out to them initially. And that happens. If you have listened, heard, and validated others' perspectives; if you understand what they care about and demonstrate you care about their professional development and fulfillment; even when things don't go as planned, they will be as loyal to you as you are to them.*

Box 9.13   Helene Gayle: To Get People to Follow You, Really Hear Them First

"You have to have a guiding philosophy. Why are you doing what you're doing? For me, that was always the motivator. I like people and enjoy working with people. I've generally been moved up managerial chains because I work well with people, teams, and I am willing to work as hard as I expect other people to work. So I think I'm good at bringing people along and listening. One of the biggest leadership skills is the ability to actually listen and hear what people are saying so that what you do is aligned with the people that you're working with. Often, hearing others is as important as what you do. It's an important part of being able to get something done. People will follow you if they feel like, 'That person listened to me. They actually heard me. And I feel validated.' Too often, people listen, but they don't hear."

**Box 9.14   Paul Weisenfeld:
The Higher You Go, the Less You Talk**

"The higher up you go, the less you should talk. It's a little bit over-stated, but it's true for a couple of reasons. First, if you're the senior person in the room and you set out your view, a lot of people will then say, 'Oh well, the boss has decided.' This is especially the case with overseas local staff. So they don't say anything, even though they may know more than you do about the issue. Second, good communication is as much about listening as it is about talking. You need to understand your audience, what's going to motivate them, what their interests are. This is something you focus on in a negotiation class, or in law school, the whole 'Getting to Yes' model. Do you really understand what they're scared of, what motivates them, what they're interested in? Are you tailoring what you say? People think good communication is all about talking. I think it's as much about listening. Well-functioning teams function because there's a lot of mutual loyalty. But you can't just ask people to be loyal to you. You have to operate in a way that generates trust, in a way that demonstrates to people you have their back and that you're trustworthy. That starts with listening."

Sundaa Bridgett-Jones had the privilege of watching a master of empathy in action. She was working in the Department of Political Affairs in the UN Secretariat when a devastating earthquake hit Kashmir (2005). She traveled with UN Secretary-General Kofi Annan to visit the region and mobilize support for recovery. She served as note taker in a series of meetings. She reported, "I was the proverbial fly on the wall, soaking in every word and gesture. I noted how in his interactions, the Secretary General embodied empathy. He made small jokes that put his counterparts at ease. He knew secret handshakes. And most importantly, he led with compassion; he listened more than he talked. This wasn't the kind of note I wrote down, but it has been on my mental notepad ever since" (Bridgett-Jones 2018).

When you have these skills and that kind of presence, you may be asked to take on the greatest challenges, the ones that can only be addressed when others believe in you personally, in your integrity, and in your good intentions. Dr. Jacob Gayle took on such a challenge. He shared, "I had a great opportunity when Nelson Mandela became president to be able to almost lead a public health revolution, getting all the old guard senior leaders of public health in South Africa to agree over one weekend that their resignations would be the greatest contribution they could make to South African history. Believe it or not, I gathered them all together on Friday night, and by Sunday afternoon I had everybody's resignations. How did I do that? We were all friends. It was because people believed in me. I had sponsors who said, 'You need someone to facilitate the impossible. We think Jacob Gayle can do this one.'"

Our giants emphasized listening a lot. Of course, communicating to others—whether verbally or in writing—is also an essential leadership skill. And you can't just trust that your written and spoken words will hit the mark or travel accurately. Ambassador Rea Brazeal shared that as ambassador in Kenya, she wrote her own speeches. "I would always have a text because the press was not always accurate, and I wanted them to have a hard copy. In addition, having a text meant we could disseminate what I had actually said to audiences and groups around the country who may not have been at the event. Eventually, I was in the media a lot: newspapers, weekly editorials, excoriated by the government newspaper, all kinds of things, during the time I was there. . . . This was a gauge of how our message was getting out and to which people" (Brazeal 2007, 90). Ambassador Brazeal also reminds us that not every stakeholder can be persuaded to be a follower. As a leader, you need to develop a thick skin and anticipate being severely criticized, especially in the local press, as some of our giants shared in Chapter 6.

Confidence and Humility

It's no wonder leadership is often characterized as more an art than a science. And an essential thread that crosses all of these elements—taking responsibility, building your team, creating the new, and developing a followership—is maintaining both confidence and humility. ■ *All of the giants exhibit an overall sense of confidence in who they are. They had to be very secure in themselves in order to be successful. And they also demonstrated humility about what they achieved. Despite their tremendous accomplishments, when we spoke with them, none of them voiced an attitude of "Because I'm brilliant, I was able to achieve this." All were very humble in talking about how they arrived at where they were.* Ambassador Ruth A. Davis described the attributes of successful diplomats, but they apply equally to leaders. She said, simply, that they "must have integrity, courage, and self-confidence, preferably laced with humility" (Davis 2016).

You cannot effectively take responsibility, and people will not follow you, if you are not confident. As our giants demonstrate, that confidence comes from you, and it also comes from the contributions of your team—their expertise, experience, and reliability. If you don't project confidence, your team and others will be less likely to want to follow you. When you are a leader, the world is watching. And as much as people may complain or disagree, in the end they want to know that someone is responsible, that someone will take charge and ensure we all get to where we need to go. It's a basic human need. It is the foundation for psychological safety. Confident leaders are especially crucial during crises, as we saw with C. D. Glin at the African Development Foundation (Box 9.3).

At the same time, effective leadership requires humility. You have to know when you've made a mistake and own it, as Paul Weisenfeld did (Box 9.2). You need to practice humility in order to connect with people. When we asked Alonzo Fulgham what skills he thought were necessary for a successful career in US foreign policy, he included being thoughtful and humble—"because arrogance never gets you where you want to go in this work." Sundaa Bridgett-Jones agreed: "Humility is so important. It allows us to relate to others in ways we could not otherwise." And humility allows you to recognize what you don't know or aren't good at, so you know what you need to learn, and so you can access what the work requires from other sources. Or, as Ed Grier put it, you have to "know your flat side" (see Box 9.15).

Box 9.15   Ed Grier:
Learning and Knowing Your Flat Side

"Everywhere I've been, I availed myself of people at different levels to find out what needs to happen. It's just learning. And I never stopped learning. I never pretend. If I don't know it, I don't try to pretend like I know it. It's okay to say you don't know. You can find out, and then you'll know what it is the next time. That's been very helpful. It can be tough when you get feedback. Sometimes it can be stinging. And if you don't get better from it, you'll just go backwards. We all think we're very smart, but I was told, 'We all have our flat sides.' So if you're not aware of them, you backtrack. So, I need other people to help me build my flat side, things I'm not as good at, to shore me up where I just won't excel. And it's not that I won't try, but some things, you just won't be able to do well, or as well as what the job requires."

■ *The irony that Ed Grier captures so well is that you have to be confident in order to be humble. The last thing in the world that you want is an insecure leader, somebody who won't admit they don't know something and refuses to bring in somebody who does.*

The higher you go up the ladder, the more humility becomes important. One great example is Ambassador James Joseph in South Africa. He was a master of servant leadership. He personifies that. As much as he has done, he is always humble and a great listener. Like him, we, Black leaders, especially, have to be good listeners and be willing at the same time to speak out when it's needed. Black Americans, and people of color in general, are often seen as being reluctant to speak out. We need both confidence and humility.

Success Is Not Always Possible

Another reason to be humble is knowing that success is not always possible. You can still do the right thing. You can still have great ideas and lead people in the right direction. You can still celebrate that you've done the good work. And you never know if the current setback will lead to future successes. Sometimes you learn the hard way that, regardless of what you may think about the work, success is in the eye of the beholder. In Box 9.16, Aaron provides an example of not being able to meet the objective, even after taking every initiative to do the right thing.

Box 9.16   Aaron Williams: Hitting the Wall on HIV/AIDS in South Africa

"When I was the USAID mission director in South Africa in the 1990s, it was widely recognized by the CDC, World Health Organization, and national public health officials that the rapid increase in HIV rates was becoming a public health disaster for that nation. As a part of US government support for the Mandela administration, we wanted to provide an estimated $30 million to the Department of Health with the goal of supporting the minister of health in what we anticipated would be the development of a national strategy to combat HIV/AIDS. So, we thought this was an outstanding idea that would be readily accepted by the South African government.

"However, the minister was opposed to working with the United States. It wasn't apparent at first, but after three iterations of presenting

continues

Box 9.16   Continued

a funding proposal to the minister, it became clear that she would not accept USAID assistance. She was anti-American, which you could understand, given President Reagan's policy of constructive engagement with the apartheid government. But she was also ignoring this very real threat to her nation. Further, we didn't know at the time that the deputy president, Thabo Mbeki, was supporting her stance.

"In order to illustrate our flexibility, I informed the minister that she could hire consultants from nearly everywhere in the world. We did not insist on solely American consultants. I said, 'Just let us help you do this.' This was also the era of the Gore-Mbeki bilateral commission that provided a forum for creative joint approaches to South Africa's major challenges, and I led the secretariat for those meetings. So I had to explain to Vice President Al Gore's staff a couple of times why we were making no headway on our special HIV/AIDS initiative.

"I think this was an obvious, major setback. It's interesting that no one within the US government considered that to be a failure on my part. I thought it was. I was fortunate that I worked for and with reasonable human beings. They understood what I was fighting with, what I was up against. She was an immovable object."

Leaders may direct, but they are not in control. Humility entails understanding and accepting that there are many factors beyond your control. Not being able to corral everyone is not necessarily a reflection of your leadership skill. You will work in contexts with a long, living history for those you would persuade. Even if you had no part in it, in US foreign policy, you are a party to it.

Leadership is so challenging because, among other reasons, leaders have to make decisions when there is no good answer. People often say that there are winners and losers with every decision. But what happens when there are losers in every option? How do you choose? Sometimes doing the right thing means you will knowingly do things that will make your own work more difficult. This was Philip Gary's experience in Nepal, as he describes in Box 9.17.

■ *What's striking about Philip's experience is that many of us have worked for horrible managers. Everybody knew he or she should not be in that position and was creating suffering for the subordinate staff. But they didn't say, "Let's change the bureaucratic structure because this person is a horrible manager or leader." You had to work through it. In the case of the deputy director in Nepal, they decide to bypass her. And so what Philip did was absolutely right and certainly consistent with the*

Box 9.17   Philip Gary: Doing the Right Thing and Paying for It

---

"I always tried to make things better for other Black folks in the agency by thinking about the system. The agency is extremely hierarchical. One of the ways you get promoted is by the number of people you supervise. That system is inherently more dangerous for people of color. One of the things I would do at any post was to try to flatten the management structure so that you didn't have this layering of supervisors. All of the staff would report to the deputy director or the director. So all of the officers had access to the front office and to programs. By flattening management, you could get people into skill areas and participating in programs in ways they had not. For instance, the controllers in AID usually deal with budget and stuff. They generally are not involved in the program side of the agency. The same thing is true with the general service officers, who do a lot of the leasing and travel work. Disproportionally, it seemed to me, minorities were represented in those fields.

"When I went to Nepal, it was a mission in hostility. It had a lot of senior office directors. The deputy director was a Black woman. The office directors were hostile to her. They couldn't get along with her. My predecessor had allowed the office directors to report directly to him. He had basically sidelined her. I had talked to my predecessor and other people, and I'd been told, 'She has a very difficult personality.' I had been advised to keep the structure as it was and work with these office directors so that everybody could be happy.

"I gave it a lot of thought. And the first thing I did was revert to the traditional AID structure and said, 'Every office director reports to the deputy director. The deputy director reports to me.' Predictably, it didn't go well. I believe that anything you do causes a reaction and that sometimes causing the right reaction is more important than the moment. And I believed that it was absolutely essential, especially as a Black mission director, that I send the message that we weren't going to play this game. This Black woman had earned the right to be there, and I wasn't going to allow her to be sidelined.

"I think that was a good decision because of the statement it made to the agency. I knew, for me, it was going to be a bad decision. It led to other confrontations with the officers. The combination of that and the confrontations I had with the ambassador made it, for me, a great failure."

---

way AID operated. As a leader, he also demonstrated a sophisticated understanding of how the system operated and how it put people of color at a disadvantage. He was proactive about challenging that system whenever he had the authority to do so.

Sometimes that brutal kiss of failure can lead to better opportunities (as we saw with Ambassador Ertharin Cousin in Box 5.9). And, while you may not recognize it at the time, it may lead you to future successes. Ambassador Johnnie Carson experienced great success regarding HIV/AIDS prevention programs in Kenya (see Box 6.12), and his work there eventually changed US government policy worldwide. But his initial efforts were not successful, as he describes in Box 9.18.

Ambassador Johnnie Carson later risked his career to implement in Kenya the very recommendations that had already been rejected by senior officials in the Department. This early experience convinced him that the US government was simply using the wrong criteria and made him more determined than ever to make sure the government eventually did the right thing. When he had the opportunity to exercise authority as a leader, he took it.

The definition of success is often subjective. Philip Gary failed in some respects, since the work was made more difficult and his tenure in Nepal was cut short, but from his own perspective, he did the right thing. That is not a failure. Ambassador Johnnie Carson similarly tried to do the right thing on HIV/AIDS. He initially failed. When he later succeeded, through

---

Box 9.18   Johnnie Carson: When Arguing for the Right Thing Is Not Enough

"I had been ambassador to Uganda from 1991 to 1994, and I saw how HIV/AIDS was ravaging the country. And then I was ambassador to Zimbabwe, where we watched people die in large numbers. I came back to Washington as deputy assistant secretary for African Affairs, and I told the assistant secretary, Susan Rice, 'We need to do something. Africa has a major issue with HIV/AIDS. We should do something to help. We should recommend that the department set up testing and counseling programs for its local employees and provide them with some antiretroviral drugs. And if we are using HIV/AIDS as a reason to disqualify people for employment in our embassies, we should stop it. Because it's against federal law in the United States, and it should be against the law overseas when we are selecting employees.'

"So, we sent forward a memo to the undersecretary for management and administration, and they said, 'Thank you. No thank you.' And, quietly, 'Hell no. Don't bring this back to us again.' They were using business criteria to turn down this proposal: 'First, we don't know how many employees or people might have HIV/AIDS, and therefore we don't know how much money would be involved in this. Second, there could be some regulatory issues. And third, if we do this in Africa, we would probably have to do it globally for local employees and potential hires in every other bureau.' It never got far inside the State Department."

his work in Kenya, others might have perceived what he was doing as a total disaster—initially. Now, no one would argue against it. When you are flying high from success on your own metrics and others only see failure, it can be hard to swallow. That happened to Sundaa Bridgett-Jones at the Rockefeller Foundation. She tells the story in Box 9.19.

■ *When you know that you did something that was extraordinary, but it wasn't good enough for your boss in his or her perspective, that's tough. And it happens.*

It's ironic that Sundaa Bridgett-Jones's "failure" was for a program on resilience. While she shared that it hurt, she focused on how she grew from the experience and what she learned—for example, in terms of building partnerships—which she can take into her future work. It is precisely these tough moments that remind us of the importance of our personal resilience and help us to build it. Sundaa Bridgett-Jones later concluded,

---

Box 9.19   Sundaa Bridgett-Jones: Perceived Failure

"When I joined the Rockefeller Foundation, the president started working on the notion of resilience. She was thinking about 'What does resilience look like in communities?' We were off and running. She demanded a lot. And she had a big idea that she wanted to partner with USAID on a resilience project. She wanted us to explore the whole notion of how to use resilience as a concept to bridge long-term development and humanitarian assistance. I was one of the few at the foundation with an international background. She asked me to take the lead on developing what became the Global Resilience Partnership. It was a long, iterative process to get to create this partnership with USAID. We leveraged $50 million from the Rockefeller Foundation. We had a $160 million effort to bridge the gap between humanitarian assistance and long-term development in parts of Asia and Africa.

"After a year or so it had failed in the eyes of the Rockefeller Foundation because it did not produce the kinds of solutions in a very short period that we were looking for. So, therefore, it was a failure for me—even though it continues; even though USAID, the Swedish International Development Agency, and [the UK Department for International Development (now the Foreign, Commonwealth & Development Office)] continue to work on it. But in the eyes of the foundation, this is not what we wanted to invest our dollars in. Just before Raj Shah's start at the foundation, the current president asked me to close out the foundation's share. I think we were at the two-year mark. I really learned that no matter how hard one works and how much effort they put in—the fact that I helped to raise over $110 million to leverage this with some very serious partners—it can still be deemed as a failure at the foundation."

"One thing I know for sure: leaders are not born. They are constantly learning, questioning, and challenging themselves. Leadership—especially transformational leadership—is something we must commit to every . . . single . . . day" (Bridgett-Jones 2018).

Resilience

As we discussed in Chapters 6 to 8, resilience is essential to your success in US foreign policy, particularly as a leader. And it derives in large part from your Black identity and personal experiences. Philip Gary shared, "I was active in a lot of what is now thought of as the civil rights movement, the revolutionary movement. I was in the Student Nonviolent Coordinating Committee (SNCC). The kinds of societal hostilities that I dealt with—being very, very young, as a teenager, and in my early twenties—I think these experiences steeled me a lot for dealing with some of the challenges that came later. And so, the community that I came from really prepared me for just about every challenge that came later." In their generation, many of our giants took inspiration and learned resilience from the civil rights movement of their time.

You now have your own experiences to draw from, including activism through Black Lives Matter. We have experienced our first Black president and have recently embraced our first Black woman vice president. The struggle is not over, and it happens on many fronts. As you encounter the frustrations of not succeeding in efforts you lead—even when you are doing the right thing and have done everything right—the giants remind you to recognize that these moments are inevitable, they do not necessarily reflect your capacity and worth, and they may give you the resilience to succeed in the future.

Cecilia Muñoz reminds us of how long change can take. She admonishes us to find joy in the work and to learn to love the journey. As she puts it, "We want to be the wave that carries the issue to victory, but what if we are the early ripples instead? We live in a society where we get to try, and the very act of trying is an expression of faith that things can be different. Win or lose, there's joy in trying and in creating the ripple that we believe will one day become the wave that changes everything" (Muñoz 2020, 142).

Every ripple counts. What's important is that you leave your mark. As Ambassador Johnnie Carson said, "I do not want to be the person walking across the wet sand and not leaving any footprints behind. And all too many people have done that."

10

The Gift and the Charge

I learned that courage was not the absence of fear, but the triumph over it. The brave man is not he who does not feel afraid, but he who conquers that fear.

—Nelson Mandela

There are still many causes worth sacrificing for, so much history yet to be made.

—Michelle Obama

All of the giants were eager to participate in this project. They have been supporting others throughout their careers. They talked about promoting people coming behind them, lowering the ladder, as Ron Brown used to say. This book was another opportunity to do that and, hopefully, to reach more people. This chapter is their final gift to you—and an expression of their expectations for what you will do next, now that you have heard their stories and listened to their advice. We offer our overview of the elements of success for a career in US foreign policy. And we present the giants' charge to you. We close with Aaron's passing of the torch to Taylor, who passes it to you.

Elements of Success

This book shares many lessons, gems of wisdom, and inspirational stories derived from experience. Some of the giants and their particular experiences may resonate more for you than others. Any summary cannot possibly do justice to the rich and nuanced contents of the previous chapters. Nonetheless, we distill here four broad areas we call the elements of success: putting in the work, being a risk taker, connecting with others, and developing resilience. We state each of these in the form of a verb. These are not checkboxes. Sustained success requires constant vigilance and action, along with practice and openness to continuing growth.

Put in the Work

■ *You have to commit to doing the work. As you move your way up the ladder, you have to be seen as an expert and as someone who can deliver for the organization, because there are a lot of other people to choose for committees, task forces, special projects, the next assignment, the promotion, and so forth. You have to stand out in the face of anticipated skepticism, because when you walk into the room, immediately, a certain instant analysis occurs. You have to confront that and be prepared to excel on a consistent basis. That's our challenge in America. We're hoping to build a country where it will not be that way, but we are just not there yet.* Ambassador Ruth A. Davis admonishes, "What you can achieve is almost limitless. First, however, you must devise a plan, and you must be willing to work unceasingly. It's not glamour and good times; rather it's blood, sweat, and tears—that's the stuff success is made of" (Davis 1996, 15).

Aside from sweat equity—the time and effort expended—putting in the work includes building knowledge and expertise at three levels: (1) being an expert at what you do—the particular position, sector, and region in which you work; (2) knowing the system, both the organization you work in and its relationship to external stakeholders, in the United States and in the countries where you work; and (3) knowing your own country, informing your comparative understandings of the way things are done in other countries, and enriching your relationships with foreign partners and citizens.

Be an expert at what you do. Ambassador Johnnie Carson demonstrates what it means to be an expert in your particular portfolio. He was adamant about hard work as the ticket to opportunity, no matter your background. We summarize three of his points in Box 10.1.

Box 10.1   Johnnie Carson on Expertise and Hard Work

"I always felt that it was my job to know more about Africa and what was happening in Africa in any room that I walked into in the State Department. Somebody might know more about HIV/AIDS or maybe a particular economic issue, but it was my job to know more about every country on the continent, all forty-nine of them, in greater depth, greater analytic understanding, and greater policy focus than anybody."

"I've never had imposter syndrome. What I have felt is the impact of being the only Black person in the room, where there are twenty or twenty-five others. I've felt outnumbered, but I haven't felt as though I've not belonged there."

"I am as far away from an elite background and a privileged upbringing as you can get. But I firmly believe that while opportunity may be limited, talent is more broadly and equally distributed. If you work hard, if you have a real determination to succeed, and if you take what you do seriously and you apply all of your energy to it, then you can be successful."

Ambassador Sylvia Stanfield demonstrates expertise of another sort: a skill with a challenging language, which opens the door to both greater cultural understandings and opportunities.

■ *To achieve that level of expertise, you have to work hard. There is no substitution for hard work. There is no magic. There is no mentor who can magically make it happen. There is no shortcut.*

Know the system. Knowing how the system operates is essential to your career trajectory, successfully executing your purpose/task, and understanding how you can best support others and contribute to more sustainable solutions. Ambassador Rea Brazeal used her understanding of the State Department system to explore and prepare for different career options (Chapter 5). She negotiated a leave without pay, pursued further training and development at Harvard University, and made sure she had a position to land in when she returned to the State Department if she decided to do so (she did). She said, "If you don't learn the system you're in, you don't know how to go around it or over it, under it or whatever. I've met many Foreign Service officers, Black and white and other, who somehow always felt like they were being acted upon. You have to know about the system you're in, so you can have some maneuverability."

Dr. Jacob Gayle needed to gain an understanding of politics and policymaking to maximize his impact on global public health. He shared, "Being in Washington gave me a better understanding of the mechanics of the central leadership of our government and how it all comes together, both foreign and domestic policies and action. Many of us naively go into public health focused only on how we want to keep people healthy. I learned that health was much more of a political entity than I realized. You have to understand the political and bureaucratic aspects too." ■ *When you think about HIV/AIDS, malaria, and now the Covid-19 pandemic, I don't care how well-intentioned you are or how much you're focused on the health improvement outcomes, you cannot win if you don't understand the political battle and how to win that battle. This is how you will secure the resources and support you need. The same is true for areas beyond global public health.*

Knowing how the system works is the only way to understand how you can best support others. Philip Gary exemplified this beautifully in his understanding of organizational hierarchy and promotion incentives (Box 9.17). He used that knowledge to ensure that everyone had an opportunity to connect to senior officials, develop relevant project skills and experience, and not be sidelined unfairly. As directors general, Ed Perkins, Ruth A. Davis, Harry K. Thomas Jr., and Linda Thomas-Greenfield all used their position and system understanding to promote diversity within the State Department. This included Ed Perkins sitting in on and supervising meetings to send a strong message—and incentive—that he expected fairness and equal opportunity for all. Ambassadors Johnny Young and Sylvia Stanfield learned more about the State Department by serving in the Inspector General's Office; Dr. Katherine Lee did so by serving as a career counselor and chief of the US Information Agency's Career Development and Training Division.

Part of knowing the system is understanding its people dynamics. Several of the giants mentioned the importance of "corridor reputation"—what people are thinking and saying about you in the halls of the workplace. Your corridor reputation is something you need to develop proactively and protect vigilantly. Ambassador Sylvia Stanfield advised, "Continue to meet people. Be open to work with your colleagues. Make sure you're listening to what's going on and seize opportunities." In other words, be proactive, analytic, and positive. Ambassador Ertharin Cousin advised that protecting your corridor reputation requires "the ability to prioritize and understand what's important and what's not. This is part of knowing the value add that you bring, that you are someone who can help the team stay on task and on mission. Too often will you see people driving an issue that may be interesting, but not relevant. There is nothing more annoying. This may be your pet thing, but it's not important to what we need to achieve today." Make sure you are seen as someone who supports the mission and supports others to do so.

Know your own country. Ambassador Brazeal had the good fortune of participating in (and later leading) the State Department's Senior Seminar. She reported, "Career Foreign Service Officers by and large spend large blocks of their professional life outside of their own country. A purpose of the seminar was to re-familiarize senior officers . . . about their own country. If you don't know what's happening in your own country outside of Washington, it's very difficult to represent it in a way that's going to impact at policy levels. You need to understand how foreign and domestic policy intersect" (Brazeal 2007, 100). In Chapter 1, the giants talked about how service overseas and service at home in the United States inform each other. To be effective in both places, you have to know our own history. Chris Richardson calls on you to "explain America in a realistic way."

Be a Risk Taker

■ *You have to be a risk taker. Many of us are taught that in order to be successful in America, you have to minimize and avoid risk. But to be successful in US foreign policy, you have to become a risk taker.* Ambassador Ed Perkins wrote that Foreign Service officers, among other things, have to be daring. "They must be not only unafraid of change, but welcoming of it. As noted theologian Presiding Bishop John Hines once said, 'You either seize change by the hand, or it will seize you by the throat'" (Perkins 2006, 167). You will need courage to know when to fight the good fight (Chapter 6), and you will need to take risks to do the right thing (Chapter 9). As we discussed in Chapter 5, especially at the beginning of your career, you have to be willing to take assignments that either are inherently dangerous or have seemingly little reward—the ones that no one else wants but will make you stand out. And as leaders (Chapter 9), you will need to envision change and have confidence and faith that your skills and relationships will enable you to persuade others to follow you.

Dr. Jacob Gayle shared three things that helped him "to be able to go into cultures or languages that were unfamiliar to me, and into bureaucracies and organizations that sometimes were not only unfamiliar, but in some cases almost threatening; and that enabled me to maintain my integrity and individualism and yet still contribute." These are the things that helped him to avoid imposter syndrome (Chapter 3) and bring his whole identity to the work with confidence (Chapter 8): "Number one, I had been told by my parents, both of them amazing social activists in their own right, that we can accomplish anything that we put our minds to. Second, we belong anywhere God plants our feet. And the third that I think is really, really important is that we have to think for ourselves."

Connect with Others

Connecting with others is multifaceted and essential to every element of your career. It encompasses cultivating networks of support, building teams, managing up and out, and developing strong communication skills.

As we discussed in Chapters 4 and 7, you need to develop a cadre, a network, of people both inside and outside your organization who can help you in terms of your career goals but also serve as a sounding board and a source of wisdom and inspiration to you as you move forward. You need to develop and support people to serve on your teams (Chapter 9). And you need to learn to connect with and manage your superiors both inside and outside your organizational unit. For example, Verone Bernard succeeded in defusing an ugly situation in the field by appealing to her superiors and having a response plan ready (Box 6.8); Ambassador Rea Brazeal was a master at managing up, sometimes coordinating with friendly colleagues in other agencies (Box 8.10). Building rapport and relationships with people in the countries where you serve is also essential to understanding not just the local culture but also how things work and what is going on. Ed Grier learned more from his Japanese colleagues over dinner than he ever did in a boardroom (Box 9.11). Ambassador Linda Thomas-Greenfield knew the schedules of a country's leadership before the ambassador did because she became friends with his second wife (Chapter 8).

The giants developed, sustained, and called on these relationships strategically. Most of the time, they were just nice to people. Alonzo Fulgham stressed, "You have to make people in positions of power comfortable with you as a person they can trust. I know that's not fair, and it's probably not right. But you have to continually put yourself in a position to compete." He added that making other people feel comfortable with you also applies to Foreign Service nationals, foreign ministers of state, and secretaries general in those countries, and so on. "If you don't have that skill set, you're not going to be very successful representing our country. You're not going to get very much from counterparts as well. Yes, there will be an *a* and *b* conversation. But not *c*, *d*, and *e*. You won't get invited to their houses. You won't get invited to parties and weddings, and so forth."

Before he even became a Foreign Service officer, Ed Perkins became known as a "polite marine." He stood guard at the front gate and was "extraordinarily nice" and "paid attention to people." It led to early promotions. He wrote, "It taught me these lessons: people want to be noticed; it does not cost anything to say nice things; people will reciprocate" (Perkins 2006, 118). Ambassador Linda Thomas-Greenfield developed a similar reputation when she served as gatekeeper to then director general Ed Perkins. Ambassadors vying for time with the director general later told her, "You were always so nice." With that same niceness, as assistant secretary for Africa, she came to know African leaders across the continent. She shared, "I want 'She was nice' on my gravestone. That defines how I approach my leadership." Paul Weisenfeld recalled an important lesson Aaron taught him: "As you move up, do favors for anyone who asks you. Don't give it a second thought. Reach out; help whoever asks you. You'll find this to be rewarding throughout your life."

Good communications skills are necessary to every endeavor in life. They are particularly important in US foreign policy careers, where you will be communicating across a broad range of cultures and stakeholders. And you need skills that encompass every form of communication. Ambassador Ertharin Cousin explained, "You need the ability to communicate, both orally and in writing. Written communication style encompasses the language and tone of everything from your emails to official reports. Neither your written nor your verbal communication style should detrimentally impact the messages and substantive information that you seek to deliver."

Good writing skills are so imperative that writing can become intimidating. Ambassador Linda Thomas-Greenfield admitted, "I lacked confidence about my writing skills. And if you lack confidence, you're afraid to write. I would write, and every time I'd get a red mark on a paper, I would cringe. It's one of the most important skills you need. I had it. I just didn't know that I had it." She finally realized she had these skills when a cable she wrote while serving in Pakistan was nominated for a reporting award.

Exceptional writing skills make you stand out. Paul Weisenfeld had good training as a lawyer. When he wrote an email explaining some complicated issues, the deputy assistant administrator for Africa picked up the phone to tell him, "When I opened this email, I thought I really don't want to read this because this issue is hairy and complicated. And then your email just crystallized what the issue was in concise terms where I got it and I understood what the options were, and I can make a decision to move on." He explained, "Being able to concisely communicate complex issues for decision makers and lay out options separates folks. And then as you get higher up yourself, your oral skills are important too. When we hire people, I think about, Can you send someone to a meeting with a minister without worrying about it?" Ambassador Ruth A. Davis summarizes the point: "In the Foreign Service, we need excellent communicators, both orally and on paper. Good writers are in great demand. The ability to express oneself well is a capital asset that a Foreign Service officer must have" (Davis 2004).

Communication skills also encompass speaking a foreign language. Many of our giants emphasized how important it is to speak not only a second language but even a third or a fourth. Dr. Katherine Lee and Ambassador Sylvia Stanfield were attracted to Foreign Service careers precisely because of their love of language (Box 2.3). Recall that Ambassador Harry K. Thomas Jr. intentionally sought out a hard language in order to differentiate himself. He chose Hindi (Chapter 5). Ambassador Ed Perkins's Foreign Service languages were Japanese, French, and Thai. He reported that he "fell in love with the Thai language. Languages are fascinating puzzles to me: once I find the key, a new culture springs open. Some people think I have an affinity for languages, but I have to study hard to learn them" (Perkins 2006, 143). Of course, learning other languages is hard work. The Foreign Service supports that training.

Speaking other languages is essential not just for the transactions that inform everyday work and diplomacy. It is the key to understanding other cultures. Philip Gary shares his experience in Box 10.2.

Ambassador Harriet Elam-Thomas summarized the point by citing Nelson Mandela: "If you talk to a man in a language he understands, that goes to his head. If you talk to him in his language, that goes to his heart" (quoted in Elam-Thomas 2017, 83).

Be Resilient

▶ Being resilient is important in every industry, but especially in this one because being Black in this field is not easy. You're going to come against things at every turn, especially as you become more successful, as you're getting noticed more and appreciated for the things that you're doing in whatever organization that you're a part of. Resilience is so important to not forgetting your purpose and your mission. You have to have discernment about whether something is truly impacting who you are as a person to your core to the point that you just cannot go on, or it is temporary. To meet the purpose, you have to stay the

**Box 10.2   Philip Gary: To Understand,
You Have to Speak the Language**

"Having foreign languages allows you to connect with people in ways we may not otherwise. If you only spoke English, you could get by in whatever capital city you were assigned to. AID didn't teach regional languages. So, unless you were in a Spanish- or French-speaking post, you didn't get languages work. All of my previous posts had been English speaking. I joined an Arabic class, and after six months of Arabic training, I landed at Sana'a airport. The first thing that strikes you is there isn't a single sign in the airport in English. Some of the ministers spoke English. But if you didn't speak Arabic, you were in deep trouble. So my Arabic got much better, much quicker, and I really had to work at it.

"Arabic language is very much tied to Islamic culture. You have to understand the culture to learn the language. Once I learned the culture, I was really disappointed in what I had not known in all of those other places, by not having known the local language—how much I obviously had missed that I didn't even know I had missed. In Yemen, I was truly, for the first time, completely inside the culture of the country I was dealing with. That gave me an opportunity to genuinely understand the perspective the Yemenis had on the region, on development, on a whole host of issues. I became aware of how little I had understood and what a mediocre developmentalist I had been. Previously, I was doing development work from the US perspective, allegedly from the country's perspective. But that country's perspective was informed by the English-speaking folks in that country who were elite."

course, push through, and fight. As the giants shared, you don't get the instant gratification that you may get from a lot of other fields. You're not going to get your roses automatically. Your roses will come. And when they do, it will be well worth the wait.

■ *That's exactly right. Being resilient is important, having that grit to ride out the tide. We all know that everybody has failures and disappointments in their career. You have to just know that this is not the end. You're going to get through this, you'll get over it, and you'll be able to move on. You just have to be resilient.*

Resilience requires faith, confidence, determination, and stubbornness. Ambassador Ed Perkins shared, "I'm certain that I could come up with excuses for why I could not succeed in certain things. I decided that I would never ever look for excuses, that I would always look for a path to overcome it." Ed Grier stated simply, "No matter where your beginnings, you can find a path. Don't give up."

Ambassador Linda Thomas-Greenfield spoke eloquently about the power of adversity and resilience in her TED Talk (2018): "I didn't have successful educated role models in my life. But what I did have: I had the hopes and the dreams of my mother, who taught me at a very early age that I could face any challenge or adversity put in my path by being compassionate and being kind; that I could conquer the world. . . . Adversity is a source of strength. Every single time you're tested, you flex your adversity muscles, and you grow stronger. But you also have to add a measure of kindness, and a measure of compassion with that as well. And a smile. And so, anytime you face some challenges in your life, you just pull out those muscles. And you remember how you dealt with it in the past. And you move forward. That is the legacy that I want to leave to my children, to my grandchildren, and to your children. That's the legacy that I inherited from my mother."

The Charge

The giants we interviewed have made a big investment in you. We asked them to step out of their comfort zones to share personal stories and experience, some of which were painful and they might rather forget. They are not accustomed to talking about such things. For many, in their generation, that just isn't done. Typically, near the end of one's career and in retirement, one focuses on the achievements. It's time to enjoy the roses. They held their breath and pushed themselves to look back on the less glamorous times. They made themselves vulnerable. They did these things for you. Because they believe in you.

Now it's time for you to take up their charge, continue the collective race, and run your own race to places farther and higher than they reached or maybe even aspired to. The women who wrote *For Colored Girls Who Have Considered Politics* shared an amusing but relevant story about civil rights leader Amelia Boynton Robinson, who is considered the matriarch of the voting rights movement. When then attorney general Eric Holder met the 103-year-old Robinson, he said to her, "I'm so glad to meet you. We all stand on your shoulders." She replied, "with a slightly wicked smile, 'Get off my shoulders! Get off and go do something'" (Brazile et al. 2018, 235).

As you read the giants' charge, keep in mind that they did not start out with this wisdom. They honed it through their direct experience and learning and through relationships with and support from many others. At the same time they worked hard, they also maintained personal lives, families, and, as Philip Gary emphasized, humor. You will need to do that too. The giants want to see you succeed. Not surprisingly, then, their charge starts with the assumption that you will pursue excellence, which means continuously cultivating the four elements of success described above. Beyond that, they have an eight-point charge for you. After a brief introduction, we present each point in their own words.

Represent Your Whole American Self

US foreign policy serves and represents the United States. You are American, you have something unique to offer, and it will be valued.

• "You are as American as anyone else who possesses a passport, having been born here, naturalized, however. You can be anywhere, stand shoulder to shoulder with anyone, and demand your right in that space" (Victoria Cooper).
• "China, Russia, Europe, Africa, and Latin America, all places, are going to need constant engagement, and they're going to need diversity to help them navigate their relations with the United States for their future. You, young African Americans, people of color, need to understand that you have something to offer" (Alonzo Fulgham).
• "You are a part of the larger world, and you need to be engaged" (James Joseph).

Work for the Public Good

US foreign policy, by definition, is a realm of public service. From the beginning, this book and our giants intended to support you not only as an individual for your career success but also so that you could continue to make and expand opportunities for others. James Joseph took inspiration from words Martin Luther King Jr. spoke, in 1961, to the movement he was a part of in Tuscaloosa, Alabama: "He called on us to help transform both individuals and society" (Joseph 2015, 267). You need to remember where you come from and make good on your history. You need to see yourself as a part of something larger and take inspiration from that. The giants are passing the torch to you.

• "Never forget where you come from and give back to those communities" (Lauri Fitz-Pegado).
• "Lift as you climb, be great ambassadors, and don't ever forget that you stand taller because you stand on the shoulders of those who went

before you. And so you owe it to those who went before you, who sacrificed, who were lynched, who bled and died and who were afraid. You owe it to them to exercise your God-given abilities, to vote, to advocate, and to be a champion for others. See yourself as something greater than yourself. If you lose sight of that, you will die from it" (Barrye Price).

• "If you've decided to pursue a career in this field, in this industry, always remember that the work is so much bigger than you. Let that motivate you. Let that humble you. And let that inspire you" (Verone Bernard).

• "This is your moment. A lot of attention is given to our movement in the 1960s, but those were different times. We accomplished a lot, and we left a lot undone. This is your opportunity to complete the American Revolution" (James Joseph, *Sarasota Magazine*).

Support Those Who Come Behind You

Part of working for a public good means helping those who come behind you and, more generally, opening the space and fighting for diversity in every context in which you work. As Toni Morrison said, "When you get these jobs that you have been so brilliantly trained for, just remember that your real job is that if you are free, you need to free somebody else. If you have some power, then your job is to empower somebody else. This is not just a grab-bag candy game" (Morrison 2003). The authors of *For Colored Girls Who Have Considered Politics* call this the Bank of Justice, "a concept built on a promise: once you get to a position of influence, you pay it forward" (Brazile et al. 2019, 133). You need to lay the groundwork for others, advocate forcefully, care for one another despite competition, and actively and personally support those who ask for your help.

• "When I was ambassador, the Chinese ambassador said something once to me: 'We have this saying in China. We plant the trees, others enjoy the shade.' I am keenly aware of the history, both my own family history and societal history, that brought me to this point. And I am therefore also keenly aware of my responsibilities to help plant trees for the shade of others going forward" (Reuben Brigety).

• "My father told me when I was a kid, 'When you grow up, if you find when you look to your left and to your right that you don't see anybody who looks like you, it's not because you're so special. It's because they may not have had the opportunities you have.' He said, 'You advocate. And don't just crack the door. Take the door off the damn hinges'" (Barrye Price).

• "Rather than crabs in a barrel, you need to take a different approach and say, 'Listen, I've fought tooth and nail to get here, and I've probably gone as far as I can go. But my job now is to make sure that the next generation behind me can go even further" (Dominique Harris).

• "We always have to be mentors to each other and to look after one another in competitive environments. You have to be able to say, 'I am competing, but not to the point where I'm going to look down on, or destroy, or not stand up for my fellow [B]lack officer'" (Chris Richardson).

• "Give the gift of time. Share time with people who reach out to you, particularly for African Americans who are interested in this space. Hear their impressions and thoughts" (Sundaa Bridgett-Jones).

• "Help others think things through and give them a person to connect with to help them more. We need our Green Book for these careers" (Victoria Cooper).

Welcome the Support of Others

Don't expect that you always have to play it tough and go it alone on this path. It would be impossible to get anywhere that way. All of our giants benefited from the support they received from others. There is a Bank of Justice waiting for you. And you need to be worthy of their support by heeding the charge.

• "There are people like me who are sitting in places looking for people like you. You are wanted. There are people who literally have it as part of their personal development goals to bring more people like you along. We are putting down the ladder as we're climbing. We know that we want people, not underneath us, but beside us. We're looking for that next generation to join us as we rise" (C. D. Glin).

• "Recognize that most people don't get to where they've gotten without some support and kindness on the part of others. You should always be worthy of that support" (Johnnie Carson).

Be Humble and Flexible

Even as you work hard to become an expert in your chosen area, you need to remain humble and flexible, recognizing that you don't know everything. And even if you did, you couldn't control all of the moving parts. This work happens through relationships, and relationships require humility and flexibility. These traits also enable you to be more empathetic, to learn and understand more, to appreciate and enjoy difference, and to be more patient and accepting of diversity.

• "Be humble, because arrogance never gets you where you want to be" (Alonzo Fulgham).

• "Hubris can get many of us in a lot of trouble. We're in a business where we are more often than not proposing to be supportive of people deemed to be vulnerable or marginalized or in situations where they might need to have some support. The idea that anyone can come in and immediately understand what the issues are, can analyze the problems and offer solutions, without understanding the issues. . . . You have to listen and engage, from the time of problem definition to coming up with solutions" (Sundaa Bridgett-Jones).

• "Observation taught me that there are many ways to do the same thing and that it isn't only our American way that's the best or the fastest, or even the correct way; there are many ways that people do the same thing. And it also taught me that people are operating off of the same emotions, but their culture makes them express those same emotions in different ways. . . . [A] closed mind is a dangerous thing" (Brazeal 2007, 30).

• "When you go overseas, don't think about, 'Well this isn't like New Jersey. This isn't like home.' You have to take it for what it is. Enjoy what you like about it; ignore what you don't" (Bob Burgess).

Be a Forever Learner

The world is dynamic. You will be working in an ever-changing environment. You don't just need to understand the substance of a situation. You need also to have the analytic frameworks, including history, to size up that situation and understand the options, the pros and cons. That means taking advantage of the many sources of learning available to you, understanding that every situation is different and there is no singular road map, keeping an open and curious mind, and always assuming there is more to learn.

• "We need you to be intellectually, interpersonally, and substantively prepared to take on roles of leadership" (Ruth A. Davis).

• "Make sure that libraries are friends. Almost everything that you would want to do, there's some reference somewhere to that. My grandmother would say, 'Don't forget. The answer is in yourself. The books provide the railroad, but you are the one that has got to travel it'" (Ed Perkins).

• "Remain curious. I am cynical of development and its effectiveness, but I have been able to see firsthand how the work that we do really does transform lives. Don't believe everything you think. Continue to ask questions and remain curious about the work" (Verone Bernard).

• "Continuously learn. Recognize that you don't know what you don't know. And accept that not knowing something is not a reflection of your abilities but an opportunity for you to expand on your base of knowledge. Know that no matter how much you succeed, you will always need to learn more. Be a willing student of every experience, whether it's good or bad. And know your experiences, alone, will not provide you with enough intellectual capital. Be a forever reader. You need to be able to support your experience with evidence and data drawn from academia, foundations, and other research institutions. Seek out, embrace, and learn from scholars studying your issues. You will find your advocacy, diplomatic engagement, and program development ideas are more effective and well received when you support them not just with experience and anecdotal evidence but also with data and scientific research" (Ertharin Cousin).

Be Courageous; Embrace Challenges

The one obstacle you have most control over is yourself. The giants urge you to be courageous. Don't listen to self-doubt or the doubts of others. Know you are made for broad impact in the world. You are never too late for the next adventure. You instinctively know much of this already—you just have to believe it. They also want you to be comfortable with the uncomfortable and even embrace those moments of challenge and fear in order to grow, learn, and become more impactful.

• "Be fearless about the possibilities for yourselves and really go after them" (Sundaa Bridgett-Jones).

• "If you get a shot, take a shot. Keep your eyes open. Don't automatically eliminate possible chances to go overseas and work there. You have a chance to influence more people. You have a chance to grow faster" (Bob Burgess).

• "Don't be a victim of the thought police. Go anywhere; do everything you want to do. I didn't learn to swim until I was thirty-six. You're not going to like everything, but try everything. It shouldn't be, 'We don't do this. We don't do that.' Try languages" (Harry K. Thomas Jr.).

• "Your generation is much more equipped than you realize to deal with everything that we're going through right now. You have a fearlessness. You call out a lot of the things we were taught to accept. Just believe in what you already know. Use the information you already have. Question everything, as you have been, and then just change it. Don't be afraid to do what you know needs to be done" (Sanola A. Daley).

• "Embrace the difficult, uncomfortable, booty-clenching moments. In those moments when you're the most uncomfortable, when you're clenching, find your power. Find your confidence in those spaces. Embrace those moments because those are your learning moments" (Verone Bernard).

• "Don't think in terms of comfort. Think in terms of challenge and how you can meet the challenge and be known for excellence in your work. Look for the places that will allow you to shine. Sometimes that can be in very difficult places, obscure places. You never know" (Johnny Young).

• "Read your history and take strength from the challenges that our forebears have overcome. And apply it to your current circumstances. Keep fighting" (Reuben Brigety).

Maintain Your Identity and Moral Compass

The giants provide you with models of integrity, grit, and ethics in action. They want you to know that you do not have to compromise who you are or what you believe in order to succeed in careers in US foreign policy and to have significant impacts in the world. In fact, it is through activating your whole selves that you will be most impactful. And that includes your understanding of what is morally right and morally wrong. Combining the last point with this one, they show you that you can be fearless. And you should be fearless in pursuing what is right for your fellow human beings. It is your responsibility to use every opportunity to advance what is right.

• "The best way to advance is to bring your whole self to the table and allow people to experience that. At some point in time, people will not only believe in it but will want it. They want a fresh perspective" (C. D. Glin).

• "The ability to stay true to your own ethical compass will determine not just how high you go but who you are inside as you go there" (Ertharin Cousin).

• "There is a verse in the book of Isaiah that says when the Messiah comes, if men are silent, the rocks will cry out. . . . . People who are in positions of responsibility, who have an option for a voice, have to take some stands to help shape the agenda. Or why should you be in the room?" (Reuben Brigety).

Where should your moral compass come from? Ambassador James Joseph has explored this question throughout his lifetime and across many experiences, both personal and professional. We share a snapshot of his wisdom here, and we urge you to consider reading his great work, *Saved for a Purpose: A Journey from Private Virtues to Public Values*. He writes, "The issues and problems of our aggregate existence are greatly aggravated by the fact that we are constantly dealing with people and systems with which we have no direct personal relationship. Personal responsibility is in many ways diluted. The directors of a business are individual persons, for example, but they are being asked to think as directors and shareholders" (Joseph 2015, 267). Private virtues are not enough, Ambassador Joseph argues. Moral guidance must also come from critical public values. He identifies ten: empathy, compassion, altruism, justice, trust, tolerance, respect, freedom, equality, and reconciliation. Ambassador Joseph draws from historian David Chappell's 2003 analysis of Black southern activism, which identifies "two very different kinds of optimism and confidence: one came from a strong sense that one was morally right, while the other came from a sense that one had been called to set things right" (Joseph 2015, 28). We hope you will find that calling in the foreign policy arena.

Passing the Torch

■ *The twenty-first century is your century. Just as we "baby boomers" took the baton from the World War II "greatest generation," we are looking to your generation to assume the mantle of leadership in the decades to come. We are convinced that you will become the diverse leaders that America and the world need to take on the current and future challenges of this century. We sincerely hope that this guidance and these stories will provide useful insights for emerging Black American and other leaders of color who may consider pursuing a career in international affairs, and more specifically in the Foreign Service. The face of America around the world must reflect the diversity and strength of our country, and I hope that this book will inspire you to embark upon or continue a career in this important cause.*

▶ The time has come for us to take up the mantle and continue to blaze the trail that the giants have created for us. I hope that you see yourself in these pages and are inspired to bring your talents to the world stage. You deserve to take up space, and you are integral to the future of international affairs. Don't ever let anyone make you feel "less than," and don't ever second-guess yourself. Have the conviction to speak truth to power and set the trail afire, knowing that there are ones who came before you to provide proverbial shade in the sun when we need it most. Our time is now.

Notes on the Giants

Gina Abercrombie-Winstanley. Abercrombie-Winstanley was the first Black woman US ambassador to Malta. With expertise on the Middle East, she served in a variety of positions in the State Department, the National Security Council, and the White House. In 2021, she became the State Department's first chief diversity and inclusion officer, reporting directly to the secretary of state. (Personal Interview)

Verone Bernard. Bernard is an international affairs professional with more than ten years of experience researching and designing programs to promote sustainable development. In her current role as senior business development specialist at RTI International, she supports the design and development of programs related to energy and natural resource management. She has experience working in more than twelve countries and specializes in establishing strategic partnerships. (Personal Interview)

Aurelia E. Brazeal. Brazeal is the first Black woman US ambassador from the career Foreign Service. She was appointed by three different presidents to serve as the first ambassador to Micronesia, ambassador to Kenya, and ambassador to Ethiopia. (Personal Interview; Association for Diplomatic Studies and Training [ADST] Oral History)

Sundaa Bridgett-Jones. Bridgett-Jones is director of communications, policy, and advocacy, and previously senior associate director for resilience, at the Rockefeller Foundation. Prior to joining the Rockefeller Foundation, she was director of public diplomacy at the Bureau of Democracy, Human Rights, and Labor at the State Department. (Personal Interview)

Reuben Brigety II. Brigety served as ambassador to the African Union, as permanent representative of the United States to the United Nations Economic Commission of Africa, and as deputy assistant secretary of state for African Affairs. His appointment as US Ambassador to South Africa is pending Senate confirmation. (Personal Interview)

Robert Burgess. Burgess was the first and, until he retired, the only Black senior executive in the manufacturing operations of GTE Sylvania (and its successor companies). He led their rapid expansion in the Caribbean and Central America during the massive export and investment expansion in that region, the precursor to the North American Free Trade Agreement. (Personal Interview)

Johnnie Carson. Carson is senior advisor to the president of the US Institute of Peace. He served as US assistant secretary of state for African affairs; as national intelligence officer for Africa, National Intelligence Council; and as US ambassador to Kenya, Zimbabwe, and Uganda. (Personal Interview)

Victoria Cooper. Currently senior vice president of the East and Southern Africa regional business unit of Chemonics, Cooper has decades of experience managing complex development projects for a variety of donors and governments, largely from West Africa, where she lived for several decades. She is a former partner in Pricewaterhouse-Coopers, Accra, Ghana. (Personal Interview)

Ertharin Cousin. Cousin is the founder and CEO of Food Systems for the Future. She previously served as executive director of the World Food Programme and as ambassador to the US Mission to the UN Agencies in Rome. (Personal Interview)

Sanola A. Daley. Daley is a gender specialist with over fifteen years of experience working primarily in Latin America with the Inter-American Development Bank, among other organizations. She is currently the global platform lead for gender, manufacturing, agribusiness, and services at the International Finance Corporation. (Personal Interview)

Ruth A. Davis. Davis was the first woman of color to be appointed director general of the Foreign Service, the first Black American director of the Foreign Service Institute, and the first Black American woman to be named career ambassador. She also served as ambassador to Benin. (Personal Interview; American Foreign Service Association 2016)

Valerie Dickson-Horton. Dickson-Horton served as the US Agency for International Development's deputy assistant administrator of the Bureau for Africa and mission director to Swaziland. (Personal Interview; USAID 2013)

Harriet Lee Elam-Thomas. Elam-Thomas was ambassador to Senegal and served as acting director of the US Information Agency. (Elam-Thomas 2017)

Lauri Fitz-Pegado. Fitz-Pegado is founder of InTheDash.live. She served as assistant secretary and director general of the US and Foreign Commercial Service. Prior to that she was senior vice president at Gray and Company/Hill and Knowlton and a Foreign Service information officer for the US Information Agency. (Personal Interview)

Alonzo Fulgham. Fulgham is USAID's first Black director for South Asian affairs, mission director to Afghanistan, chief operating officer, and acting administrator. (Personal Interview)

Philip Gary. Gary served as USAID mission director in Nepal, held office director positions in both the Asia/Near East and Africa USAID bureaus, and served on the faculty of the National War College, among other posts. (Personal Interview; ADST Oral History)

Helene Gayle. Dr. Gayle is the president and CEO of the Chicago Community Trust. She served twenty years at the Centers for Disease Control and Prevention, focusing on global health and infectious diseases, including HIV/AIDS. She then became the AIDS coordinator and chief of the HIV/AIDS Division at USAID and subsequently the director of the HIV, TB, and Reproductive Health Program at the Bill & Melinda Gates Foundation. She was also CEO of the international humanitarian NGO CARE. She was named one of *Forbes*'s "100 Most Powerful Women" and one of the *NonProfit Times*'s "Power and Influence Top 50." (Personal Interview)

Jacob Gayle. Dr. Gayle was head of AIDS programs for USAID and senior public health officer for the US Centers for Disease Control and Prevention. He later served as the deputy vice president of the Ford Foundation and the vice president of Medtronic Philanthropy. (Personal Interview)

C. D. Glin. Glin is vice president and global head of philanthropy for the PepsiCo Foundation. He is former president and CEO of the African Development Foundation, former associate director for Africa for the Rockefeller Foundation, and previously the first director of intergovernmental affairs and global partnerships at the US Peace Corps. (Personal Interview)

Ed Grier. Grier is dean of the Leavey School of Business, Santa Clara University, and former dean of the School of Business, Virginia Commonwealth University. He served as a top executive during a twenty-nine-year career with Disney, including as president of operations, Walt Disney Parks and Resorts; president, Disneyland Resort, Anaheim, California; and executive managing director, Walt Disney Attractions Japan. (Personal Interview)

Dominique Harris. Harris has been with Cargill, Inc., since 2012, with increasing responsibilities and scope. She is currently a strategic account manager. Before that she served as strategy and business development lead for Alternative Protein and as Cargill's director of international business relations in Washington, DC. She previously served as a congressional affairs specialist, Bureau of Oceans, Environment, and Science, at the Department of State and was a program associate at the Partnership for Public Service. (Personal Interview)

Taylor A. Jack. Jack is a program manager at Chemonics International. She is a returned Peace Corps volunteer, graduate of the Elliott School's international development studies master's program, a public speaker on diversity in international development, and coauthor on this project. (Personal Interview)

James Joseph. Joseph served as ambassador to South Africa. He also formerly served as president of the Council of Foundations, undersecretary of the interior, chair of the Corporation for National and Community Service, president of the Cummins Foundation, and vice president of Cummins Engine Company. (Personal Interview; Joseph 2015)

Katherine Lee. Lee served twenty-six years with the US Information Agency, including as director of its Career Development and Training Division. She also served as diplomat in residence at Spelman College. (Personal Interview; ADST Oral History)

Edward Perkins. Perkins served as US representative to the UN Security Council and as ambassador to the United Nations, Australia, Liberia, and South Africa; he was the first Black American director general of the Foreign Service. He is perhaps best known for having been appointed by President Ronald Reagan as ambassador to South Africa during the apartheid regime. (Personal Interview; Perkins 2012)

Colin Powell. Powell was a four-star general and first Black secretary of state (2001–2005). He also served as the national security advisor and chairman of the Joint Chiefs of Staff. (Powell 1995)

Barrye Price. Major General Price served thirty-one years in the US Army, including as commander of various posts in the United States and abroad, and as director of human resources policy at the Pentagon (where he worked on "Don't Ask, Don't Tell" and expanded the role of women within the army, among other things). He was the first Black American to earn a doctorate in history from Texas A&M University. He currently serves as CEO of Community Anti-Drug Coalitions of America. (Personal Interview)

Susan Rice. Rice is currently director of the United States Domestic Policy Council. She previously served as national security advisor and ambassador to the United Nations. (Rice 2019)

Christopher Richardson. Richardson served in Nigeria, Nicaragua, Pakistan, and Spain as a consular officer. He resigned in protest due to President Donald Trump's Muslim ban and derogatory statements about African countries. (Personal Interview)

Sylvia Stanfield. Stanfield served in a variety of political and economic posts in the diplomatic corps before becoming the first Black woman US ambassador to Brunei. She recently served as president of Black Professionals in International Affairs. (Personal Interview)

Harry K. Thomas Jr. Thomas served as US ambassador to Zimbabwe, the Philippines, and Bangladesh and as director general of the

Foreign Service. He was special assistant to US Secretary of State Condoleezza Rice. (Personal Interview; Xi 2013)

Linda Thomas-Greenfield. Thomas-Greenfield is US ambassador to the United Nations. She previously served as assistant secretary of state for African affairs, director general of the Foreign Service, and ambassador to Liberia. (Personal Interview; TED Talk)

Paul Weisenfeld. Weisenfeld is executive vice president at RTI International. Previously, he was a career minister in the Senior Foreign Service at the US Agency for International Development. At USAID he served as director of the Bureau for Food Security, led the Haiti Task Team for the 2010 earthquake response, and served as USAID mission director in Peru and Zimbabwe. Weisenfeld received the USAID administrator's Distinguished Career Service Award, the agency's highest award. (Personal Interview)

Aaron Williams. Williams has extensive experience working in international affairs through the public, private, and nonprofit sectors. At USAID, he was a pioneer in public-private partnerships, mission director for the Eastern Caribbean region, the first Black person to lead the Latin America and Caribbean Bureau, and mission director to South Africa (when Nelson Mandela became president). After his career at USAID, he was the first Black person to hold the following positions: vice president of the International Youth Foundation, executive vice president of a business group at RTI International, and the first Black male director of the Peace Corps. (Personal Interview)

Stacy D. Williams. Williams is deputy director in the Office of the Haiti Special Coordinator, State Department. He has served as chair of the Diversity Council in the State Department's Bureau of Western Hemisphere Affairs and as president of the Thursday Luncheon Group, the oldest employee affinity group at State. (Personal Interview)

Johnny Young. Young served as ambassador to Sierra Leone and Togo. He was also the first and, to date, only Black US ambassador to Bahrain and Slovenia. He is one of only four Black Americans appointed career ambassador. (Personal Interview; Young 2013)

Acronyms

ADST	Association for Diplomatic Studies and Training
AFSA	American Foreign Service Association
AID	Agency for International Development
ASEAN	Association of Southeast Asian Nations
CDC	Centers for Disease Control and Prevention
CEO	chief executive officer
DCM	deputy chief of mission
EER	employee evaluation report
FSNs	Foreign Service nationals
HBCU	historically Black college or university
IAF	Inter-America Foundation
ICAP	International Career Advancement Program
LSU	Louisiana State University
NEA	Near Eastern Affairs Bureau
NGOs	nongovernmental organizations
OAS	Organization of American States
PEPFAR	President's Emergency Plan for AIDS Relief
PMF	Presidential Management Fellows Program
PWI	primarily white institution
SADC	Southern Africa Development Community
SNCC	Student Nonviolent Coordinating Committee
TLG	Thursday Luncheon Group
UN	United Nations
USAID	US Agency for International Development
USIA	US Information Agency

References

American Foreign Service Association. 2016. "A Foreign Service Trailblazer—Ambassador Ruth A. Davis." *Foreign Service Journal*. September.

Angelou, Maya. 1991. *All God's Children Need Traveling Shoes*. New York: Vintage.

Angelou, Maya. 1994. *Wouldn't Take Nothing for My Journey Now*. New York: Bantam Books.

Association for Diplomatic Studies and Training (ADST). 2016. "African American Ambassadors." ADST. April. https://adst.org/african-american -ambassadors.

Blyden, Nemata Amelia. 2019. *African-Americans and Africa: A New History*. New Haven, CT: Yale University Press.

Brazeal, Aurelia E. 2007. Oral history. Interview by Daniel F. Whitman. Association for Diplomatic Studies and Training. September 22.

Brazile, Donna, Yolanda Caraway, Leah Daughtry, Minyon Moore, and Veronica Chambers. 2018. *For Colored Girls Who Have Considered Politics*. New York: St. Martin's Press.

Bridgett-Jones, Sundaa. 2018. "Transformational Leaders." Speech upon receipt of the 2018 Distinguished Alumna Award, Graduate School of Public and International Affairs, University of Pittsburgh, April 25.

Brinkerhoff, Derick W., and Jennifer M. Brinkerhoff. 2005. *Working for Change: Making a Career in International Public Service*. Boulder, CO: Lynne Rienner Publishers.

Burns, William J., and Linda Thomas-Greenfield. 2020. "The Transformation of Diplomacy." *Foreign Affairs*. September 23.

Chappell, David. 2003. *A Stone of Hope: Prophetic Religion and the Death of Jim Crow*. Chapel Hill: University of North Carolina Press.

Davidson, Joe. 2019. "Federal Employees Loved Rep. Elijah Cummings—and He Had Their Back." *Washington Post*. October 24.

281

Davis, Ruth A. 1996. "Not for People like You." *State Magazine* (August): 14–15, 46.

Davis, Ruth A. 2004. Former director general US Department of State. Remarks to the Princeton University Junior Summer Institute, June 28.

Dixon-Fyle, Sundiatu, Kevin Dolan, Vivian Hunt, and Sara Prince. 2020. "Diversity Wins: How Inclusion Matters." McKinsey & Company. May. www.mckinsey.com/featured-insights/diversity-and-inclusion/diversity-wins-how-inclusion-matters.

Elam-Thomas, Harriet Lee, with Jim Robison. 2017. *Diversifying Diplomacy: My Journey from Roxbury to Dakar*. Lincoln: University of Nebraska Press.

Elliot, Jonathan. 1836. *The Debates in the Several State Conventions on the Adoption of the Federal Constitution as Recommended by the General Convention at Philadelphia, in 1787*. 2nd ed. Vol. 3 (Philadelphia).

Fapuro, Elisabeth. 2020. "We Need to Talk About the Pressure of Black Excellence." Refinery29. October 21. www.refinery29.com/en-gb/2020/10/10098749/why-is-black-excellence-important.

Gary, Philip-Michael. 2017. Oral history. Interview by Carol Peasley. Association for Diplomatic Studies and Training. January 9.

Garza, Alicia. 2020. *The Purpose of Power: How We Come Together When We Fall Apart*. New York: One World.

Givhan, Robin. 2021. "Vernon Jordan Made Being a Black Man in America Look Effortless." *Washington Post*. March 2.

Hirsch, Afua. 2018. "Review of 'Michelle Obama Live.'" *The Guardian*, December 4, 2018. http://www.theguardian.com.

International Career Advancement Program (ICAP). N.d. "Homepage." www.icapaspen.org.

Joseph, James A. 2015. *Saved for a Purpose: A Journey from Private Virtues to Public Values*. Durham, NC: Duke University Press.

Joseph, James A. 2020. "US Ambassador James A. Joseph on His Lifelong Fight for Equality." Interview by Heather Dunhill. *Sarasota Magazine*. September 3.

Kendi, Ibram X. 2019. *How to Be an Antiracist*. New York: One World.

Kenyon, Cecelia M. 1955. "Men of Little Faith: The Anti-federalists on the Nature of Representative Government." *William and Mary Quarterly: A Magazine of Early American History*: 4–43.

Krenn, Michael L. 1999. *Black Diplomacy: African-Americans in the State Department, 1945–1969*. Armonk, NY: M. E. Sharp.

Lee, Katherine. N.d. Interview with AAFP. [provided by Katherine Lee].

Lee, Katherine. 2005. Oral history. Interview by Charles Stuart Kennedy. Association for Diplomatic Studies and Training. May 16.

Lewis, John Robert. 2017. *Across That Bridge: Life Lessons and a Vision for Change*. New York: Hachette.

Lorde, Audre. 2017. *A Burst of Light and Other Essays*. Mineola, NY: Courier Dover Publications.

McCormick, Ty, and Tendai Marima. 2018. "An Emissary to Tyranny." *Foreign Policy*. January 6. https://foreignpolicy.com/2018/01/16/an-emissary-to-tyranny-zimbabwe-african-americans.

Morrison, Toni. 2003. "The Truest Eye." Interview by Pam Houston. *O, The Oprah Magazine*. November.

Muñoz, Cecilia. 2020. *More Than Ready: Be Strong and Be You . . . and Other Lessons for Women of Color on the Rise*. New York: Seal Press.

Obama, Michelle. 2020. "Protests and the Pandemic with Michele Norris." *The Michelle Obama Podcast*. August.

Obama, Michelle. 2021. *Becoming*. Crown.

Perkins, Edward J., with Connie Cronley. 2006. *Mr. Ambassador: Warrior for Peace*. Norman: University of Oklahoma Press.

Powell, Colin L., with Joseph E. Persico. 1995. *My American Journey*. New York: Random House.

Rice, Susan E. 2019. *Tough Love: My Story of the Things Worth Fighting For*. New York: Simon & Schuster.

Richardson, Christopher. 2020. "The State Department Was Designed to Keep African-Americans Out." *New York Times*. June 23. www.nytimes.com /2020/06/23/opinion/state-department-racism-diversity.html.

Roosevelt, Franklin Delano. 1934. Radio address from the White House. September 30.

Saad, Nardine. 2021. "Poet Amanda Gorman Leaves CNN's Anderson Cooper 'Transfixed' by Her Personal Mantra." *Los Angeles Times*. January 21. www.latimes.com/entertainment-arts/tv/story/2021-01-21/inauguration -poet-amanda-gorman-hamilton-cnn-anderson-cooper.

Sales, Ruby. 2020. "Where Does It Hurt?" Interview with Krista Tippett. On Being. January 16. https://onbeing.org/programs/ruby-sales-where-does-it -hurt.

Shultz, George. 2006. "Foreword." In *Mr. Ambassador: Warrior for Peace*. By Edward J. Perkins with Connie Cronley. Norman: Oklahoma University Press.

Steele, Claude M. 2011. *Whistling Vivaldi: How Stereotypes Affect Us and What We Can Do*. New York: W. W. Norton & Company.

Thomas-Greenfield, Linda. 2018. "How I Found Strength and Compassion Through Adversity." TED. November 30. www.ted.com/talks/linda_thomas _greenfield_how_i_found_strength_and_compassion_through_adversity.

Travis, Danika J., Jennifer Thorpe-Moscon, and Courtney McCluney. 2016. *Emotional Tax: How Black Women and Men Pay More at Work and How Leaders Can Take Action*. New York: Catalyst: Workplaces that Work for Women, October 11.

USAID. 2013. "Behind the Scenes: Interview with Valerie Dickson-Horton to Discuss Her 24 Years in Foreign Affairs for USAID." USAID. July 31. https://bloguat.usaid.gov/2013/07/behind-the-scenes-interview-with-valerie -dickson-horton-to-discuss-her-24-years-in-foreign-affairs-for-usaid.

Walker, Rheeda. 2020. *The Unapologetic Guide to Black Mental Health: Navigate an Unequal System, Learn Tools for Emotional Wellness, and Get the Help You Deserve*. Oakland, CA: New Harbinger Publications.

Weisenfeld, Paul. 2020a. "Calls for Racial Justice Are a Wake-Up for the Global Development Community." *Devex News*. June 17. www.devex .com/news/opinion-calls-for-racial-justice-are-a-wake-up-for-the-global -development-community-97480.

Weisenfeld, Paul. 2020b. "Let's Have an Uncomfortable Conversation." *Devex News*. July 29. www.devex.com/news/opinion-let-s-have-an-uncomfortable -conversation-97810.

West, Cornel. 1997. *Restoring Hope: Conversations on the Future of Black America*. Boston: Beacon.

Xi, Joyce. 2013. "An Interview with Harry K. Thomas, Jr., Ambassador to the Philippines." *The Politic*. August 14. https://thepolitic.org/an-interview-with-harry-k-thomas-u-s-ambassador-to-the-philippines.

Yoshino, Kenji. 2007. *Covering: The Hidden Assault on Our Civil Rights*. New York: Random House.

Young, Johnny. 2013. *From the Projects to the Palace: A Diplomat's Unlikely Journey from the Bottom to the Top*. Oral history interview conducted by Charles Stuart Kennedy. Bloomington, IN: Xlibris Corporation for the Association for the Diplomatic Studies and Training.

Index

285

Fitz-Pegado, Lauri, 10, 11, 37, 48, 58, 64, 77–78, 78, 121–122, 144, 166–167, 173, 174, 175, 178, 201, 203, 265

Foreign service. *See* service, foreign

French, 190, 262, 263

Fulgham, Alonzo, 9, 10, 14, 22, 24, 46, 55–56, 63, 69, 79, 83, 85–86, 94–95, 96, 105, 115, 119, 126, 128, 142–143, 144–145, 156, 157, 248, 260, 265, 268

Gary, Philip, 110, 127, 131, 138–139, 148, 160–161, 177, 200–201, 204–205, 205–206, 210, 250–251, 252, 254, 258, 262–263, 264–265

Gayle, Helene, 10, 11, 14, 16, 17, 18, 47–48, 58, 62, 63, 64, 65, 68, 99, 109, 147, 153–154, 181, 186, 199–200, 204, 245

Gayle, Jacob, 11, 25, 62, 89, 92, 98, 107, 154–155, 175, 183, 184, 192, 211, 212, 223, 246–247, 257–258, 259

Gender, 16, 37, 63, 68, 71, 138, 139–140, 143, 156, 175, 196, 198, 199, 207, 208, 210

Germany, 21; German, 35, 140

Ghana, 24, 47, 51, 111, 118, 139, 189, 207

Glin, C. D., 11, 14, 21, 28, 32, 39–40, 46, 51, 52, 78–79, 81, 102, 106, 114, 155, 188, 196, 201, 201–203, 213, 220–221, 222–223, 226, 228, 230–231, 234, 248, 267, 270

Grier, Ed, 10, 11, 40, 52, 58, 69, 96, 97, 125–126, 135, 172–173, 175, 178, 186, 187, 219, 236, 243, 244, 248–249260, 263

Guinea, 81, 97, 119

Haiti, 19, 22, 33, 46, 77, 113, 128, 144, 233; Haitian, 198

Harris, Dominique, 54–55, 62, 65, 70–71, 76–77, 78, 80, 97–98, 100, 101, 104, 111, 123, 125, 131, 140–141, 179, 180, 182–183, 204, 215–216, 220, 267

Health, 48, 112, 178, 198, 204, 229, 249, 258; global, 25, 47–48, 257–258; mental, 28, 171, 171–176, 178–180, 183, 187, 198, 200–201; public, 47–48, 109, 204, 241, 246–247, 249, 257–258

Heritage, 4, 26, 32, 114, 211, 219, 221

Historically Black College or University (HBCU), 9, 27, 31, 36–41, 201, 212–213

History, 2, 6, 8, 20–21, 22, 34, 37, 45, 83, 115–116, 124, 141, 143, 153, 154, 157–158, 172, 199, 200, 216, 225, 236, 246–247, 250, 255, 259, 265, 266, 268, 270

HIV/AIDS, 10, 48, 155, 165, 186, 229, 241, 249–250, 252–253, 257, 258

Humility, 6, 226, 247–249, 250, 267; humble, 59, 133, 247, 248, 249, 266, 267–268

Humor, 148–149, 156, 177, 206, 264–265

Identity, 21–22, 28, 77, 82, 110, 195–223, 259–260, 270–271; Black, 14, 39–40, 127, 128, 174, 199–201, 208, 219, 221, 222, 225, 254; gender, 175, 199, 208–210; racial, 175; sexual, 175

Inauthentic, 206, 210–213; inauthenticity, 206, 210–213. *See also* authentic

Impact, 22–23, 26, 34, 53, 107, 109, 114, 114–115, 117, 123, 125–127, 141, 159, 171, 230, 231, 235, 257–258, 259, 269, 270; impactful, 197, 216, 221; institutional, 80

Imposter: syndrome, 27, 57, 58–66, 68, 70–71, 113, 171, 177, 206, 257, 259–260

Injustice, 3, 6, 26, 137, 143, 157, 222

Inter-America Foundation, 129, 148, 167

Inter-American Development Bank, 68, 140, 179

Internship, 27, 31–32, 33–34, 42–50, 51, 52–53, 73, 88, 124

Intersectionality, 86, 140, 196, 208; intersectional, 196

Jerks, 27, 53–54, 137, 141–143, 169, 171

Jordan, 115

Jordan, Vernon, 73, 148–149

Joseph, James, 9, 10, 11, 14, 20, 47, 57, 82, 107, 144, 159, 182, 187–188, 221–222, 223, 232, 249, 265, 266, 271

Justice, 6, 17, 18–19, 27, 138, 145, 271; bank of, 266, 267; racial, 141; social, 109, 130

About the Book

Young people of color confront a myriad of challenges that deter them from considering, pursuing, and succeeding at careers in international affairs. The authors of *The Young Black Leader's Guide* address these challenges, drawing on the experiences of Black American giants in the field to provide systematic, practical advice.

From getting started to learning to lead, from overcoming imposter syndrome to acing performance reviews, from dealing with racism to knowing when to say no, the invaluable tips and hard-earned wisdom in the book go beyond standard resources to provide an essential guide for Black Americans seeking to play a much-needed role in the global arena.

Aaron S. Williams has extensive experience in the public, private, and nonprofit sectors, including posts as USAID mission director for South Africa, vice president of the International Youth Foundation, executive vice president of RTI International, and director of the US Peace Corps (2009–2012). **Taylor A. Jack** is a program manager in the East and Southern Africa Division of Chemonics International, an international development consulting firm. She served as a Peace Corps volunteer in Senegal. **Jennifer M. Brinkerhoff** is professor of public administration, international affairs, and international business at George Washington University.